FIFTY SHA

MW00944204

Sometimes
the Most Powerful Messages
Come Wrapped in Surprising Packages.

First Edition

CHAPTERS

Foreword

Life can change in an instant. One minute you see things a certain way, and the next everything is different. As a new avenue of seeing the world merges with an open mind, you feel compelled to dive deeper, to try to understand these new thoughts and feelings swirling around in your brain... and heart.

Such is the purpose of art of any kind. Be it music, visual arts, film, or the written word, the goal is to make you think, to feel, to love.

The next step is to congregate with others who share your interest, to commune with like-minded people. People to laugh and cry with. People who support you and people who challenge you. People who expand your thinking, who get you to see the things in new and different ways.

If you're a fan of the *Fifty Shades of Grey* series, this book will enhance your love for E.L. James' books in an even deeper and more meaningful way. It might even help you explain to the doubters out there why the books aren't just entertaining and intriguing – they're *important*.

If you're not a fan of FSOG and you're scoffing, or perhaps mimicking Ana and rolling your eyes at the thought of the books being either deep or important, then we challenge you to open your mind and heart, and take another look at the series through our eyes.

Believer or skeptic, the goal of this book is to get you to think. To feel. To love.

With much love,
Brownell

Dedication

This book is dedicated to E.L. James. Thank you for your talent, your wisdom, and your inspiration.

This book is also dedicated to the passionate, intelligent, insightful, beautiful souls in the Fifty Shades Deeper group.

Editor's Note

Due to the limitations for page size for a printed book, this is an abridged version of the e-book. At an estimated 600 "printed pages" in the e-book vs. over 400+ pages in this version, the e-book version is, in a word, Deeper. Still, there's a wealth of deep topics to read and think about in this version. Let's call it the "best of the best."

This book will be edited and updated regularly. The first edition was collected and published just before the film Fifty Shades Darker was released; therefore, the comments herein are based on the first three novels in the FSOG series, plus Grey, the first book in the series from Christian's point of view.

Stay tuned for more!

Introduction

Why We're Writing This Book

First and foremost, our primary reason for writing this book is to show support and love for E.L. James and for the fans of the series by helping them dig deeper into the messages and insights in the Fifty Shades books. To show the naysayers that they might've missed something in their prejudice against the books. And to maybe open the eyes of new people to uncover what we saw in the books.

What This Book Is – And What It Isn't

This book is a labor of love in its most literal sense. We are here because of our love – for Fifty Shades, for E.L. James, and for each other. Captured over nearly two years of around-the-clock interaction and discussion, this book represents the community we have built. It is not intended to force beliefs. Instead, our goal is to stimulate thinking so you can formulate your own views.

As you'll see throughout this book, we encourage diverse opinions; we love lively, deep discussions. In fact, we have enough stories to fill two or three books! And we have a *lot* of fun!

We should let you know that we look at these characters as being actual people. Go ahead and laugh at how seriously we take these books. We can take it! Heck, we've got a sense of humor, too! We also know that while these characters might be fictional, they are also quite *real*.

Brownell says, being an author herself, "When you write, the characters become their own people. They speak to you and tell you what to say. Yes, we 'hear voices.' What keeps us from going crazy is writing down what they say! Ask any author and he/she will tell you that the characters they write are *very* real."

Who We Are

Author Bios

Brownell Landrum is an author, speaker, entrepreneur and innovator. Brownell's writing includes four novels in the "metaphysical romance" *DUET* *stories* series, two children's books in the *Wonderactive Books!* series: *Sometimes I Wonder* and *This Isn't My First Time*, one nonfiction book entitled *Five Reasons Why Bad Things Happen: How to Turn Tragedies into Triumph* as well as several screenplays for film and television, short stories and blogs. Brownell has also co-written a few songs, one of which, "While You Can," was featured in the film *Almost Home* in 2015 and is available on iTunes.

Brownell has a Master's Degree in International Business and is also the inventor of DrawSuccess, a breakthrough process for employee development to accelerate performance, and DrawSuccess 4 Students, a transformational anti-bullying program for students and schools.

A recurring theme in all of Brownell's work and writing is delving deep into the "why." When she read the Fifty Shades of Grey (*FSOG*) series, she was compelled to explore all of the deeper "whys" in the books, from "Were Ana and Christian destined to meet?" and "Had they known each other 'before?'" to "What would have happened if Ana hadn't left (at the end of the first book)?" and "How did Christian's being born to a crack whore influence his life?" These questions – and dozens more – prompted her to create the Facebook discussion group *Fifty Shades Deeper*, from which this book is derived.

Brownell is single and lives in Aspen, Colorado.

Kaydee Fergus is a stay-at-home mom who educates her two young children in her home in the Southern United States. Kaydee has a Bachelor of Arts degree in Psychology and is a licensed Elementary and Middle School Teacher. She and her husband, who were high school sweethearts, have been happily married for over 20 years. She grew up in the center of the Bible Belt and stands firmly behind her belief that reading *Fifty Shades of Grey* can enhance married life for curious and/or stagnated couples. Kaydee is adamant that reading *FSOG* changed her life and marriage for the better because of the message contained therein of unconditional love and feeling free to fully express love without reservations. She has written many unpublished poems over her lifetime and hopes this book will become the dawn for future writing endeavors.

Jewell Hennessy is an administrative assistant who works for a hospital in the Greater Toronto Area, in Canada. She was born and raised in Montreal, Quebec, until her family moved to Toronto. Jewell's parents instilled a passion for reading at a very young age. This passion has given way to the dream that Jewell hoped to one day pursue writing. When she read the FSOG trilogy, she realized that the story has very meaningful messages, which she hopes to share with everyone. It is a complex love story that deserves exploration and discussion. This is Jewell's first foray into publishing, and she hopes to continue writing for years to come. She continues to live in Toronto, Canada, and has been married to her husband for the past 33 years.

Welcome to Our Group

The Fifty Shades Deeper group is a Secret group on Facebook comprised of women and men from around the globe. We come from a wide range of ages and experience levels with a variety of religious and social backgrounds. What we have in common is our passion for discussing the deeper messages and insights of the Fifty Shades of Grey (FSOG) books and film series. The way we explore everything from the pros and cons of the BDSM lifestyle to the impact of child abuse and addiction to subtler spiritual messages, makes the Fifty Shades Deeper group stand out among the dozens of other FSOG fan pages and groups.

We're Different

I was just reading the messages in another group, and I was reading about how the group was becoming more and more negative, which I admit is totally true. That's why I want to say that I love this group. I never wanted to be part of a group that was full of yes people always agreeing with each other, loving EVERY part of the books or EVERY part of the film and not daring to disagree. That's just not real life. I love that I can come here, and feel safe in saying how I feel and what I think, and hear what you all have to say about it. So in short, thank you. Thank you for giving me a safe place to express opinions, good or bad. And thank you for being the kind, respectful people that you are. Oh, and thank you for not always agreeing with me. That's really nice too.

- Thank you for being here. This is the kind of place where we hope to attract people like us who can agree to disagree. Something like this group was long overdue.
- There's a difference between expressing a negative opinion, and being negative. I've seen people complain about everything, and frankly that's irritating.
- Just knowing people like that is a drag. I avoid them like the plague!
- There are a ton of groups out there that are getting to that point. I'm all for voicing an "unfavorable" opinion, but to bash the actors, and everything about the films or the books is ridiculous.
- There's a difference between disagreeing and being disagreeable. The distinction, I think, is respect and honoring differences.
- I'm all in when it comes to what you just said. I will say this though, I just don't like the FSOG haters. I feel they come into the group, and show hate for it when they don't even really fully understand the whole story.
- There are respectful ways to say you don't like something. Many people miss that.
- I'd like to thank all you wonderful Deeper members for your support. I know Christian is a fictional character, but I feel the need to set these people straight. There are

8

enough Fifty Shades of Grey haters out there and with comments like "Christian is dark," I feel they're being misinformed. These people should take notice of people like us, who will give them a true, unbiased opinion. I'd also like to say thanks for inviting me to join this group. I love the laughs and lusting we do over our beloved Christian, but I also love these in-depth conversations.

The Message

Which was the message E.L. James wanted to convey to her readers? Was it "And they lived happily ever after?" Could it have been "Eventually, passion and love always win?" What about "If we dream it, it will happen?" Or was the message something *Deeper*?

- I like to think it's a love story with a kink about an abused boy and teenager who overcame his many, many demons thanks to love, patience, and understanding. BDSM was just thrown into the mix to show an extreme spectrum.
- How true soul-connected love can heal and transform.
- I think she wanted to touch on the pain of abandonment and his childhood abuse to set up the parameters for his inability to recognize his self-worth.
- I think she wanted to relay that with love and trust, even the darkest, most wounded heart can change when a strong connection and patience is there.
- The happily ever after! How their true connection allowed them to cure the pain and abandonment they both suffered, and to deal with all the factors that surrounded them, such as their past and present (Elena, Ana's inexperience, etc.). In a few words, yeah, they're soulmates and they found each other and they battled everyone and everything to stay together.
- The power of love will cast away deep demons.
- I think that whatever our deepest wishes and obsessions are, love conquers all for the souls that are destined to meet and find each other. The story shows that lasting love is possible. It's probable even. But sometimes, you have to go through pain to find your true love.

Sometimes you have to fight for what you want. Sometimes you have to change who you are. Sometimes you have to sacrifice. But when the pain is over, the joy is immeasurable.

- The power of forgiveness and being forgiven.
- I think it was that no matter how broken someone is, love can help repair that.
- Even the most unlovable person can be changed by genuine unconditional love.
- That we can only know we are truly loved when we share our darkest secrets.
- Love can conquer the hardest of hearts if you believe.
- That sometimes the knight can be saved by the princess.
- Love really does conquer all.

What Made You Read the Book for the First Time?

- I was just *curious*.
- When I read the book, I hadn't heard that they were going to make a movie. So I read it because of the feedback from my friends.
- I saw an episode of Dr. Oz where they spent the whole hour talking about it. I got curious, bought the audiobook, and BOOM! Instant addict.
- I heard about it from other people and was very curious. I wasn't disappointed!
- I saw the film first and I *had* to read the books then!
- A friend told me about it three years ago.
- I saw the movie, loved it, and then read all three books in a weekend.
- My friend told me there is a book series just right for me and my kink. Soon after that she told me it would be made into a movie. She read the first book and then cooled off. I'm still hot, for the books.
- What initially made me pick the book up was the hoopla surrounding it and its ties to *Twilight*. However, I could never get past the first couple of chapters. It wasn't until I saw the film that my interest was renewed. I wanted to see how the film compared, and then find out how the story continued.

- I read it as an e-book but didn't like it. I thought the BDSM was tame! I went to the airport one year later saw the book on display, bought it and enjoyed it! Everyone was reading it and hiding the book in paper bags or inside the cover of another book. It was so funny!
- I read the books before the movie was announced. I was getting tired of all the buzz about it everywhere. At the airport on a long flight to Europe I decided to buy it just to not be bored in the plane. And, oh my! My husband got to have a fantastic honeymoon on that trip! I read the book in just a few days and I struggled trying to find *Darker* in English in Europe, so I did have to buy it online. I loved it!
- I read the books before the movie came out. I was intrigued with what everyone was talking about. I've enjoyed reading all three books - more than one time! I enjoyed the movie, too!
- I read the books about 15 times before I saw the movie. I can't say any specific person told me about because EVERYONE I met had heard of it, except me!
- I had heard about it from various friends, but never really got in to it. Book one sat on my dresser for over a year. I saw the first movie trailer and had to read the book. And, I read all three books in one weekend! Couldn't put them down.
- The very first time I heard about the book, I was at my sister's place. A bunch of her friends were going on and on about this really hot book that just came out, and I asked what the name of the book was and one of the women blushed a bit and said "Fifty Shades of Grey." I responded by saying it sounded rather naughty, and she agreed. At that time, I started to hear about the book EVERYWHERE. I even tried to sign out the e-book from the local library, but all copies were signed out with no available copies to be had at all! Finally, a friend of mine took pity and pointed me in the direction of Google Play, where I downloaded the entire trilogy. The rest is history, where my love for the story is concerned.
- My husband got it for me for Christmas; he got me the boxed set. He wasn't sure what it was about, but he'd

11

heard all kinds of women were reading it, so he got it thinking I'd like to read it. I read it and was hooked!

- I read the books first. When I first heard about it, it was called "mommy porn," and I wanted no part of it. Then about a year later, it was still all the rage. I decided to find out what it was all about. I read the trilogy in three days. I couldn't put it down. It was a love story I couldn't quit reading.

- I went out with my girls to the cinema. They had already read the book, but I hadn't, so I had no idea what I was going to see. Unfortunately, I didn't like the film. It was too raw for me, so they urged me to read the book. And now I'm here.

- I got interested because of the film and wanted to read the book before watching it.

- I heard about it on talk shows, and I also heard it was called "mommy porn." I knew it was written for me. I love a good dirty book and a good love story.

- My son had gotten a new Kindle and gave me his old one, and FSOG is the first book I bought for it.

- I heard about it through various talk shows and seeing E.L. James in interviews. Then my BFF and my niece asked if I had read these books. I was hooked after FSOG. When I heard they were making a movie my only concern was what rating would it get.

- My sister kept trying to get me to read them, but I wasn't a reader. Hubby and I saw the movie on Valentine's Day and I begged my sister for the books that night. I had to see what happened to Ana and Christian. I stayed up very late every night reading them until I finished all 3 of them. I've never stopped reading them in some form.

- My friend offered to let me borrow them back in the summer of 2014. I tried reading, but decided Christian was an asshole and couldn't get past the first chapter. Just didn't think it was the story for me. Fast forward to October 2014, and I happened across an article about the movie. Well, that settled it; I was going to watch Fifty Shades! I decided that since I planned on watching, I should also read the book, too. This time I couldn't put it down, and bought my own set before I had finished *Darker*! It was a Godsend for my libido in the midst of going through infertility. My little one was conceived while I was reading them!

- All it took was hearing my minister mention Fifty Shades in a sermon, calling it "smut" and "sinner's pornography," and I went to the bookstore immediately after church. Thanks, minister!
- That sounds like something I would do.
- It is ironic, isn't it? That the more something is forbidden the more we're attracted to it. Wow. It sounds like I'm talking about Christian!
- I was curious about it, and then once I read the first one I was hooked, and had to read more.
- I heard about it so often on the news. One day E.L. James was on a talk show and I thought, "What's with all this craziness from a book?" The title didn't convince me much; I thought it was about colors. Then I went to the store, and suddenly it was in front of me. I read a bit, and could not stop my addiction after that day.
- I had heard about it from a casual friend. I think this was the summer of 2012. Long before there was a movie announced. My story is similar in that the thing that intrigued me was the naughtiness. Ironically, the person who told me about it is a fundamentalist Christian.
- So, I'm one of the people who actually read it first when it was Twilight fanfiction. I remember anxiously awaiting emails saying that a new chapter had been posted. After it was pulled and published as FSOG, I, of course, read it right away!
- My co-workers got the book on tape, so there were like five of us who kept passing the CDs. Since I liked it so much, one of my sons brought me the whole set for Christmas.
- I read it before it became Fifty Shades. I just loved Master of the Universe (MOTU).
- I heard about MOTU, and couldn't find it online at the time. So I read the books, then watched the movie, and then read Grey.

- My sister kept telling me about this series! I had just finished reading *Twilight*. I told her I wanted to read something else, and she just kept on and on and on about Fifty Shades. She sent me the first book, and the rest is history. I'm so thankful!
- My friends and coworkers were reading it and talking about it. I thought not much about it until the news about the movies came out and I borrowed one book. From reading the first chapters, I was drawn in, addicted, and knew what all the fuss was about.
- I remember it so vividly. A friend started talking about it. She'd heard about it on a talk show one night when we were out to dinner. She said, "You guys should check out this new, hot book: Fifty Shades. They say it's supposed to be very sexy and dirty." We all chuckled and discussed it awhile of course and moved on. I, not being a reader at all, bought FSOG that weekend, and my life hasn't been the same since!! A true fact: that friend, who mentioned the books, still to this day has not read them. My other girlfriends have read it, and they liked it, but no huge spark.
- The hype.

Why Fifty Shades?

Why do you think Fifty Shades hit such a nerve in so many people? It was definitely not the first erotic novel to ever come out. But it certainly did rewrite the genre. What made it different?

- I liked it immediately for the love story. I've read all three books multiple times, and I've found that I started to skim over the sex parts to get back to the story. This is probably heresy to say, but I think if you removed all the sex scenes in the books, it would still be a great romantic love story.
- I totally agree. Erotica has been around for quite some time with stories from Anais Nin, Anne Rice, etc. I think this book put the story on the map because of the evolving times it has come into. Women are getting kind

of bored and want some excitement, but don't want to say that aloud because anything other than the "norm" is considered "taboo." This is the time to come out! Though I truly don't understand how E.L. James managed to bring it to the forefront when there was already so much erotica existing. Maybe it was the timing, on the tail end of the *Twilight* saga. Either way, I'm glad the word is out!

- I love the romance of it. But I have church friends claiming it's abuse, which I see as a massive insult to my intelligence. One particular friend knows my story. I've been through every form of abuse, and yet she knows I'm a fan of FSOG. You'd think that would tell her something. Prior to Fifty Shades I don't remember a book like this (BDSM) being popular. So some people just don't understand it. But for me it's definitely the romance.

- I think it's also a departure because you always read about the damsel in distress. This time it was the *man* who needed rescuing. Usually it's the woman who's been abused, cheated on, etc. Rarely do we read about a man who has been so badly hurt; so badly abused. Yes, Ana needed *rescuing* of her own, but as they say, "She rescued him right back."

- Your story is inspiring and very important. I'm really honored by all the openness and honesty of the Deeper members. Thank you.

- Your response hit me straight in the heart. You're so right. Very poignant message. Still reeling with feeling.

- Do you think the rise of e-readers had anything to do with its success? Women could read it on their Kindle in public and nobody would know.

- If the books had come out a few years earlier, before e-readers, and if the books featured a hunky man on the cover, do you think it still would have taken off like it did?

- In addition to the emergence of e-readers, there were two other factors: First, it started out as *Twilight* fanfiction as you know, meaning it got a huge fanbase out of the gate. And because it was controversial, it got even more buzz.

Second, she gave it for FREE online for a long time, which also built a huge audience. The e-readers were the extra jet fuel in something already set to take off!

- The abuse of men is so rarely, if ever, touched upon; how could you not be affected by it? This guy was so badly hurt, so badly abused by a woman no less, that he couldn't even handle the slightest touch. That's not something you see anywhere really. So E.L. James put a modern spin on a tale as old as time, and I for one, feel it was a refreshing change. I can't speak for all women, but most of us have a need to nurture, to fix what is broken, and you couldn't get more broken than Christian. That's why I feel it struck a chord with a lot of women.
- Because it teaches that sex for women should not be taboo.
- I'll be the first to admit I read it because all my female friends were talking about the kinky f*ckery, and I wanted to see what all the craziness was about. I read all three books numerous times and loved them. I felt it was a great love story with the kink as an added bonus. Fifty Shades was the first erotic novel I ever read.
- She did kind of have a built in fan base with the *Twilight* fans. I'm sure that helped. But I think there was more to it than that. I think timing had a lot to do with it. The popularity of e-readers helped, as well as the rise of women willing to explore more of their sexuality. It just seemed like a perfect storm.
- I definitely think being able to e-read was a plus for many.
- Wow, these are intense questions. Personally when I first started reading the book I didn't like it and put it down. When I saw the movie and the elegance it entailed, I started reading the books. Somehow the way Christian was played in the movie was so much more elegant than what I got from the book. On the other hand, there are a lot of details in the book, i.e. emails, that you miss from the movie. But I certainly wouldn't have picked the book off of the shelf if I hadn't seen the movie.

- I think most people who saw the movie were already fans of the book. Why do you think the movie caught your attention more than the book? Since you read the books only after having watched the movie first, how do you think the movie affected the books for you?
- I kind of felt sorry for the people who just saw the movie and didn't read the books. The ending would've both confused and crushed me if I were them!
- I've had to explain the whole book to people and then they go, "Oh, right. I get it now."
- I believe it's the age of e-readers. FSOG was the first that captured over one million in downloads for e-readers. So I think that's the key.
- I saw the movie and ordered the books right afterward. I loved it on its own, and of course was floored by where they left it. But somehow I knew that they were leaving room for the other two books to make them into films. I loved reading the stories and then I went back to see the movie twice more. I, too, loved the grace that the actors brought to the characters, but yes, the books and the story of their love is what made me fall in love with the series.
- As for me, I'm not an ardent reader. I'd never read much romance before, but after hearing everyone's reviews on the kinky stuff, I had to read FSOG. It took me until the interview where I fell in love with Ana and her subconscious. I just couldn't stop reading, so I read all three; falling more and more in love with their connection. Just like Ana, the kinky stuff was new to me, so I also learned a lot. And, let's just say after reading FSOG it opened me up to many new romance novels.
- When I was 14, I picked up my first Rosemary Rogers and Jackie Collins books, and I've never looked back. I've had favorites that I've read again and again, but I loved Fifty Shades from the first page. I think what I liked was that it wasn't written by a novelist, it was written by someone that had an idea and wanted to share it. Her writing is basic and honest, and I didn't need the Kama Sutra to work out the sex scenes. Plus, she touched on a taboo subject, BDSM, which wasn't

remotely mainstream. It was still very much underground. If you lived that lifestyle or indulged in it, you were a freak, a weirdo, a deviant in league with the devil. Secretly, some of us were a bit intrigued by it, but would never admit it. Before these books, could you sit over a cup of tea and talk about silver balls, or flogging or wooden crosses or bondage? She allowed us to peek behind the curtain, and this kink appealed to the dark side of our psyche. The story follows a time-tested formula: a feisty young girl, a jaded damage hero, the battle of rescuing each other, and of course, what all us girls love to believe in, which is that love really does conquer all.

- It is real and emotionally believable!
- It was a hit from the start because it tapped into the deepest desires of all women. The author knows what's going on in our minds and bodies. It wasn't porn, but instead a beautiful love story. Deep in our minds, we all long for a Christian Grey. E.L. James made him come alive for us.
- The story of a damaged man who needs to be rescued by the love of a good woman is as old as time. But there was something different about the way E.L. James told this story that made it stand out. I think part of it was the simple writing, part of it was the kinky element that was still taboo, and another part of it was the availability of e-readers that allowed women to read this without embarrassment or judgment. Combined, it was a storm waiting to be unleashed. The publishing world will never be the same.

Closeted Fandom

Does anybody else suffer like me? I'm a "closeted" fan of FSOG. I wish I could simply be very open on my Facebook page, but unfortunately my family, friends, and peers aren't very supportive. To avoid cat fights with them, I just keep my love of FSOG in the groups and on my profile to a minimum, but definitely wish I could simply scream North and South about how much I love this fandom.

- You're not alone. I think many of us here are in the same boat!
- If I talk about FSOG, my girlfriends look at me as if I'm a pervert.
- I just keep it all to myself unless I am in my Fifty's groups.
- My family knows how I feel. One daughter is very supportive. She does not partake, but she gets it. Others are not understanding at all. I don't even discuss it around them. I have a growing list of friends who I share with. I guess because of my age, people are shocked that I'm into Fifty Shades.
- I try to keep FSOG stuff off my timeline, too. I'm not ashamed; I love all my FSOG friends dearly. I just have to manage my business life, and that can be a delicate balance.
- People around me just make fun of my interest in FSOG. They don't understand, and I feel weird and abnormal when they ask me about it. I usually don't speak about it.
- I have friends on Facebook who would be shocked if they knew I read FSOG. I homeschool my kids and there are a lot of religious people that I interact with on a regular basis. I love this group because it is secret, and I can be totally open here without judgment. Very rarely do FSOG posts end up on my personal Facebook page. I just don't want to deal with the judgmental people who are on my friends list. I am getting bolder by feeling that I just don' t care who knows if I love FSOG. But I'm not quite there yet.
- I keep my wall limited to anything in a gray area. There's a reason I am in a "secret" group.
- I keep FSOG and anything pertaining to sex off my timeline. It just makes life a little simpler.
- I've decided at 46, I no longer care what people think about what I enjoy reading. I love erotic romance stories. It's healthy. It's normal. I don't apologize for it. There, I said it. Plus, there must be a lot of closeted FSOG fans given its unrivaled success.

- It's always been a taboo to speak of our sexual preferences. This is still true in most of our circles.
- Well, I for one am glad there so many of us that are on the same page.
- I must be weird because I've never been a closeted fan of anyone or anything. I don't share the BDSM items only because I have a number of friends who would be flat on the floor, so I save those for my groups. And just for clarification, I am not in nor am I looking to be in a BDSM relationship. I have lots of questions, and can appreciate the beauty in some of the photos that are shared. Being a domestic abuse survivor makes me leery of anything that would trigger or remind me of my past. Oh, and I'm 62, but can fangirl with the best of them!
- I'm not really a closeted fan, I just keep the "deeper" things off my wall, for many reasons. I just don't want the drama from some of my friends and family. I'm from a very religious family. They would never appreciate the things we talk about in this group. I'm 56. I do what I want, when I want, and how I want, but I avoid the drama.
- I'm a closeted fan of FSOG. Most of my friends are church friends that just wouldn't understand.
- Everyone thinks I'm crazy for still obsessing about FSOG. There are very few outside of my Facebook life that I can talk to about it. That's why I love all of you.
- Believe me; I'm with all of you. I just don't get why people get so judgmental about what you like to read. It just forced me to hide what I read. Or just hold back on commenting. So I just keep to my favorite group. I love it here.
- I have a lot of people in my life that wouldn't understand and a hubby that thinks FSOG and the people who read those kinds of books are perverted. He saw that I had the FSOG trilogy books loaded on my e-reader, and got really mad at me and started wondering about me and our marriage. I won't go into all of the details, but suffice it to say that I've removed all FSOG related items off of my real Facebook page and made a fantasy profile to put

all of my FSOG, BDSM, and sexy stuff there. Now I don't have to worry about anyone seeing something they shouldn't see.

- It's sad we have to censor ourselves around so many. These groups allow us to be who we are and discuss what we like. My closest friend who I've been friends with for over 30 years is very religious. I can't share my love of this book and others because she looks down on them. It's so sad that I have to keep this private from someone, who I shared so much with. Glad I have this group!

- I never post anything Fifty related to my page. I don't know if anyone I personally know likes FSOG. I've been a part of this group since around the time I first read the books, so it never dawned on me to post about it to my page. I always posted anything Fifty related to these pages.

- The way I look at it, I'm not ashamed of it, but I don't need to wave it in other's faces who aren't open to it.

- I got tired of the eye rolling. If someone is eye rolling, I've gotta put that to good use. Haha.

- I'm not ashamed, but I simply try to avoid the eye rolling by not advertising on my page about the level of my fandom. Here's a quick funny to share: During a presentation for women at church, I mentioned that I had read a trilogy that no one seemed to have heard of because no one was discussing it. I grinned, and then said the title of the books and how much I enjoyed reading them. There was quite a bit of giggling and smiling. After the seminar and for weeks later, you wouldn't believe the number of ladies who privately told me they had read them also.

- Saying that reading the Fifty Shades books makes you a pervert or sex freak would be like saying that reading *Twilight* makes you a vampire or reading *Gone with the Wind* makes you a Southern Belle.

Sweetest Taboo

Why do you think FSOG was so controversial when it came out? Do you think it still is?

- I think there was a lot of controversy because kink was not so out in the open. Yes, people participated in it, but it was not openly talked about by the majority. When I first heard of the book, all I heard was that it was "mommy porn." I'm not a prude, but I thought, "I don't want to read that!" Sometime later, the hype was still going and I decided I wanted to see what it was all about. I was immediately hooked by the love story, and read the trilogy in 3 1/2 days. I couldn't put it down! And this is what I've shared with other women since then: The sex is amazing, but you have to look past the sex and comprehend the story. It's a beautiful love story that many of us can relate to.
- People are close-minded and judgmental, and some are just afraid of what they don't understand.
- I want to yell, "Come on people! What are you afraid of? That maybe you will like what you read?"
- I think anytime you tap into something that is different, it causes controversy. But I think when you throw in sex, people lose their minds.
- Maybe it was controversial because the movie openly told people it was R Rated, and there was sex in it. There are plenty of movies out there that had as much sex and violence as it did. I think these were people, who never bothered to look into the books or movies, and knew nothing about them except what other people told them. Of course they also had selective hearing.
- BDSM is/was controversial and E.L. James made it mainstream. Here we have a woman telling men how to please women. I think many men think they already know how to please a woman, and certainly don't want to be told how to do it. "Who does she think she is anyway telling me how to please a woman?"
- Yes, but E.L. James wins in the end. She has countless fans, one of the most read books in history, and a record-breaking movie. Who cares what the critics say?
- I started reading it, because I heard it was "mommy porn." I love a dirty mind and lots of sex. I did quit

reading it when I got to the Contract. I was really mad and hated Christian. I thought he was a controlling, possessive stalker and a manipulative, sick pervert. I didn't read the book for a couple days. I kept seeing things on the TV about the books, and picked it back up. I'm so glad I did. I see Christian in a whole different light now. I love the love story and the sex. However, I have to admit I wouldn't enter into a serious relationship with a guy like Christian. I'd have a good time with him, and then discard him. As far as E.L. James' writing style, it isn't that bad. It's very British, so it's different than what we may be used to, but it isn't bad. Of course, I've read much more well written pieces. I read a book this week that was very poorly written; one of the worst I've ever read. It sounded like a junior high kid wrote it. E.L. James' writing isn't that bad!

- I didn't like Christian at first either. He came off as a creep. I'm also glad I kept reading. *Darker* and *Freed* were so worth it!

- I think is was controversial when it was first released because it caught on so quickly and spread like wildfire. I'm sure there were books with similar content out there already, but FSOG just took off. I think it still has some stigma, but it has definitely left an impression on how open or close-minded people can be about erotica.

- I think it was the first peek into the BDSM lifestyle for a lot of people. Now that they've heard of it, and maybe dabbled in it, it's not so risqué.

- I think it's controversial because people mix everything in it, saying it's a story of woman being beaten, or just a sex tale. People stop at the cover without seeing what is within it, which is the story of a tortured man encountering love.

- I do think the content should be limited to those mature enough to handle it. I've seen some stories about younger kids, who think it's okay to be beaten, etc. They need to know how to distinguish a Dominant from a misogynist.

Dominant? Or Misogynist?

Is there a difference between a Dominant and a Misogynist? If so, please help me understand the distinction.

- A Dominant is NOT a Misogynist. Never confuse the two. A Dominant needs his submissive to be strong. A misogynist expects the women to be weak or works to bring them down so that they feel weak and powerless. Women are drawn to dominant men because they complete them but also complement their submissive tendencies and deep aches. Women are also drawn to misogynists, for other reasons, but the two are not the same. Not even remotely. A Misogynist is a person who dislikes, despises, or is strongly prejudiced against women. A Dominant is a person who likes (loves) women, and is energized by a strong submissive woman, but doesn't like a weak woman. A Misogynist may welcome a doormat, but a Dominant prefers to open the door to the play room; to push the frontier of erotic edge with consent.
- This is so very true. I love this. Thank you for explaining it to others!
- I think the definition of misogynist says it all: 1. a person who hates, dislikes, mistrusts, or mistreats women. Ideally, a Dominant likes or even loves women. Quite a clear distinction.
- I can totally understand that the threshold and desire for pain differs for different people. And I can also totally understand someone exerting that pain to someone else who wants or enjoys it. I just don't think that makes that person, the Dominant, a misogynist. I agree that it has to do with whether the man/Dominant likes or hates women.
- A Dominant is hardly an abuser. Not if they're a true bona-fide Dominant!
- I've lived with a misogynist. I've lived with an abuser. I've lived with a Dominant. I can tell you now that actions speak louder than words. Whether or not the misogynist/abuser says they love the woman is neither

here nor there. Their actions denote that they do not. A Dominant's actions quite clearly show, they do indeed love.

- We may not recognize it right away, but there is definitely a difference between a misogynist and a Dominant. There are definite signs.

To the H8ers

I posted this quote on my timeline, and thought I'd also post here: "You think it's cool to hate things. And it's not. It's boring. Talk about what you love and keep quiet about what you don't." By Unknown.

- Isn't it sad that people put down Fifty, especially when they haven't even read it? It's fine if they're not interested in reading it, but to me it is NOT fine to put something down that you don't even try to understand! That is called prejudice.
- Too right. No hate, no judgment.
- Really makes me mad. I remember when the books first came out that a lot of guys made very sarcastic comments. I just asked them if they had read the books. I think maybe they felt threatened by the books. Afraid that they would be compared to Christian in the bedroom. I also get mad with the people who say it's about abuse! I hated it when Christian beat Ana with the belt, but she asked him to. I am totally against woman and child abuse, and the only abuse I could see was Elena's treatment of Christian.
- It's so true. Know your facts before making accusations. Elena took advantage of his situation.
- I was talking a few months ago to an extreme feminist who kept going on and on about how Christian was abusive. The only "abuse" I saw Christian inflict was the scene with the belt, and even that wasn't abuse more than it was Christian losing control of himself. The out-and-out abuse I saw was Elena's abuse toward Christian.
- It blows my mind how many people are outspoken against a "love story with a little kink" (as E.L. James

25

calls it), but they jump up and cheer at violence and murder!

- I was like, "Shut the f*ck up. You need to be reading the books again and this time stop seeing f*cking abuse everywhere." Especially in *Darker*, Christian *constantly* asked Ana if this was what she really wanted, or said, "We'll try this and if you don't like it, just tell me to stop." The biggest indicator that Christian had changed, was on his birthday. Ana gave him the Dom jeans, butt plug, and nipple clamps to get him back into the playroom. She asked, "How should I behave?" Christian responded, "Behave any way you want to." To me, this signified that Christian was seriously letting go of his need to dominate and control.
- I tell the haters, the ones shouting out against the books or movie who haven't read or seen them, even if it spoiled the ending, "Hey, everyone - SHE LEFT!" That's the POINT! Ana didn't take it!
- Exactly! And *that* was the catalyst for him to realize that he couldn't live the way he'd been living. He could either have his punishment kicks or he could have the girl. He chose the girl, which showed an immense amount of growth on his part.
- As an abuse survivor, I must admit that the first time I started reading it, I was more than a little bit triggered, especially when I got to the contract. At that time, I hadn't yet received any counseling, and I wasn't able to see beyond the BDSM aspect, which in my opinion now is such a small part of the whole story. After counseling and some wonderful support, I decided to try it again. And I fell in love with the whole story. I could finally see that it wasn't "abuse" in the truest sense of the word. Some of his actions, some people would interpret as such, but I disagree with them.

Impact of Fifty Shades

How did FSOG get you to "see things differently?"

- I see sex differently now. The next time I have sex, I think I'd like to have it a bit rough or little kinky. It depends on the guy of course, whether he likes it, too. Or we could just watch FSOG together and he might understand my intentions.
- I see how sex meets different people's needs in different ways. I also wonder how one's past experiences impact what drives them sexually. And it also gave me a lot of fun ideas to try!
- Made me accept that my desire for a rough, kinky, dominant man was okay.
- I can't say that I see the things differently. I see things for what they are. I'm happy it's been brought out in the open. These inner fantasies have always existed, and E.L. James was bold enough to put it out there. Though I truly don't understand how she managed to bring it to the forefront when there was already so much erotica existing. Maybe it was the timing, on the tail end of the *Twilight* saga. Either way, I'm glad the word is out!
- I see sex differently; I love spicing things up in the bedroom. I feel confident about my sexuality where I didn't before. And having a loving, trusting husband is a plus. I learned that a little kinky f*ckery is awesome.
- I think there were a lot of factors influencing the success of FSOG. The *Twilight* connection was HUGE in getting fans to read it. Also the fact that it was controversial, both in terms of it being or not being true to *Twilight*, but also because the subject matter spurred the discussion. And of course, what's even more profound are the "deeper" reasons people resonated with the books. The discussion of pain vs. pleasure, the repercussions of abuse (his mother and Elena), Ana's leaving when it went too far, and even the relatively simple writing made it easier and more relatable. Of course, the power of LOVE to transform was the most important topic in these books. As I saw it, the powerful, life-changing soul connection of Ana and Christian, and how the fates conspired to help them reach their highest path/destiny.
- I'm always open to all possibilities in the bedroom, thankfully so is my husband. This book changed my life,

27

not so much the sex, but the connection Christian and Ana had. It sparked a fire in my relationship, and really got me through some rough times.

- I thought my husband and I had a pretty varied sex life but all of this has made us consider adding some things to it that we might not have otherwise considered!
- Sexual awakening is all I need to say. I always knew what I liked and now it's much more acceptable to communicate that to your partner with no judgment. Success of this series was the start of the e-book. Erotic fiction has been a genre I've read since my late teens in the 1970s. Yes, I'm the older demographic in this fandom.
- When you get married at 18 and 21 you have to find things to keep things exciting!
- I read Anais Nin and *The Story of O* and only fairly recently the *Sleeping Beauty* books by Anne Rice (A. N. Roquelaure). FSOG is different in a lot of ways. That's why we're here, discussing them!
- True, it is different, but I think it's the archetypes E.L. James used and her development of plot that make it different.
- The books changed me by allowing me to see the connection that there should always be with your partner. I don't know much about the kinky or Dom/Sub stuff. All my hubby and I ever looked at was porn, so BDSM was all new to me. Although I've read about it, we've never gotten around to trying any of it. It's always vanilla sex for me. Hopefully, I will try it one day.
- For me, it actually freed me from the "submissive" mindset. Having been exposed to the lifestyle at such a young age, I thought that was what I wanted most in my relationship(s) in the past, but especially with my husband. I tried for years to entice him to become more Dominant in our relationship (of course I know just how skewed that viewpoint/finagling is), and I was always missing that element in our relationship. It's funny (strange) how E. L. James' stories released me from that mindset, and I've come to know that I am not a "true submissive," but that I just enjoy the playtime. As a by-

product of the movie, my hubby likes to spice it up even more now.

Giving the Wrong Message? Or the Right One?

Why do you think critics believe so strongly that the Fifty series promotes rape? Some fans think the book is purely fantasy, and say that critics take the material way too seriously. Realistically, could you deal with a Christian Grey personality (rich or poor)? Be honest.

* Safe, sane, and consensual. Ana could walk away at any time. And she did.
* Why do critics believe the Fifty Shades series promotes rape? They're uninformed, haven't read the books, are fearful of sex and their own sexuality, and don't understand BDSM. I've dealt with a Christian Grey personality in my life, and it was difficult. I'm no longer involved with him, and we're not even friends anymore (my choice). He was involved in a BDSM lifestyle, and I didn't know it.
* I think it should be a soul connection with that man for me to be able to handle him. Because I'm a fragile personality, so I'd be easily crushed. I'd rather find a nice romantic, sensitive man.
* The critics don't bother to read the story behind the BDSM scenes. These naysayers say the books suggest that women want to be treated violently. I disagree. Rape is violent and not at all similar to the actions of Christian. Christian is very concerned about Ana's feelings and thoughts, while a rapist is not. If only they read the beautiful story, they would know it's far from a rape story.
* There are two key components that distinguish this story, which the critics don't know or try to understand:
1) The openness in which they discussed EVERYTHING,
2) the fact that she LEFT.
Without these two factors, I might have agreed with them.

- As far as whether I'd be interested in a Christian Grey type man, I guess I'd say that if it was a true soul connection, then I'd probably have as much courage as Ana.
- Safe, sane, and consensual. That's the part people seem to miss. Ana could always walk away. And in fact, that is what she did. Christian's response wasn't to browbeat her into submission, but instead to try a real relationship Ana's way. That doesn't sound abusive at all to me. Don't get me wrong, that doesn't change the fact that Christian Grey is more than a bit overbearing, however, Ana is able to keep up with him. So again, at the end of the day, it's about the choices that you make. Everyone isn't for everybody. There is nothing remotely abusive about his treatment of Ana, physical or otherwise. Most people argue that it's emotional abuse, but one's own personal views and belief system is what dictates abuse.
- To deal with a Christian in real life? I don't know. In the books and movie, it had been romanticized a great deal. It appears exciting to me; never boring. But maybe it would also put a heavy strain on my emotions.
- As a person who is not in love with a Christian Grey. I can easily say NO. There is no way in HELL I could put up with that. Rich, poor, homeless, whatever. But with that said, it's about a soul connection. When you really love someone, you don't know what you are willing to deal with until you have to go through it. This relationship would indeed be tiring to the psyche (as most relationships can be after a while), but it comes down to what you are willing to put up with. Again, it's about choices. Experts may say that no one should live like that; that it's unhealthy. But at the end of the day, you love who you love and to hell what other people think.
- This is a consensual relationship. Neither forces themselves on the other.
- Those tarnishing and bashing the movie and the books don't seem to realize that she waited for him for the longest of times, unaware that she was waiting. This is not just some love story. It is, as my mentors so

eloquently put it, a soul connection. Nothing is disconnected. Everything is linked. It doesn't matter if you meet up with your soulmate and never see them again, or see them again when you're much older. Everything is linked and others fail to understand that. There's a reason for every union.

- I'm sorry but there is no abuse in this series. I was abused for four years. I had the sh*t beat out of me for four years by an ex-boyfriend. So I know abuse. I can tell you that my husband saved me. So I'm sorry, but Christian Grey is not abusive. He just has an alternative lifestyle. And like you say, Ana could walk away at any time. And she did! She and Christian got back together. They're adults and they try stuff; and if she didn't like it, they didn't do it again. And I'm glad that he got rid of the canes because she'd never have gotten past that. My ex used to beat the sh*t out of me every day. I was told that I was nothing. I was told that I needed to do stuff that pleased him. That if I didn't have sex with him when he wanted to, then I got my ass kicked. Now *that's* abusive and *that's* taking someone's will away from them. So I know what that's like. I'm sorry to get so deep, but it pisses me off when they say that this story is about rape. Bullsh*t! People have the right to do whatever they want in the privacy of their own homes. And if that's what they want to do, then let them do it. It just upsets me so much that people think that she's being demeaned. I was demeaned and I put up with it when I shouldn't have, but I was told that nobody would want me and nobody would love me the way he loved me. I guess I thought that was love, but thank God my husband saved me, because my ex probably would have killed me.

Abuse

Abuse is a recurring theme throughout the Fifty Shades books, from Christian being abused physically, verbally, and emotionally as a baby/toddler to his relationship with Elena and perhaps more. Some see Christian's behavior toward Ana in the first book as being a form of abuse, either physical, emotional, or perhaps both. Others see it differently. This chapter highlights some of the discussions our group has had on this fascinating, complex, and controversial topic.

Is It Legal?

If Christian had been 16 (the legal age in Washington State) instead of 15, would you have felt differently about Mrs. Robinson? Or, could it be that it was not just his age, but the indoctrination into the BDSM lifestyle that impacts the "age of consent?" Thoughts?

• I don't have a problem with teenagers when they're both of "legal age," but your question involves an adult, and this topic resonates deeply for me. As both a parent and a high school teacher, my visceral reaction is that for an adult to touch a *child*, underscore child, under the age of 21 is wrong, not only legally, but morally and ethically as well. Sexual relations involve an emotional component that children aren't equipped to handle, especially when "relationships" end. I confess to being such a child, although I wasn't wounded for life. However, that's a rare exception. I wasn't scarred, thank God, but looking back, the adult should not have set his sights on me in the first place. Adults must respect boundaries in order to protect the innocent.
• If Elena is 40 or so in the books, and Christian is 28, there's a 12-year age difference, making her 27 or 28 when she seduces him. When I was 16, I had a few men in their late 20s asking me out. I went out with one of them, and it was no big deal. But a couple of the others were like, "You want to go for a drink?" and I replied, "I'm only 16! I can't go for a drink!" Their response was,

"Don't you think you look 21?" In hindsight, I didn't have any idea what thoughts were going through their minds. It was fun, but very innocent.

- But you know now as an adult, and that's the problem. They knew then, what you know now. And so they would've had the advantage over you, just as Elena did over Christian. Looking back, we realize the inequality of partners, and that's precisely why I object to the construct. Granted, FSOG is fiction, but the truths it tells are thought-provoking because of how well they reflect reality.

- Personally, I think this should be standardized across the country, but I also think there needs to be common sense applied. If a 16-year-old boy has consensual sex with his 15-year-old girlfriend, I do not think he should have to register as a sex offender for the rest of his life. I don't know how this can be done effectively, but I think smarter minds than mine should try to figure it out.

- I heard about an interesting case. The boy was a year older than the girl, who was legally underage. She got pregnant and wanted an abortion. He didn't want her to get one, but if she did, they could prove it was his and he'd go to jail for statutory rape. Talk about complex!

- This is what I meant when I said that sexuality among the underaged presents a sticky wicket. Even adults find relationships problematic. Everything is compounded for the young, who don't have the emotional or financial resources needed to confront the inevitable difficulties.

- I feel she took advantage of him when he was vulnerable in many ways, and she knew it. She is a predator. He could've said no, but since he had a horrible childhood, how could he? She knew that. Yes, it's BDSM, but some people use this to their advantage to get what they want and prey on people, like Mrs. Robinson did.

- Whew. This hits me in so many places. I'm going to try and keep it away from me, and look at it as "an outsider" if you will. Regardless of the age of any State, an adult over 21 should not entice a younger person into the position of making adult choices. They're vulnerable, and someone Mrs. Robinson's age, that should know better, to me is a predator. She took advantage of a confused, troubled boy for her own pleasure and entertainment. She taught him that BDSM was the way to let go of his frustrations, instead of trying to get him help to address his issues. Young adults of that age still have a lot of growing up to do, but it's not okay for an adult to take advantage of their sexuality.

- It occurs to me how interesting it is with boys that age, especially, in many ways, they're so immature. Yet we seem to excuse sexual exploration more with boys that age than we do with girls, who are at least a little bit more emotionally mature. What a weird world we live in.

- In some ways it's worse for boys, who don't have the same support as girls do. I think boys suffer more sometimes because they're so alone, and less likely to seek help, or they write it off as a necessary sexual initiation. Sad.

- As a man, I've got mixed feelings about this. If a hot sexy older teacher seduced me back when I was a teenager, I would've thought I'd died and gone to heaven. I'm not sure it would've damaged me at all.

- You do have a point. If she didn't hit you, smack you, or make you do things you didn't want to do, and you had to accept them to be her submissive; then yeah, I can see that. But I think in this case in my opinion, she took advantage of him in that way. But if it was like you're saying, like the schoolteacher who got pregnant by a minor boy. She went to jail, and they were in love. That's different. I totally agree with you in that case.

- The teacher whose "victim" was 12 years old? I still can't believe it, and yes they're apparently married now.

- But the reason I'm mixed up about this is that I wouldn't feel the same way at all if it's a teenage girl and an adult man. I know it shouldn't, but somehow it just seems different.

- Any teacher who touches a student inappropriately should be fired, and I've seen colleagues dismissed because of it. I've always thought they were crazy to give up their careers and all their schooling for adolescents whose music isn't even good. Lol.

- My issue isn't the age of consent, though I think it should be 18 across the U.S., it's that he still wasn't an adult. I'm going on the age of 18 since that is the legal age in the states; and as someone in her middle-to-late 20s, Elena knew it was wrong. I think she was attracted to Christian, and she used whatever excuse she needed to get her claws in him.

- Do you think your reason for thinking differently about it being *wrong* for an adult male to have sex with an underage girl would have anything to do with the fact that she could get pregnant? It's like we feel we need to "protect" our daughters from predators, but don't feel as drawn to "protect" our boys from them because it is the girls, who if they become pregnant, will have to deal with those repercussions for longer than boys will. I'm just curious about your thoughts on this subject.

- I would still think she was wrong. I mean Christian had a lot of emotional things going on with him, then Elena comes along and takes him "under her wing," so to speak. Even if he had been the legal age of 16, but still the same young Christian.

- Maybe pregnancy has something to do with it, but I think it's more than that. Maybe it's just because I'm a man, but if an older female teacher had seduced me when I was 15 years old, I would have thought I'd won the lottery. I honestly don't think I would have felt abused in any way. This may not be politically correct to say, but I think women generally hold the keys to consensual sexuality. I cannot have sex with my wife unless she consents to it, and sometimes she doesn't. But I can't think of a single time she approached me for sex, and I said, "No." But a little girl cannot give consent like that. She does not yet realize the power over men that she will one day wield. Does any of that make sense?

- Legal or illegal, the age difference at their ages between Christian and Elena is too big.

- Do you think there's a difference between seduction and the control she exerted over him with BDSM? Between a damaged, phobic 15-year-old and a "normal" 15-year-old?

- It's interesting that you mention that "women hold the key to consent." While that may be true a greater percentage of the time, a LOT of men do reject sex, too. And honestly since they're the ones who need to "perform," it's more complicated. There's some interesting research about "sex-starved wives." With the prevalence of low testosterone and ED (a lot of which is correlated to online pornography), the problem is increasing.
- Let's be clear here. I'm not excusing or defending any abuse of a child of either gender. I'm just saying that sexual abuse of a young girl by a man seems more serious to me than an adult female abusing a young boy. But that does not mean it's okay for the woman to abuse the boy. In the case of Christian, he was a very fucked up boy to begin with. It was terrible what Elena did to him, but, in hindsight, she may have helped him more than hurt him.
- Not being *able* to perform is different than not *wanting* to perform.
- It's still rejection, though, isn't it?
- I suppose, but if a man can't get it up for whatever reason, it's impossible for him to perform. If a woman is just not in the mood, then that's a choice.
- Well, it would depend on the definition of "perform." A woman being a receptacle vs. being in the physical/mental condition to climax is different.
- I believe Elena was 15 or 16 years older, not 12. It's only four years, but at those ages, four years is significant. And while there are occasions where that age difference might be innocent, in the vast majority, there's something "not right" on at least one side. I'm 40 and just going to the mall is annoying. I wouldn't want to be in a relationship with a teenager.
- My husband has rejected my advances before. So it does happen.

- What you said does make sense. May I go a step further and propose that the "rape culture" exists because men feel that women hold the key to consensual sex? I am in no way judging or stating that I believe this to be factual. I'm merely asking the question. Is that why we have this culture of rape in the world? That is where my mind jumped to when I reread your answer to my question above.
- I have a funny story to share. I had a fantasy about picking up a younger man. I was 28 at the time. I went through with it, but he turned out to be 21 and a LOT more experienced than I was! So much for my "older woman" fantasy!
- I did an interview with John Berger who wrote the book *Dateonomics*. I think he would say part of it is an inequality in the sexes. You'll see rape go up areas where there are more single men than women. The woman will generally be more promiscuous to attract men. Men then get the idea that it is normal, and expect it. Then you see an increase in sexual assaults.
- I'm also a cop, and years ago I did quite a few initial interviews for rapes, and they would fall into a couple of categories. There were the girls who were forcibly raped. And then there were girls who could tell the perfect date/acquaintance rape story, like they knew the law too well and nothing felt quite right. Those were rare, but those are the ones where you want to know the real story. Most fell into this weird, "We met at the bar, went back to the hotel/apartment, and he raped me" category. The scenario was that both had been drinking, not necessary drunk, but that varied. Occasionally the girl came in with her boyfriend. These all fell into the category of "Drank and made bad choice, then guy took advantage of girl." Now, some were just that. Bad choice, guy took advantage, girl was either mad or felt victimized, and called it rape. Some were raped, either because they were too drunk to give consent or because they said, "No." But this group feeds very much into the Jon Berger theory.

- Wow! Thank you for sharing your perspective. It's eye-opening to hear from someone firsthand how rape is viewed by law enforcement. It makes total sense and seems very logical. I just wonder about the first category you listed. What makes someone think it's okay to rape someone? Is it like you said, that it becomes normalized and then expected by these men, who are around promiscuous women? I know that does not make up all of the forcible rapes though.
- Those are bad men. Having studied a lot of serial killers, I learned that a category of killing is for sexual gratification, and a lot of rape is about power. I was listening to something tonight, a story about a drunk man, as in a drinker. He didn't have money, robbed a liquor store, things went bad, and he killed a man. He went to jail for life. The story then followed his two sons. One got married, had kids, and had a legit life. The other ended up like the father. When asked separately about why they turned out the way they did, they both said, "How else would I turn out with a father like I had?" The point of the story is that it's not about your situation, but the story you have. I suspect these rapists had a history that made them believe it was okay. And not just subtle social queues, but an environment that allowed them to fundamentally believe that's okay, which is different than getting used to women putting out, and then expecting it.
- Very different.
- Society has a huge influence on behavior as well. When rape and sexual assault are tolerated (or even celebrated), especially by celebrities or sports idols, then it becomes more of the "norm." Women are afraid to come forth out of fear of being labeled or condemned, and the problem is perpetuated and then escalates.
- Media/societal awareness of an issue has a potent effect, which can be either good or bad. FSOG has raised awareness of BDSM, which can be extremely healing for many people, and destructive for others. That's one of the reasons I love this group. Our purpose, as it was, is to discuss the pros and cons of the issues; to shine a light

on the positive messages in the books; and to delve into the "darker" sides of the characters to explain their motivation, behavior, and lessons in a productive way.

- For me it was Christian's being under 18, but also that she introduced him to the lifestyle.
- To me, if you're not old enough to vote, you're not old enough to consent to sex, especially with an older adult. Having said that, given that consent is legal at the age of 16 in Washington State, I'm not sure I'd have quite the same issues that I do, that he was raped at the age of 15. Yes, I'm going there. Elena had no business with Christian at that age under any circumstances! If she really wanted to seduce him, she should have waited until he was 16 years old before sinking her disgusting claws into him.
- This has been a very interesting and thought provoking discussion, and one of the reasons why I really love this group! Here's a link to some very interesting data which came from a published report that discusses the prevalence of false reporting of rape (https://icdv.idaho.gov/conference/handouts/False-Allegations.pdf). The report talks about 136 cases of sexual assault reported over a 10-year period, 8 (5.9%) are coded as false allegations. These results, taken in the context of an examination of previous research, indicate that the prevalence of false allegations is between 2% and 10%. I'd be interested in everyone's thoughts on this.
- I just had a thought come to mind from what I learned in sexuality training with ASECT (Association of Sexuality Educators, Counsellors and Therapists). Many times those who sexually abuse have been sexually abused as well, even to the point that they repeat the offense at an age that it happened to them. One has to think of what might have happened to Elena at age 15. Was her abuser a male who was 27 or 28? Sexual abuse and rape have to do with power, anger, dominance, control. No means no. I believe the person who is being abused or raped should always be listened to and believed until proven otherwise. The person doing the interviewing should be well-trained in the nuances of human behavior to

39

understand why, for some, it is easier to fabricate than be honest. They should observe body language. The statistics show that the incidence of lying is very low. So, the police or rape counselor needs to look beyond and be savvy enough to encourage discussion and thus the truth. I don't believe in inequality of the sexes. I have never felt inferior to any man. The men in my life treat me as an equal. I feel very uncomfortable with what appears to be your "blaming women" for causing sexual assaults....women ... more promiscuous to attract men... men think it's normal... sexual assaults increase. So, in your view, any time I like dressing in an alluring dress that shows off my breasts, I'm "asking for it?" I'm not at all comfortable with blaming. Boys will be boys is not how I view sexual assault. Boys and men take responsibility for their behavior. Should women only dress as nuns (I'm not castigating them) so they won't be viewed as rape bait? In my view and from what I have learned through my work experience, rape is always forcible. It doesn't matter whether or not they met at a bar, had a drink, or were inebriated. No is no. Rape is rape. Assault is assault.

- Thanks, but the example you used of a mother molesting her twelve-year-old son is a bit different than I had in mind. That is more than just an older woman seducing a young boy. There is incest, and all kinds of other issues involved with that sick story. I'm talking about the hot neighbor, or the hot looking teacher, seducing a teenage boy. I agree with you that a boy that age probably does not have the maturity to handle a real relationship like that. However, I still think most boys in that situation would not feel like victims, or like they had been violated. But a young girl in that situation would be much more likely to feel that way. I'm not sure if that's cultural, biological, or something else. Fortunately, (or unfortunately I suppose) I never found myself in that situation. So all I can go by is how I think I would have felt at the time. I probably would not have wanted it to end after only a one-night stand, and my self-esteem probably could not have handled it well if she had humiliated me in some way. So you have a point there. However, my point remains. I still think the harm, in general, is far less in young boys molested by older women, than the other way around. Just my opinion.

- Is a 15-year old boy prepared to support a child? Is he emotionally mature enough to handle a relationship, especially one with an obviously troubled if not deranged older woman? How would it affect his relationships later on in life? It certainly tarnished Christian's perspective on relationships. And if the woman gets arrested for rape, she'd be in jail and he'd have to raise the kid with no help - financial or otherwise. I think it might "sound" okay, but there are serious repercussions...

- There are some who are mature, wizened, and ready for life in an adult world at age 16, 17, and 18, and some who are not mature enough to be considered an adult at age 30! Adults who are truly emotional, intellectual, and physical adults, have an advantage over children in that they have life experiences under their belt. No adult should exert themselves over children sexually AT ALL, no matter their age. I get quite upset with the issue of authority, control, and power because from those behaviors can come dominance. This worries me because those characteristics can be used abusively. Elena knew that she was taking advantage of a needy young man with raging hormones, and it thrilled her sexually to have control over him. She was a sexual predator, a pedophile.

- There are progressive-minded police departments in our country and then there are some that are abysmally ill-trained. It's difficult to speculate how the police in Seattle would have reacted. Having said that, my impression is that Seattle is a progressive city and therefore one would hope they would hire and train police who are sensitive to the ill effects of abuse and rape; not blame the victim, but do a thorough job of investigating. Not much is given in the books to give much information with properly answering this question. I think the Greys would have had to take Christian to the police headquarters kicking and screaming in order to make the report. He was quite resistant in wanting to define his relationship with Elena as having had a negative effect on him. We do know that Christian's parents were well-known in the community and appeared to be involved and caring. I believe they would have fought very hard to bring justice for Elena's wrong-doing. And, I think the Greys would have been believed because of who they were. My guess is that Christian would not make a good witness. When I worked for Planned Parenthood, the statistics maintained by the Guttmacher Institute showed that 1 in 4 girls or young women were sexually abused and 1 in 5 boys or young men were sexually abused. Reporting was very difficult for males. Not as much so with females. The reasons warrant a different discussion. I think the net effect of Elena's arrest would have been for Christian to have retreated further into himself, possibly do harm to himself. I don't think he would have taken it well at all. My hope would be that Elena would have been convicted and appropriately punished with a very long-standing psychiatric evaluation and treatment.

Intimate or Not?

Do you think Christian and Elena ever had any kind of sweet sex scene or did they always include whips and restraints and violence? Do you think Elena ever restrained him with underwear or anything soft like that, or was it always cuffs and rope?

- I think she seduced him by keeping him on edge, vacillating between sweet and fiery. She knew it would make him infatuated with her, wanting to please her. And by being inconsistent, he had to be extra-attentive. So yes, I think she was "sweet," but only as a way to manipulate him. Just like that first kiss. Kiss first, slap second.
- So do you think he was in love/lust with her? I think he was heavily infatuated with her, more than he admits even to himself. That's probably why she still had a hold over him after so many years.

- When Christian said, "You never said you loved me," indicated that he loved her. Or at least he craved her love.
- Of course he did! There are all kinds of love. He considered her his savior, his lifeline, his awakening. Whether she reciprocated with sincere love is not really relevant. It was his feelings that were real.
- Elena was so very calculating and divisive; every interaction she had with Christian was to train him into being exactly what she needed to fulfill her needs for that particular moment. I, personally, do not think she ever truly took Christian's needs into consideration. She gave him the structure he needed to uncover his true inner-self and to help him see beyond himself, so that he could start on his ultra-successful journey in business. Beyond that point, there was nothing that she contributed. Her words at his birthday party that "Love is for fools," said it all.
- They were into punishments only.
- I don't think they were ever into "sweet" sex. They both loved it rough; the rougher the better. Christian experienced "sweet" sex, a.k.a. vanilla with Ana, and he discovered how incredible it could be.
- There's nothing sweet in Elena.
- No, sweet sex would involve holding. He said she never held him. I don't think they were ever intimate, just a Dom/sub sexual relationship.

Making Promises

In the beginning of *Darker*, Christian says, "Don't leave me again," Ana responds, "Okay." Does anyone else wish she had replied, "Don't hit me again?" How could she make that promise at that stage without making sure he had changed?

- She loved him regardless. She was miserable without him. Even though she wasn't his submissive, she didn't realize that a submissive has all of the control.
- She was overwhelmed with her emotions all over the place. She wasn't certain, but knew he needed to be reassured. Did she still have doubts? Certainly. She was

especially afraid that he'd hurt her again, emotionally or physically.

- I think she was willing to give him the benefit of the doubt. Plus, he had already said he wouldn't do it again in a sense. His demeanor had already changed so much; he was displaying promise on his end. I think it was the feeling behind the intention at the time that she said that.
- I think she really hoped he had changed, so she said yes. I do agree that maybe she should have waited before saying she wouldn't leave him again.
- I'd never leave such a gorgeous man!
- They had just finished hot, getting-back-together sex, and her mind was elsewhere. Wouldn't yours be?
- She liked some of the hitting/spanking. And she asked him to show her how bad it could be. He did so, and she "forgot" to use her safe-word. I think she realized that she held at least some of the responsibility for what happened. Not that this entirely discounts the fact that she was a newbie in this lifestyle, and Christian should have used better judgment. But it's not like he slapped her around, or that she was a battered woman.
- I respectfully disagree. I think he was both emotionally and physically abusive in the first book. Christian knew exactly how to lure her, and get her to do what he wanted. I understand how you feel about her not using the safe-word, and I disagree there, too. I think she was young and immature. And even if she was older, she thought she could tolerate six hits, or certainly thought he'd stop. I put 100% of the blame on Christian.
- Well, we have to agree to disagree. I think even Ana would agree with me. I don't think she ever saw him as abusive. She saw him as damaged and in pain, and she wanted to help "bring him into the light," so to speak. At the beginning he tried to treat her like one of his regular submissives. It wasn't until she left him that his eyes were opened, and he realized he had to treat her differently. She'd never be a submissive, but he had to have her anyway. It was the first time in his life that he wanted a "regular" relationship with any woman.

- Of course Ana would agree with you. She took on way too much of the blame, if you ask me.
- Beyond the final belt-whipping, when else was he physically abusive to her? And how do you think he was emotionally abusive to her? How did he change? Remember the hickey scene was in one of the later books. I thought that was pretty abusive, or at least childish. He never really stopped "stalking" her.
- A few examples of emotional abuse include separating her from others (by making her swear not to talk), his push-pull behavior, double standards (things he was allowed to do but she'd get punished for, i.e., eye-rolling), his "mercurial" mood swings, trying to control what she wore, ate, and did, etc.
- I know what emotional abuse is, but I don't know how you see it in Christian. We are all human, and we all make mistakes. I'd certainly not call myself emotionally abusive, and neither would my wife, but I've probably screwed up at some time in the last 31 years and done something emotionally abusive to her. And she has probably done the same thing to me. I've never really seen Christian and Ana's relationship as abusive at all. He screwed up a time or two, and paid a heavy price for it. He learned that she was not like his former submissives, and he learned a new way to be with her. Would you call him abusive to his submissives? They were adult women who went into a relationship with him with their eyes wide open. As long as he did not violate the agreements he made with them, and I don't think he would, then I don't think he was abusive to any of them either. It seems that you have a pretty negative opinion of Christian Grey. I thought you liked the books. Am I missing something here?
- Maybe everyone does some of these behaviors on occasion over many years. But to be so manipulative and cruel to her in such a short period of time was undeniably abusive in my book. Heck, the constant threat of physical punishment was abusive in and of itself. Whether it happened once or twice, or a hundred times, it was still cruel. Especially to someone who clearly said

"No." To me, one of the major things in these books, especially the first book, is that she could see he was abusive and she left. If she hadn't left, then I would hate these books. The key message is that because she left, he changed.

- As most of you know, I do have a lot of respect for people who are in a true BDSM relationship. What I mean by true is that it is safe, sane, and consensual. I can understand the need people may have to be in this kind of relationship, and can appreciate that position. I can even relate to several aspects of it. But Ana was not in the lifestyle and clearly abhorred punishment, and he knew that.

- Abuse comes in more than one form. Christian is a man of many talents, and emotional abuse was on that list. Maybe he did it subconsciously, but nevertheless he manipulated her and he knew it. He played on her vulnerability and desire to "rescue him." Maybe he didn't "slap her around," but he should've given her more time in the lifestyle to become comfortable before getting into punishment. Just look at how he wouldn't let her talk to Kate, making her hide the abuse from the ones closest to her; how he blamed her for not safe-wording; how he told her that if she left there was no coming back; and the constant push-and-pull. These are the hallmarks of abuse.

- Yes. Isolation is one of the hallmarks of abuse.

- That's because the abuser knows that if you tell those who are close to you what's going on, they wouldn't stop until you were away and safe from the abuser.

- But how did he change? Sure he said he'd never hit her with a belt again, and he treated her with kid gloves when they first got back together, but he was still controlling. He still stalked her. He gave her hickeys as punishment without telling her. He acted terribly when he found out she was pregnant. Once she asked to return to the RROP, he was way more careful with her, but beyond that, I don't see where he really changed all that much from the Christian in the first book. He was "mercurial" as Ana described him, but that's part of what she fell in love with.

- I can't believe some people don't think he changed! He got rid of all the instruments of torture. He was infinitely more gentle with her. He basically gave up his lifestyle. He allowed her to touch him. These are huge milestones.

- In *Darker*, Christian made really big changes for Ana. Even though he acted like a jerk about the pregnancy, there's no telling just how far he would've gone to hold on to Ana and the unborn child. He would've done anything to keep them.

- I'm not saying he didn't change after she left him. Sure he changed, but I don't think he was a monster in the first place. All I'm saying is that he was not all that bad in the first place, so there wasn't all that much to change. Sure, he got rid of a lot of his toys in the RROP, and he was willing to get rid of the whole thing for Ana, but she liked his "kinky fuckery," so she didn't want him to get rid of all of that. My point is that he was a decent human being to begin with, and he was a decent human being afterwards. He was just into some kinky shit; shit he was willing to give up if he had to in order to keep Ana. But he was always controlling, and I doubt that would ever change. Plus, I doubt Ana would want it to change. He was always a bit immature at times, but that probably came from his fucked-up childhood and the effect Elena had on him. He had no idea how to have a normal relationship with a woman, so he had to learn how to for Ana. In that regard, he certainly did change. He was willing to entirely give up the only lifestyle he knew, and learn something else, in order to keep Ana. She became his touchstone, his magic pill, if you will. Just being with her made him calmer. He could sleep better with her. He was a confused and fucked-up man, who became less fucked-up and more confident when he was with Ana. But his basic nature never really changed all that much in my opinion. He was always a decent and honest person, and he remained a decent, honest person. And as for her being afraid to tell Kate, that's because she was embarrassed, plus she had signed that non-disclosure agreement. When she asked him if she could talk to Kate, he reluctantly agreed. He didn't like it, but he didn't try to stop her. She chose not to discuss it with Kate, although I think she probably would have eventually, if Kate hadn't found those emails in the coat pocket.

- I don't know about "monster," but look at the definition of an "abuser" and look at Christian: controlling, stalking, punishing, telling her how to dress, what she could eat, and even who she could talk to!
- Just to be clear, are you claiming that Christian was an abusive and controlling man in the first book, but became a "normal" man in the later books?
- In abuse cases, the "monster" is the stronger party. While yes, Ana could've walked away and the warning signs were there, Christian was the stronger and more powerful (dark) billionaire with control over her. Not many women could resist that, much less a young, inexperienced college student. Of course, we know she ultimately did leave him, which was the catalyst for his dramatic change.
- If you really feel this way, then why do you like the books? Do you see them as "dark" romance? An evil billionaire who takes advantage of an innocent young girl and leads her to the dark side? Did she not have any responsibility or control in their relationship at all? Was she just a dupe who fell for the rich handsome man in spite of all the warning signs telling her to run away?
- I liked the books because of two factors: (1) She left and (2) he changed.
- I still don't quite understand where you're coming from, but I don't have to understand it. You have a right to see these characters however you want to see them, and so do I. The world would be a boring place if we all agreed on everything.
- Why have a discussion group if we all have the same view point?
- Basically, I see the books as telling the story of the transformative power of love.
- It was a sweet surrender.

- I wouldn't appreciate Ana saying, "Don't hit me again," right after the dialogue above it. It shows indirect anger that should be dealt with in a more direct, adult manner, not with a snarky remark.
- At Jose's show she had already addressed it in that manner.
- You're probably right, though I do think she could've said it to herself. It bothered me how she took too much of the blame. It also bothered me that she'd make this unconditional promise to him when it was, in fact, conditional.
- Maybe the promise meant something different to her and something different to Christian.
- She was just glad to be back in his arms again. When they spoke in the car after their reunion dinner, he asked her what she didn't like, and she said that "the whips and canes scared the living sh*t out of her," so he agreed never to use those or a belt on her ever again. She took a huge leap of faith to trust that he was being honest with her.

Which Hurts More?

Which is more painful, emotional or physical pain? Whose agony was more painful, Christian's or Ana's?
- Emotional pain. Christian's pain. Physical scars disappear more quickly than emotional scars.
- It's the greatness of the emotional pain that makes us feel physical pain. Like that hole in your chest when someone leaves you, and tells you that they don't want you anymore. The emotional pain can be so powerful that it can cause headaches, chest pain, etc. Sadly, I speak from experience.
- Emotional pain. I know from experience as well.
- Emotional pain. I'd even go so far as to say that what Christian experienced was spiritual pain. The tearing of his tenderly young spirit that seared/scarred him forever. Ana just happened to provide a healing salve that he could've never hoped to find on his own.

- I've been asked this question quite a bit, for I've suffered (since the age of 7) emotional, mental, physical, and sexual abuse, and out of them all it would have to be the emotional and mental pain that hurts the most. I always say that you can heal from the physical scars, but those emotional and mental scars are there for life. It's just a matter of how you learn to handle them.

- For me, it's Christian's pain. He's finally allowed himself to develop some feelings for another human being, but knows that he's sabotaged everything with his need to punish.

- Emotional Pain. That can stick with you for years and years if you don't seek the right help, and even then it can still hang around. I've experienced both in a relationship (in the form of emotional and physical abuse), and it took way longer to come to terms with the emotional side of things than the physical. I'm still not "normal" because of some of the emotional stuff. I don't think Ana's pain was any worse than Christian's, and vice versa. Everyone handles pain differently in all its different forms. Sometimes the emotional stuff doesn't stick with people and the physical stuff does, and vice versa. I think each person is different. Just from reading FSOG, I don't think you can clearly judge exactly how much pain Christian is feeling. The first books are told from Ana's side, so we sort of have a fair idea of exactly how it's affecting her, but other than what we learned in *Grey*, we just have to make assumptions about how much pain Christian is or isn't feeling. He says a few comments about being hurt especially in regards to the break up, but we have way more information on how Ana is feeling.

Christian's Indoctrination

Do you think Christian would've practiced BDSM if he hadn't met Elena? Was it his childhood that triggered it all, regardless Elena?

- I don't think he would have. She introduced him to it.

- Bitch Troll Mrs. Robinson introduced him to the lifestyle. Though I think he was right, that he'd probably have ended up like his birth mum if she hadn't.
- How would Christian have coped, since he had Haphephobia (fear of being touched), if he hadn't met Elena? If we could ask him, he'd say he would have self-destructed. That he was on his way to a life of drinking, fighting, and perhaps drugs. It's safe to say that he desperately needed discipline of some kind. And Elena did force him to focus. So, would he have discovered BDSM otherwise? Perhaps, because it did provide him with an outlet that was safe for him. I do think that it turned him into the sex expert we all crave.
- Don't you think he would've been a sex expert without practicing BDSM? I preferred Christian outside the Red Room of Pain, personally.
- Maybe, but I doubt it. I think his training helped him immensely with the mechanics, especially the focused attention. Now, when it comes to love, there's only one way to learn that.
- We all know Elena "beat the sh*t out of him," but it wasn't a cure. It actually reinforced the negative behavior, and he continued it by beating the brunettes (his 15 submissives). Wouldn't an enormous portion of love have been enough to free him?
- The only reason why he got into that lifestyle was because of Elena. So I don't think he would've gotten into it without her.
- Given the clues that E.L. James puts into the books about Christian's teen years, Christian's life could've gone sideways before he even got a chance to be introduced to BDSM. It's likely he'd have gone to juvie for beating the sh*t out of somebody before then. So it could really go either way. Fifty Shades of Grey (BDSM) or a really bad episode of Criminal Minds. (Or Paul Spector in The Fall). Your guess is good as mine.
- Elena was the catalyst that led Christian down the path to BDSM. I don't think he would have found it otherwise. The lifestyle (especially before FSOG), was

pretty underground. I do think that if he hadn't met Elena, he would've continued on the dangerous, self-destructive direction he was already headed in.

- Okay, we blame Elena, but don't you think somehow she saved him from self-destruction or becoming a villain? So maybe she isn't such a bitch troll?
- She definitely saved him. I'm not denying that. But she sexually abused him, which in my mind makes her a bitch troll. Whether or not he knows it, she had a negative effect on him. I was sexually abused, so I know how it feels to have a monster hurt you. Yes, being sexually abused helped me on some level, but it also destroyed me.
- I did a role play as Elena (with a teenage Christian), and it was very interesting to get inside her head. She had a lot of issues herself, an abusive husband for one. She's not "pure evil," and in a lot of ways I think she felt like she was helping not only Christian, but Grace, too. Her friend was struggling with her out-of-control teenage son, and Elena made a world of difference to him. Was it "wrong?" Of course. She took advantage of a vulnerable, needy, troubled teenage boy. (I played it like she didn't think he was 15, but 16 instead, making it legal in Washington state). Her biggest offense, in my opinion, was her inability to infuse any love or caring into the relationship. But that is probably not her fault. I'm guessing she had a pretty difficult childhood herself.
- There would've been a lot of potential paths for him, with BDSM being something that he might or might not have discovered. I agree that it's a hidden lifestyle, but I also think as soon as he found out about the idea of bondage, he'd have been intrigued.
- So Elena saved him from self-destruction, but she was a child abuser, right? Showing him no love, Grey grew up convinced that BDSM was the only way to interact with women. Until he met sweet Ana.
- This might be a long shot, but I think I side with Christian to some extent on this. I think Elena helped him in some sort of a way, when therapy wasn't working. Granted, she molested him and that is never condoned, but what if

he had been 21? Would it still have had the same effect on him? I think he would have eventually landed on a similar path on his own without even realizing it, due to his Haphephobia. It's obvious that Christian is a sexual person by nature. I think perhaps it may have been a softer form of BDSM, but he still would've figured out the "Oh, I can tie her hands so she can't touch me" solution eventually.

- I don't think he would've practiced the lifestyle. But without it, I don't know if he would've become who he did in life. It was a blessing and a curse. It helped put him on a better path, but it also hurt him and caused him more emotional trauma.
- Do you think if he'd been introduced to BDSM at an older age or by someone else, he would've been the same?
- He might have, but maybe not as wealthy or famous. Or it could've backfired and he might have ended up like Jack Hyde, Ana's boss.
- Ana wouldn't have called Elena a child abuser if he had started BDSM at the age of 21.
- Very true.
- Or even 16, the legal age in Washington, I believe.
- Absolutely it was Elena who taught him about BDSM. Without her, no BDSM. But who knows what he might've turned in to, if he hadn't met Elena? According to him, he was well on his way into alcohol abuse and trouble, and he felt she saved him from that kind of life. So either way, his future was bound to turn out bad. But we all love the Christian Grey that blossomed after he met Ana.

Elena – The Confession and the Lure

In *Freed*, Christian tries to explain to Anastasia the impact Elena had had on his life. "And you know something, Ana? My world came into focus. Sharp and clear. Everything. It was exactly what I needed. She was a breath of fresh air. Making the decisions, taking all that sh*t away from me, letting me breathe."

Many of us vilify Elena, but when you read this part, did it help you understand her better? Understand why Christian needed her? Have you ever wanted someone else to call the shots?

- We all agree that a grown-up woman shouldn't be taking advantage of a young kid. Yet I can see it a bit differently now. I can see how she helped him control his anger and stay in school. My only complaint is that as an educated adult woman, she shouldn't have introduced him to BDSM at such a young age. She should've let him learn about love and prepare him for a good relationship with girls his own age.
- She was certainly too selfish, and too screwed up herself to take the high road like that.
- There are days that I really wish I could have someone calling the shots for me. Some days I feel like I wish I could be a kid again, and not have a care in the world. Sadly, that's not life.
- It's like looking back when you were younger, and you didn't have to worry about anything. Your parents made all the decisions, paid all the bills, etc.
- It did make me understand her more, but I still can't forgive what she did to him. You cannot tell me that she did what she did to him for unselfish reasons, in order to "help him." I won't believe that. Do you think Elena tried to *save* him from the beginning? Or is that a farce?
- As a f*cked-up and confused teenager, he felt that he had a lot to live up to with the Greys, and felt that he didn't belong or fit in with them. That's a lot of pressure for a kid to have the weight of the world on his shoulders. It probably overwhelmed him to the point where he just couldn't think straight. Elena entered his world, and snapped him out of wallowing in self-pity; while also taking control of his life, and making all of his decisions for him. It allowed him a chance to gain confidence in himself, and allowed him to focus, and straighten his life out. The only problem I have with all of this, is that he

could've gotten all of this from Grace. She would've been a rock for him and very supportive. If only he had given her a chance.

- No, I think she wanted Christian for a "pet project".
- She doesn't seem like the type to let anyone go, least of all Christian. He was her favorite plaything.
- I have always thought that Elena was abused as a teenager (or younger) and was submissive to Linc, and he was an abusive Dom. So when she got a chance to find someone to dominate, it was cathartic for her. It's the typical "abused becomes the abuser" cycle.
- I think that Elena has some issues that go deeper than Christian. I think in some ways, she is a damaged woman, and you know what they say about damage people. "They tend to find other damage people."
- You're totally right.

Ana the Virgin

Anastasia Steele. Twenty-one-year-old virgin; intelligent, yet inexperienced and naïve; smart, but as far from worldly as a person can be, meets Christian Grey, twenty-seven-year-old megalomaniac billionaire CEO and certifiable sex god. How did Ana's inexperience impact her relationship with Christian, for him as well as for her?

What Did I Do?

The morning after their "first time," Christian had a "pervading sense of guilt." Why did he feel so conflicted? Why the guilt? He was in too deep by now, no doubt.

- He'd never taken anyone's virginity. Perhaps he didn't feel worthy of that gift, and felt guilty because of that. He probably also didn't expect to feel as deeply as did about her and the whole experience.
- He felt he took her innocence, and was about to lead her down a path he wasn't sure whether he should subject her to.
- It's indicative of his inner struggle. He didn't understand the distinction between sex and "making love." The purely physical act vs. the integration of emotional and spiritual components.
- What about this abstract thought: Christian might have felt like he took advantage of an innocent, much as he had been taken advantage of as a small boy? Thus, the guilt.
- I was just thinking the same thing! And that may have been part of his revelation about Elena later in the series. He thought of how Ana was innocent like a child. Didn't he compare her to a child at one point?
- Interesting! I was thinking she was talking about his being abused as a toddler!
- I wasn't really thinking in terms of abuse. Just innocence and how it was taken from him, and he took it from Ana, so he thought.

- Oh. See, I went directly to Elena in my mind. How she took his virginity. I know he suffered greatly before he became a Grey, but a blessing from that time would be that at least he was not sexually abused as a toddler. Or at least as far as we know, he wasn't.
- Maybe not sexually. God, I hope not! Though it's entirely possible. But he was most definitely abused, in infinite ways, as we know.
- I think he felt that he took advantage of an innocent girl, and he didn't understand the emotions that he felt for her. He never felt guilty before because he never really loved someone that way before Ana. He was all confused about himself and the situation. He kept reminding himself that "It's just sex," but inside him there was so much more. The feelings that he kept suppressing because they were odd and unknown to him.
- I think you all have pretty much hit the nail on the head. Ana's virginity is representative of her innocence, not just sexually but emotionally. Christian thinks of himself as broken, a monster. I believe that the guilt came from him seeing himself as taking those characteristics away from her. That he had brought this girl into this world without a clear understanding of just exactly what she's gotten herself into, yet also knowing, even now, he won't be willing to let her go despite that. He was in deep with Ana, but he still didn't think too much of himself at this point. So of course, he'd struggled with his decision to sleep with her. Even then he didn't know how this was going to play out. He still believed at this point in the game that the only way he could make any kind of relationship work with her was under his typical BDSM terms.
- This tells me he'd never "taken" a virgin before.
- Yes, he said he never had. Ana was his in *every* way. He didn't want to defile her, but then again he very much wanted to.
- This leads me to another question. Why do you think Ana chose debasement? Why do you think she selected Hardy as her favorite author?

- I think it's interesting that Ana was so over-eager, especially with such an enigmatic man. She barely knew him, and he already said he wasn't any good for her. Moth to a flame?
- Yes, there is definitely that.
- *Tess of the D'Urbervilles* has some amazing similarities to *FSOG*. However, Tess ended rather sadly. One of the main similarities that is fairly easy to see is how both women are thrown into new worlds they didn't see coming. Ana is thrown into Christian's.
- Well, she said if there were only two choices, Alex's debasement or Angel's high ideals, she'd take the debasement. But we all know she just wanted Christian any way she could get him and same for him towards her.

Guilty As Charged

Why was guilt such an unfamiliar feeling for Christian Grey?

- I think Christian has trained himself to "push aside" any concept of guilt. He justifies all his actions. But I think it's always there, lingering under the surface.
- Because he didn't give a sh*t usually about other people's feelings. He was unapologetic for his ways of being.
- Yet he also was brought up to "do the right thing." Do you think he was ever conflicted?
-
- But he hid the way he lived. He's had to feel guilty on some level at some point. That may be another reason he turned his back on Catholicism because it's known for instilling guilt.
- To me, Christian built an emotional wall very early in life. In the book, it states he was withdrawn and didn't speak for years. To me, he didn't allow himself to feel so he wouldn't be hurt again.
- I don't think he was conflicted anymore, maybe when he was younger. I also think maybe he might feel concerned if it was something that might get back to his family.

- Why should he feel guilty about the way he lived? Can you define what you mean by "the way he lived?"
- I mean being a Dom. I'm not saying he should feel guilt for living that way. I just think he had some guilt about living that way since he hid the lifestyle from others. (My opinion.) He especially felt guilt about that lifestyle after Ana left him. That maybe this wasn't the way he should be living. Didn't they also talk about how he was paying for Leila's school because he felt a bit of guilt? He felt guilty because he couldn't help his birth mom, too.
- But it's okay to be private about one's sex life. I don't think he felt guilty at all about that. It's not like he was hiding a lie, he just wasn't volunteering personal information about himself.
- I think every time he talked or thought about having a "dark soul," he was reflecting as well as maybe justifying his guilt. I think he knew he led on some of his submissives, but he defended himself with the "If you leave it's over forever" talk and in-depth contracts. Maybe I'm wrong, but I think some, if not most of them wanted "more" with him, and he felt guilty about that. Hence paying for their education, letting them keep the cars, etc.
- I agree that he gave all those things to the subs because he felt guilt about the things he did to them, and maybe for leading them on. Describing himself as a "dark soul" is a good example of his guilt. I never could figure out why he described himself that way, but having guilty feelings is a good explanation.
- Because Elena taught him to ignore it. Obviously, she never felt a twinge of guilt.
- I don't think Christian had any kind of conscience or guilt.
- Do you think he was a narcissist?
- No, he was too full of self-loathing to be a narcissist.

BDSM

FSOG opened up the discussion of BDSM to a much wider audience. But what is BDSM, really? To start with, BDSM is an acronym that's a combination of practices: B/D, which stands for Bondage/Discipline, D/s, which signifies Dominance/submission, and S/M (or S&M), which covers sadism and masochism.

As this chapter illustrates, our Deeper members represent a range of interest and practice in BDSM. Some are fully "in the lifestyle" 24/7; others have enjoyed some parts of the BDSM experience, and others have little or no interest. Whichever way our interests lie, we love a good discussion about trust and faith, control vs. release, pain and pleasure.

The Importance of Trust in a BDSM Relationship

The quote, "Trust is our relationship with the unknown," blows me away in how it relates to FSOG. This makes me think about the "trust" in a BDSM relationship. The letting go. What are your thoughts?

- This is so thought provoking. Trust is always earned, in every equation. I think what we fail to realize is, trusting ourselves is just as important.
- So true! I tend to trust too soon and too easily, and inevitably get disappointed or let down or taken advantage of.
- On the flip side of that coin, waiting too long to give your trust can also create disappointment.
- I think it's important to realize that trust isn't absolute. You can trust someone to pick you up on time, for example, but not trust him or her with you pin number for your ATM card or to raise your children if something happened to you.
- Looking at Ana and Christian, she trusted him in so many ways, yet not in others. And vice versa. They had to go through a lot to build their trust.
- So very true. There are "levels" of trust.

- Trust is very important in all relationships, be they between men and women, same sexes, friendships, love relationships, bosses and employees, or BDSM arrangements.
- Trust is a necessity in any relationship, but most of all between a sub and her/his Dom! That is something that needs to be earned by the Dom because the submissive puts so much of her/himself into the Dom's safe keeping!
- Very true. Trust is a big issue in any relationship, but especially a BDSM relationship. If a woman submits, she needs to be sure she can trust her partner/Dom and vice versa. As Christian said, "The submissive has the power in a BDSM relationship." She must trust him enough to guide her through her experiences.

Hit Me with Your Best Shot

For me, it's easy to see why Christian enjoyed the S&M of BDSM when he was a submissive. He probably got pleasure and felt he deserved to be hit or beaten by Elena. What's harder for me to understand is why he'd enjoy *inflicting* pain. Perhaps he felt like the person receiving it enjoyed it as much as he had. What are your thoughts?

- Being a switch (someone who switches back and forth as Dominant and submissive), the receiving of pain is about having the desire to please your Dom and testing your personal limits. When you're the one inflicting the pain, you use it to truly enlighten a sub; to teach them that fine line between pleasure and pain.
- I think it's more about feeling numb and then doing something, sometimes something extreme (in some people's eyes). To feel again; whether it is receiving pain or inflicting it. If you feel, you know you're still alive.
- I really feel like Christian had sadist tendencies. If you look at the scene where he hit her with the belt, he was turned on by it. In Grey he says, "I drop the belt, savoring my sweet, euphoric release. I'm punch-drunk,

breathless, and finally replete." It sounds to me that he is a switch for sure.

- In that scene you also see the pain in his eyes (in the film). I keep thinking he is thinking to himself, "Why isn't she using her safe-word?"
- You can see both feelings of pleasure and pain in his eyes.
- Christian's interest in BDSM went beyond the "lifestyle;" it actually *became* his lifestyle. For him, it wasn't just a sexual experience, it was deeper. It was where he didn't feel judged for feeling the way he did. BDSM was familiar to him on a whole different level. He knew abuse and related that to the punishment in the lifestyle. One doesn't necessarily have to do with the other, but I feel he made that connection. You know, how when you have a pain somewhere, and you pinch yourself to distract yourself from the first pain. I think as a submissive, he felt that way about it.
- By administering the punishment, it kept his world in order; kept him in control. Also, I think it took him back to the times he received the pain.
- I can totally and completely understand the desire to feel pain as a way of enhancing awareness and adding to sensation that leads to pleasure. What's more challenging is to understand the desire to inflict pain when the other person doesn't enjoy it.
- That's the sadist part. For me, I always like to believe in safe, sane, and consensual. I don't think I can answer your question.
- I think in his submissive life he might've felt that he didn't deserve anyone. That he deserved to be beaten. And if by beating him it made someone happy, then he was happy. In his Dominant life, it was because he learned about sex this way. It was the only way he knew. It was also a control issue for him. He had to be in control of everything at all times.
- I think Christian equated punishment with love. It's like a small child that acts up to get attention. It might be negative attention, but it's still attention. In the same

way, when you're punishing (or being punished), you have the other person's complete attention and focus.

- Honestly, I think it came from a past life. Those kinds of compulsions are often karmic flashbacks; lessons we're here to learn and re-learn.

BDSM: What Triggers Interest?

Perhaps the BDSM traits were with Christian long before Elena. In the prologue, we read where young Christian witnessed the scene where Ella was being beaten with a belt by her pimp. What do you make of this and how it stayed with Christian into adulthood?

- I hadn't thought about that. Perhaps his mother was a masochist.
- You could be right about him; about when he was small and watched his mother get beaten, and then him being beaten. He always thought about the pimp beating him and burning him; that horror. No wonder he was so f*cked-up.
- There's a fine line there, as BDSM is supposed to be safe, sane, and consensual. Abuse isn't. His witnessing abuse must have sparked the need of revenge. Belting/whipping/caning his subs was to punish his mum for neglecting him. But I think he jumped into this cycle too easily. Using BDSM to punish for even the smallest of demeanors. In a way, he was perpetuating the cycle of abuse. And yes BDSM is not abuse, but I believe Christian used the lifestyle as an excuse to be able to use physical punishment.
- I think Christian's past prompted his need to punish, which makes it heart-wrenching.

Sadistic Needs

In *Darker*, Flynn tells Ana that sadism is no longer recognized as a psychiatric term or paraphilia. A paraphilia is "a type of mental disorder characterized by a preference for or obsession with unusual sexual practices, as pedophilia, sadomasochism, or exhibitionism." Do you think sadism is (or should be) classified as a mental disorder? Or do you think there are "degrees" - depending on the type of pain inflicted and the intent behind the pain?

- I think someone who is a sadist should not be looked at as having a disorder. I think my opinion could change if the other person in the relationship doesn't like it, or the sadism is used to inflict life-threatening pain on their partner.
- So, there are degrees of sadism depending on the amount of pain inflicted? Or the intent of the pain?
- Yeah, I would think so. If you start stabbing your partner, and they're screaming, that's not a good sign. If your partner likes to be cut and screams in enjoyment, that's a very different story. I think it just depends on what two people agree on from the beginning. Disorder to me implies something is wrong with a person. If this is something someone enjoys, who am I to make them feel bad?
- Are you familiar with the story of Sid (Vicious) and Nancy?
- Yeah, sad story.
- Tragic. I use it as an example of how two people can both be consensual, but still destructive to each other.
- I think you are right.
- It depends on the intensity of need for it to be considered a disorder. It depends on if it's an addiction rather than a choice.
- To me, it's a matter of degree. Pain can be a stimulant for pleasure, or it can just be pain. Pain that leaves a mark is obviously an extreme form of pain, and to me is when it's venturing toward cruelty and unhealthy. But pain just to stroke the flames of desire and to get you excited is not only not abnormal, it's also a lot of fun!
- It's more like an addiction as I understand it. Some people like it so much it can become destructive.
- I don't think it's a mental disorder. I think it's a preference. It's supposed to be quite a compelling urge once experienced; the fact that pain and pleasure are so

closely entwined. As Christian said, "To sides of the same coin."

- My ex-husband had been molested by his mother as a young teenager. I think this had an effect on his desire to be dominant over a woman.
- That's horrible! His mother?
- I think it's like anything; taken too far it becomes a mental disorder. It's like the difference between being moody and being bi-polar. Some sadists use pain to arouse, others use it to be cruel. There's a continuum.

What if Ana Had Used the Safeword?

If Ana had used the safe-word, things would've been different? Was she determined to see it through to end, or did she really forget?

- I don't know if she forgot or not, and I'm not sure how different things would have been. Ultimately she couldn't take the punishment, safe-word or no safe-word. She tried to "safe-word " the whole idea of punishment, but Christian said it wasn't how it worked with his lifestyle.
- I think she was wanting to see it through to the end.
- She had to prove a point to him. She wanted to see how bad it could get. She saw, and she knew that would never happen to her again. It was her turning point. She had to go through that, and in turn she left him because of it. He had to go through that too. If she hadn't left, he wouldn't know how much she truly meant to him. It was his turning point too. He had to choose: Ana or his lifestyle. Absolutely gutted me, but a poignant part to the story. Especially difficult for me in the book where he laid with her for hours holding her before she left.
- At that point it was a matter of wills.
- I guess you can say she forgot, but I don't think she did it on purpose. Ana was never meant to be a submissive, she could never get completely in that frame of mind. Her thoughts were about their relationship. Maybe by

not safe-wording she was ultimately proving to him that she couldn't be a submissive. A true submissive would've never asked to be put in that situation, let alone allow it to continue beyond her limits.

- If she would've safe-worded, I think eventually they would have ended up in the same predicament again.
- I think she got lost in the moment; was trying to absorb the pain and truly forgot her option other than getting off the table.

Aftercare 101

"Aftercare" is a key component of BDSM relationships. I have a few questions about it. What kinds of "aftercare" did Christian use with his subs before Ana? How did that affect him and them?

- There was no aftercare in that book. Not really. It's much denser. Emotionally. Spiritually. It's draining. When a sub gives their all. The aftercare takes whatever else is left. It could involve a lot of tears, sobbing, nausea. Depends on what the sub is holding on to and releasing. There is a spiritual cleansing that happens. You know how when you're down and sad for one reason or another, and you finally have a good heartbreaking cry, sobbing, snot, the whole nine yards? And then you feel better? Same thing.
- I imagine that he stayed with them in the sub's room, held them if they needed it with the provision that they did not touch him, and if needed, he'd administer lotion where he whipped/hit the women.
- See. This is why the BDSM community takes such umbrage with the book. That teeters on abuse. It portrays the community as abused and abusers. *It could not be farther from the truth.* He would've bathed them and washed their hair, dried them off. Delicately showed them affection. They wouldn't have to touch him. But he'd have had to touch them.
- That's one of the things I love about this group. We know and understand and appreciate the difference.

66

Aftercare

What are your thoughts on aftercare? Yay or Nay? What might be nice, and what might freak you out a little or a lot?

- Bathtub aftercare is awesome!
- From what I hear it's very important.
- Love the aftercare.
- Aftercare is just as essential as every other aspect of this relationship. It is a Dom's responsibility to care for his sub, to ensure her well-being and safety always.
- Cuddling yes; light kissing yes. If you are referring to aftercare after an intense play.
- Again "aftercare" for Christian has a whole other meaning. He's a nurturer. He's giving what he didn't get. What, deep in his heart, he wants; to be cared for.
- I always bring up the importance of "trust" in this lifestyle. The very next thing that's just as important as trust, and when going through an entire session is the "aftercare." Sort of like, the warming up, the actual work out and burn, and then the cooling-down period. This is aftercare. The calm, the caressing, what Christian did when he carried her to the bedroom. Something like that can be so intense with pleasures, it's completely overwhelming. You NEED the aftercare for a session that intense.
- He takes such good care of her. It's endearing.
- It would be so interesting to hear Leila's story. To see how he was with her afterward. Perhaps we might in one of the sequels.

Aftercare And You

If you were a submissive, how much would aftercare influence you? How would it make you feel? How important would it be to you?

- I am a sub. And aftercare is *extremely* important. Like breathing is. It's a must. A rule. And anyone that tells you differently is mistaken.

- There's a term, "sub drop." If you as a sub have given all and receive no aftercare, it can spiral you into a very, very dark and dangerous place.
- I only know about BDSM through FSOG, and have not researched further, but I'd think that the whole dynamic, as in Christian getting mad that Ana called herself a whore and him saying that as her Dom he'd "be devoted to her" explains why aftercare is a must.

·

- There is a societal stigma. You like being tied up, you're a whore. You let him put his cock in your ass, you're a whore. You like it when he calls you a slut, you're a whore. In a true D/s relationship there are layers of devotions. In BDSM, a Dom can have as many subs as he or she can handle. And then there are some who have one. There is no rule in that sense. A true Dom is devoted until he/she releases the sub, or the sub breaks the code. That contract is real. Before anything happens, every aspect is discussed and discussed again. Doms are vetted by other Doms. Subs are under protection of Doms until they find another. So many aspects.
- Thank you for your insights! Very "Deeper," meaningful and helpful!
- Never having been in the lifestyle, I can't really answer this question. I would hope that my Dom would be there if I needed him to comfort me. I don't think I'd like it at all if he had his way with me and then just left me in a room to recover from what he'd just done to me.
- I think the aftercare would be very confusing in a relationship that was like the one Christian had with his Subs before Ana. It would be very easy for me to confuse it with love.
- It's bound to happen. You can't share that kind of exchange of energy and NOT catch feelings. Happens on both sides. Doms love taking care of their subs, littles, brats, etc. And how you feel as a sub; allowing someone free range of your body, soul, and mind, it's hard not to fall in love.

Aftercare and the Dominant

How important is aftercare to the Dominant? What emotions does it generate in him/her?

- That it was okay to "punish" her, and that by comforting her he also comforts himself.
- Doms do not only want to exert force. Their role is to be there for the sub *in every manner*. Aftercare is *extremely* important to a Dom. Almost if not more than it is to the sub. Dom's take the aftercare to the highest level. They pick you up, hold you, cradle you, and pet you. They wash you; wash your hair. They talk it out, sit and listen to you, and talk to you. It's all about nurturing you. They dress you, hold you, read to you, and feed you. They do everything for you.
- Beautifully said.
- There so much more. So much more. Thank you. I tried to get it all in there.
- I love giving aftercare to my subs! They give me themselves and 100% of their trust, and I value that! I love to make them comfortable and rub lotion on them if needed; give them fluids and food, and hold them. It's a complete sense of happiness and satisfaction.
- It's important because it fulfills the need of caregiver for them.
- When I was in the lifestyle, I didn't realize how important aftercare was until I realized my Dom took me through some severe training. Not all at once, mind you. He slowly built my endurance. It's like if you spank your child, you kind of soothe them afterward, letting them know you did it because you love them. It seems like a contradiction, but in role play, it can take this form. That's the way I know how to explain it.

Stigma

Until Ana came on the scene, everybody, including Christian's family, thought he was gay. Elliot thought he was still a virgin. I understand he never introduced his subs to

69

his family, but why going to such lengths to hide his relationships? To a point where everyone's unsure about his sexuality? Was it because deep down inside, he was ashamed of his lifestyle? There's nothing shameful about it, and no one needs to know what sort of sex he enjoys, but I've always wondered why the secrecy?

- For starters, what would the submissives tell the Greys they did for a living?
- They would have ordinary jobs.
- It's nothing to be ashamed of, but not everyone would agree. Given his influence in the business world, he'd have to keep it quiet or risk some business deals.
- If it was found out what lifestyle he was living, I think it would've ruined his pure white reputation. They would've looked at him in a different light. Paparazzi would be following him around to see the girls he was with.
- The girls weren't suitable to be introduced to his parents. I think they would smell something was off.
- I just don't think he cared to share any of that or have to defend himself to anyone. His family was his only sacred thing. He probably saw no purpose in introducing women to his family whom he had no long term interests in or deep connection with.
- Everybody doesn't understand the lifestyle, and can be very judgmental about it. I have a friend who is beyond judgmental, and we would argue about it.
- I think he didn't want them to try to push a relationship on him. He knew his mom would love him either way, but since he had been rejected as child, I don't think he could handle the thought of her being disappointed in him.
- His subs were disposable, so why integrate them into his real life?
- Christian always had a complex about not being perfect in the "perfect" family. He probably thought that if they knew about his sexual predilections, they wouldn't understand, and he especially couldn't bear to hurt Grace.

He always felt like an outsider, and couldn't risk the possibility (in his mind) that he'd be ostracized from the family, so he kept things hidden from them.

- My ex-husband was the only relationship that my friends and family have ever known about. I've had lots of subs over the years, but until the day I decide I want "more" from my sub, they don't get to meet anyone. It's a lifestyle thing for me anyway.

- I believe Christian wanted to keep it private and didn't really care what people thought. He had to know that they knew he didn't have a normal girlfriend and wondered why. So he had his subs; each one for so long. Then Ana being so different she just came into the picture.

- I think he mostly saw the sub relationships as business arrangements. On some level he probably is ashamed of the lifestyle (especially that he likes to hit women that look like his mum with a belt). He knows he's Fifty Shades of f*cked-up. And also he feels odd and not good enough for his family. A failure. But then Ana comes along, and so it begins.

- Could you imagine Grace's face if she saw the Red Room? I think she'd be shocked like Ana was! I think she'd go into a Major Mom Mode, and maybe yell at him. It would make an interesting book from Grace's POV.

- I don't think Christian was ready yet for familial introductions because he wasn't sure about wanting more with Ana. I think it was just circumstantial that the invitation was proffered. And I think Grace's curiosity got the best of her!

- I think he would've introduced Ana to his family quite quickly. As much as he never introduced any women to his family, he was almost insistent that Ana met his mum.

- Eventually he would've introduced Ana to his family. As he said, he wanted to get the notion that he was "gay" out of their heads.

To an "Innocent"

When Ana did her research, some rather shocking images popped up on her computer. What was she thinking when she saw them? What would you have been thinking if you had been Ana?

- I would've thought he's out of his mind. *It was nice knowing you.*
- They would make me feel uneasy, scare me, and create many questions. That's why I loved *Grey* and Christian's take on that. After looking at these images, Ana emailed him with, "It was nice knowing you," and he rightfully assumed that simple online "research" wasn't enough. He was thinking to himself that he should have lent her some books on BDSM, which would give her a better understanding.
- It would've scared the crap out of me! But I would've still been drawn to him. It would have been very confusing, just like I'm sure it was to Ana.
- I loved this scene. Ana was so curious, and when she saw this she shut down her computer immediately (in the film). And it was right after this she emailed him, "I've seen enough. It was nice knowing you!" Seeing these bondage pictures scared me off too. Some tying up with a tie and spanking is okay, but this kind of bondage is too much for me. I guess because I am claustrophobic.
- That it would make me feel humiliated, and in pain as well as exposed.
- She was so young and not exposed to anything like this. She was smart enough to realize this was not what she wanted to get wrapped up into. (No pun intended). At 21, I would feel the same way. I was the same way in many ways. Pictures like that would be a deal-breaker.
- I was a little surprised because of Christian being such a control freak that he would have left it up to an internet search engine for her to search "submissive," and allow her to determine if being a submissive was what she wanted to do. I think after the, "It was nice knowing you," email that maybe he realized that doing the search

may have shown her too much too soon. I was thinking that he should have allowed her some more exposure to the RROP, and what happens in there to help her figure out if that is what she wanted to do.

- Seeing those images, I'm not sure she was really joking with her "It was nice knowing you" response. She was so innocent that it didn't surprise me that she had the reaction she did. Christian should've given her books rather than rely on her to "do the research." He even mentions that in *Grey*. If I were Ana, I probably would've reacted the same way.

- I think it was more than she could absorb in that moment. She was undoubtedly thinking, "No way!" I would've reacted the same way. I think I actually did search and found the same photos. The woman is a well-known submissive whose name I've forgotten. Curiosity led me to read more. There is a Japanese bondage called Shibari, more correctly known as Kinbaku, is an ancient Japanese artistic form of rope bondage that has many styles and uses. Fascinating images online.

- She had to be frightened, not having any prior knowledge and being a virgin. But she had to be intrigued as well, otherwise she would've called it off. At her age, I'd probably been more than a little frightened and no matter how curious I was. I would have walked away. But that's just me. Today, however.

- "What the hell is this?" I would've been very overwhelmed about it and I would've been conflicted between wanting him so badly, but also doubting my ability to do those things.

- It would've scared the living daylights out of me. I think I would have responded with, "It was nice knowing you." She had to have been thinking he was crazy for suggesting that type of relationship.

- For an innocent like Ana, it's extreme! She must have been thinking "Oh, HELL NO!" Since I understand it, and have had it done to me, it's just another walk in the park.

- My experienced self would be intrigued and want to do some, but I'd define my hard limits clearly. If I was young and newly deflowered like Ana, I would have run.
- I had just lost my virginity when I was first exposed to this lifestyle. Granted, I was not shown pictures as graphic (and frankly, beautifully done) as these, but was given a verbal description nearly as picturesque, as these pictures. I had a choice to make, do I want to walk down this path or find a way to push this Dom out of my life? There is something that really draws you, and I think if you have a proclivity towards this lifestyle, it may almost be 'beyond' your ability to walk away from it, once it presents itself to you.
- Not a hope in hell would I let anyone do that to me.
- I'm not sure which would freak me out more, being tied up like that, or being photographed!
- For me, both.
- I would've thought he was out of his f*cking mind. It scares the sh*t out of me. I know now why she didn't want to sign that contract. I think at that point in time she had reservations, and she didn't want it.
- I would've had reservations about the contract.
- As a sub, especially if was in love with my Master, I would've willingly submitted.

Crime and Punishments

Does a Dominant always have the need to punish? Is it just the way they are? Will a submissive always seek a Dominant?

- In the past I have always sought Dominants, and from the ones I've been with, it seems to just be the way they are. Punishment was always a big part of that. I guess it shows more power. Also I'm guessing that having someone submit to you, so that you can punish them would be a pretty big "high." I've never met a Dominant that didn't like to punish. However, that doesn't mean there aren't some out there!

- A Dominant shouldn't have a need to punish unless the submissive has given him/her a reason, like breaking a rule. When the limits have been broken in a BDSM relationship, the submissive has the safe-word and the Dominant has punishment. That's just how it works. Punishment doesn't always have to equate to pain, though. A sadist has the need to cause pain, which can be on its own or as a punishment. It all comes down to the agreement between the Dominant and the submissive. Every arrangement is different.
- When Christian (who is fictional) punished Ana because she wanted to know what to really expect, he seemed to have such pleasure on his face like it was so arousing and enjoyable. But I think it is definitely a part of that lifestyle.
- Yes, it seems to me that punishment is definitely a part of the lifestyle. With Christian, it seemed to me, he was often searching for a reason to punish Ana, but not in a sadistic manner. It aroused him, so I guess only in the end did it look sadistic to me.
- Just as vanilla relationships are each unique, so are BDSM lifestyle relationships. My Sir isn't on the lookout for reasons to punish me. That would be abusive. And it's one thing that bothered me about Christian. He seemed to make up excuses to punish Ana. A sadist needs a masochist, and vice-versa. They're the complement of each other. The yin and the yang. Of course, pain for the sake of pleasure is different. Punishment can be painful, or not. The main "rule" is that it should fit the crime, so to speak.
- Thank you for the enlightenment. So interesting to read it, as you explain it so clearly. So actually, it is all about agreement and understanding, which are the most important things in any relationship.
- As someone who enjoys a BDSM lifestyle, I'm happy to share information about how it works. So many people don't understand it, and a lot are not open to learning. I like how this group is so open-minded.
- I've never been a submissive, but I would think if I tried

it, I'd expect some kind of punishment if I broke the rules. It would be part of the, shall I say it? Fun. I might even test the limits. I wouldn't want anything too extreme or painful. But a bit of torment might be interesting.

- I think Christian was turned on sexually by the spankings with his hands, and it fed his need to be in control. When he used the crop and flogger, that was for pleasure. In the books, he ties Ana to the cross and brings her to the brink of orgasm over and over again and that *was* punishment; sexual torment with the intent to punish. But when he belted her, I don't think that was for arousal. I think that met his broken, dysfunctional need to punish, stemming from his mother and her pimp's abuse. All very different things.

Saying "No"
In the boathouse in FSOG, Ana said "no" to Christian's punishment. We're you surprised? How did that impact Christian? And what did you think about "for my pleasure, not yours?"

- First, don't think she deserved punishment. So I'm not surprised she said no. I think it forced him to very quickly rethink her "punishment." And while I don't think he expressed it, and nor was it true orgasm denial, he was still punishing her. It wasn't something she had refused in the past. Her issue had been with pain; this was more of a mental thing. It gave him just enough control to control himself.
- He'd always had submissives who just did what they were told without question, so for her to refuse to be spanked it probably shocked the hell out of him. I can't blame her for refusing because she was at his parents' house having dinner. You're hardly going to be able to walk back in there and pretend nothing's happened after you've had your arse spanked till it looks like a baboon's. Being in control of the women in his life has meant

76

Christian has never been challenged, everything has come easy. He said jump, and they'd reply, "How high, Sir?" To realize he didn't have that power over Ana, a battle of wills had begun, a battle for his control over her, and him having to break Ana to win it, probably made it all the more exciting and a massive turn-on. The one thing he did have total control over was Ana's body. He knew her body better than she did, and if he couldn't control her mind, he'd control that instead. When he used "sex as a weapon," took her body as he pleased, and denied her an orgasm yet had one himself, he was showing her he still had the power. He was still in charge.

- This part also made me think about how so many other men I've known are selfish in this way, not putting enough attention into the woman's satisfaction. And how Christian used it as punishment, because he knew better, while other men do it out of selfishness. Or maybe not knowing better. I'm not sure which is worse!

- I think that Christian was afraid of his feelings for Ana. (Mrs. Robinson told him love was for fools, and that no one would love him.) So when Anastasia challenged him (even though he thought it was hot, and one of the things he loves about her), he went into Dom mode.

- I think from the beginning Christian was living in this "bubble." From what he experienced with Elena and was taught as far as being with a woman, I believe it was almost robotic; an automatic response until Ana. She wasn't what he thought she'd be initially, and that intrigued him from the start. The attraction of her resistance, along with her innocence, it was almost like a new game for him. It jarred him to seeing something exciting, and not as "common" as he was so used to. It was hot.

Revenge

In *Freed*, when Ana used the safe-word, "Red." Then she says, "This is not love. It's revenge." Did you agree? We know Christian was well trained to be alerted to the use of a safe-word. Do you think he'd heard it before with other subs?

- I'm sure he heard it before, but not often. He was with experienced subs before. This was different because Ana was not a sub and was his wife. He was very much in love with her.
- Agreed! He was only thinking about himself and punishing her. Until her words brought him out of that mindset. Then he realized he went too far. He felt really horrible even though I think he still tried to justify it by suggesting orgasm denial was a normal part of sex play. That was terrible of him in my opinion.
- I think he heard it before, but maybe his subs rarely said the word because they so wanted to please him.
- I think he did hear it quite a bit. It seems that when he's "in the moment" he only focuses on his needs, almost like he enters into a trance-like state. When he's angry, I think that's particularly true. This situation was completely different because he loves Ana and has said quite often that hurting her is abhorrent to him. He didn't love the others, so he didn't care so much about their feelings.
- I cried in this part the second time I read the series.
- Before he was 100% Dominant, so it was always for pushing too far, "testing the limits" as he would say. I don't think he heard it too often but something tells me that he last heard it with Leila. This time was different because he's not full Dominant, he's in love and married. His focus isn't the same.
- I think this a powerful moment because you see a side to Christian that is not pretty. He was pissed off at her and got really carried away. I give Ana a lot of praise for being able to tell the difference. She even said at the end that, "My husband can be scary sometimes." As much as I love this character, I was actually a little worried for Ana during this part. I do agree with everyone that I don't think very many subs have safe-worded on him often, or if they did he never believed them.

78

- I was worried for her, too. I wondered if she'd leave him after that. But she's so understanding with him.
- I feel sometimes through the book she was a little too understanding.
- Absolutely she was!
- This was different, first because he wasn't his calm, collected self, he was doing it in anger. Then he was terrified that if she said, "Red," that she'd leave him (like the belt issue). And because he really didn't want to harm her to the degree of *red*. He doesn't understand how very much his anger scares her.
- He would've heard it before. But in this case, I was wondering if he'd have heard her right away. Also, if he stopped as soon as she safe-worded, how would he have handled his anger? This scene scared me a bit. I even cried.
- I'm sure he'd heard safe-words before. He was probably the kind of Dom who pushed women to their limits. Just as Elena probably did with him. Given his push-and-pull behavior, he probably also got rid of the women who used the safe-word. What makes this different was that he was *in love* with her.
- I think Christian was so detached from his other subs, just using them for sex, that they were afraid to safe-word in fear of losing him and the perks that go with him. Also, I suspect he chose women who were aligned with his hard limits, and could take whatever he gave.
- This was also different in that he didn't remind her to use a safe-word before they started. So I think hearing her say "red" really pulled him back to reality, and he saw that what he was doing was very wrong.
- I don't think he heard safe-words very often because his submissives liked the same kind of sexual activity as he did. He needed the painful component and probably had submissives who also liked that as well. This part was difficult to read because Christian suddenly was shaken out of his reverie into reality and what he was doing to

Ana. It was a wake-up call to him because he needed to be very careful from that time forward in being present sexually with Ana.

- One thing I like about this scene is that it leads to the possibility of Ana using a safe-word in other situations, too, when Christian is getting out of hand.

Haphephobia

Christian was afflicted with a condition called Haphephobia, which is the fear of being touched. As we know from reading FSOG, he was severely abused as a toddler (and probably as an infant as well). While it's not clearly stated in the books, according to research it's likely that his abuse led to this phobia.

Haphephobia and Selective Mutism

I know Grace and Carrick meant well, but I wonder if they were wrong about respecting little Christian's fears about touching. What might have happened if they had given him a hug, forcing him to confront his fears? Letting him know that touch is nothing to be afraid of? By not touching him as a little boy, did they perpetuate his phobia, thereby leaving him vulnerable to Elena? I'm not a psychiatrist, but I suspect there must be better ways to handle this fear in a small child. What do you think?

- I'm very opinionated about this. It's not just the touching. There was also his not talking until the age of six. To just hug Christian, to have him face his fear, would be just as detrimental as to demand that he speaks. It doesn't work in children and only makes it worse. I say this because I lived the "no talking" with my son – it's called Selective Mutism. So many people told me to just demand that he speak. NO! That fear, that anxiety, just makes it worse. What works? Therapy, love, understanding, and time. Desensitizing the behavior. My heart bled for Christian. It took this story to a whole other level. I saw his struggles, what Ana did for him and what he allowed Ana to do for him was monumental. It just took someone to see beyond those walls he put up and help him heal.
- I wondered about that too. I've had an anxiety disorder for as long as I can remember. All through my life people, some with the best of intentions, have tried to make force me to face my anxieties. But in doing that they made it worse. Just in the last few months I had

81

someone do that to me. It's horrible. I dread going anywhere near that person now. Unfortunately, I don't have a choice.

- Well, whatever they were doing for little Christian didn't work. Perhaps they should have realized that and tried something else?
- Time. It takes time. Those fears were so deep. Every child is different and every fear is different. As an adult he was ready and it took Ana to change it.
- I agree about continuing therapy and taking time. I think pushing Christian as a child would've been inappropriate and too much for him to handle. He was a prisoner of his stronghold, his safety net that he needed. I've never been a proponent of throwing the kid in the pool to watch him or her learn how to swim. Frankly, I got frustrated with Ana. She didn't know about the depth of Christian's problem with touch. If only Christian could've been more forthcoming earlier on, it would've prevented a lot of heartache.
- This is such a complex issue. I totally get why they didn't push little Christian into so many things. Let's face it, he didn't have a great start in life, and all he knew about touch was that it always hurt. Having said that, I would've hoped that the Greys would've found a child psychiatrist who deals with these really complex issues and finds ways to teach little Christian that not all touch is bad. Even then, it could take many years to right this horrible wrong.
- Maybe it would've been wrong, but if I was Carrick, I would have just picked him up and held him in a big hug until he stopped struggling. I would've spoken softly to him the whole time, and tried to comfort him as much as possible, telling him how much I loved him and that I'd never hurt him. While I was holding him, I would've explained to him that all touch is not bad. I'd do it for hours if necessary. Maybe I would've made it worse, I don't know, but I do know that's what I would have done. And I would've kept doing it until he no longer feared my touch. Until I finally got it through his thick head

that I was not the pimp that hurt him. Maybe it's a good thing I don't have kids of my own...

- I expect, given Grace's job/experience they had the best child psychiatrists they could find. It could even explain why they moved to Seattle. I can feel for the heartbreak of Grace and Carrick. I can also feel their joy at baby Mia causing the breakthrough. So poignant.

- By holding him against his will, to him it may have hurt. Even if it was a loving touch, it would feel hurtful to him. And I'm sure he would've screamed the whole time. I'd want to hug it out too, but I think they probably did what they were told to do by the therapists. Maybe it was the right thing, maybe not. But like Maya Angelou said, "When you know better, you do better."

- Sometimes we have to hurt the ones we love in order to help them. sure it would've been uncomfortable for him, but in the long run I think it may have been the best thing to do for him.

- Not always the best way to show touch is okay, no matter how much love there is, but we wouldn't have the story we love if he didn't work through his fears. They learned together how and what worked for them to feel love.

- I wouldn't have done that right away. I would've given him time to get to know me and to know that I was safe, but after a few months, maybe a year at the most, I wouldn't have put up with it anymore and taken drastic action for his own good.

- We also have to remember that the little boy never associated touch with anything positive. There was always something painful connected to it. If his birth mother had been kinder to him and actually held him, he might have been okay sooner, but he never knew loving touch. Then at the age of four, he got ripped away from the only life he knew, so he was doubly scared. It really didn't help that Elena perpetuated that perception with her beatings (he even called her on that - "you never once held me, and told me you loved me") ...Ana was the very first person who connected with him on that level, and that's when he started to change and heal.

83

- Sounds great in theory, looking from the outside. But living with a child like that, not as easy as you think. My son also had a touch issue (did not like to be touched, hugged etc. from non-family members). I will never know what triggered his behavior. He was not autistic, but had a true anxiety disorder.
- Christian was burned with cigarettes and was kicked by the pimp with his boot. He was yelled at and starved. I'd have to say that the degree of his fear is extreme.
- Re: "Forcing"... How would feel if you had a fear of heights, let say, and someone grabbed you and dangled you over the cliff a mile high? How would conquer your fear? It's the same concept. A fear can be so ingrained that forcing the fear would have the reverse affect. I try to educate wherever I can. This is a great discussion and we all would want the best for little Christian. That's why we feel so passionate about this story!
- Dangling me over a cliff would be dangerous, and not in the same league as hugging someone, but I get your point. I'm not saying what I would've done is the right thing to do, but I still think that whatever Grace and Carrick did for little Christian did not work, and that they should have reevaluated that lack of success and tried something else, rather than just let him continue in his fear.
- Christian mentioned that none of the therapists he had seen during his lifetime were helpful until he met John Flynn. We don't know what modalities the others tried with Christian that didn't work. As you said, I'm sure the Greys used the best resources available at the time. Nothing seemed to have worked. I'd opt for not traumatizing Christian any more than he had previously experienced.
- He was traumatized enough. I think, though, that Elena was the one who made things much worse for him by continuing and justifying the no-touching. Really Ana was the only person who was able to get through to him, not to mention Dr. Flynn. The combination of the two helped him move on and heal.

- By the time he was 15 years old and falling into the grasp of Elena, it was too late. I'm talking about a little 4, 5 or 6-year-old Christian. They should have done something to help him confront and face his fears long before he was 15 years old. Instead they placated him. They catered to his fears, thereby making them even more powerful in his mind. There must have been some small part of that little boy who craved to be held by Grace the same way he saw her hold little Elliot, and even later baby Mia. They should have done whatever they could to bring that out in him.
- I used the cliff as a metaphor which would be to the degree of the fear. The only way I could explain it.
- He definitely craved to be touched; he even says to Ana that he never been tickled but he watched Carrick with Elliot and Mia playing and he longed to join but even the thought was too much... I also believe that the key here was time and patience.
- I think with a little boy like that, you can't just rely on time and patience. He doesn't know what's good for him. He doesn't know how to overcome his fears alone. I think at some point Grace and Carrick needed to force the issue with him. But that is something they apparently failed to ever do.
- Remember that Christian did tolerate Mia touching him; I don't recall exactly where - his chest and arms, I believe.
- He didn't see Mia as threat. She was smaller and awakened protectiveness in him. She was the only one who could touch him.
- Ding ding ding. You said a key word "threat." Christian did not see Mia as a threat or his fear did not stem to his interaction with children. Only adults!
- Christian's protective nature was awakened with Mia. He also felt protective of Ana. Perhaps that was why he eventually allowed her to make the lipstick trail and then eventually to actually touch him in the no-go zones. So maybe his feelings of protectiveness - someone who

appeared powerless as he had been as a child - spurred this on.

- Don't you think he also felt protective of his submissives? I don't think he ever wanted to hurt any of them. I think he certainly seemed to feel protective of Leila.
- I don't know if he felt protective of his submissives. I think he felt guilty about seeing Leila in her depraved condition, but I didn't think of that as protective.

Ana's Touch

We all know Anastasia eventually got to touch Christian after working on that together, to the point where Christian hungered for her touch. Christian never let Grace touch him, bathe, him dress him, etc. But how is it, that upon being introduced to sex and BDSM and at such a young age and with a person he hardly knew, how was he able to trust Elena to touch him, to restrain him? She could've tied him up and touched him at her leisure, how could he trust her over his safe haven of a mother?

- The more I try to understand this, the more I don't see how Elena got him to trust her.
- Elena used sex to gain his trust. As a hormone-driven teenager, he'd probably have done anything for sex, especially sex with a more experienced woman (and friend of his mother).
- Subspace (when you're a submissive) makes you think/feel differently.
- He was sexually vulnerable and would let her do anything to him in order to have those feelings.
- There is a part in *Grey* where he talked about Elena touching him.
- I don't think that even though Elena touched him, he was ever comfortable with that. In *Darker* he talks to Ana about the fact that Elena knew where to touch him, but in *Grey*, he remembers her running her nails down his chest and him wanting to scream out in pain, but refrained for fear of whatever humiliation she might put

him through. As far as why he'd let Elena touch him over the touch of his mother, I think it had to do with the context of the touch. From Grace, he didn't feel he deserved to be loved, and her touch would've been in a loving context. Touch from Elena was purely from a sexual and punishment context. There was no love involved, so I think he rationalized it that way. Then along came Ana and turned his thinking completely upside down. Once she gained his trust, and showed that she'd never physically hurt him, his walls came down and he was able to accept her touch everywhere.

- Elena knew about him. Knew about his Haphephobia. Elena knew where to touch him. Remember in this kind of relationships there are hard and soft limits. Touching must have been one of Christian's hard limits. That's why he trusted Elena.

- I suspect she touched him "down below" first. Once that part of his anatomy was aroused, she moved on to the rest of him.

- My argument is that he wasn't familiar with the lifestyle then especially not enough to trust. He was the Anastasia in that situation.

- Elena was his escape. She taught him everything he knew. She knew about him through her connection with his family. He initially felt like he deserved the pain/pleasure she gave him. Being a submissive took away all his responsibilities in life. He said she gave him freedom; and through this freedom he didn't have to think.

- Perhaps because she didn't touch his torso (where the burns were) with her hands.

- What I think is that Elena never touched him with her hands but always used something like canes, whips and so forth. I guess that's why it was acceptable; as long as the touch didn't involve hands or an intimate caress.

- He says (in *Grey*) she did scrape her long fingernails over his chest. He also told Ana that Mrs. R. wouldn't put up with that s***.

- I thought it was that she never really touched him as a teen/submissive in a more intimate way, like giving him comforting hugs.
- He felt that he deserved what the bitch troll gave him. Because of his early years, but I always felt that Grace and Mia could hug him. I think Mia could've done anything and would've been fine. She had Christian wrapped around her finger. But also remember Grace ran up and hugged him when he returned after the crash and he hugged her back.
- I always assumed that she knew his "vest" limits and stayed away from them. I could be wrong, of course, but that's how I explained it to myself.
- I don't think Elena ever asked him permission for anything as the Dominant. She took what she wanted and he tolerated it as a good submissive just as he'd expect from his subs.
- I think that Elena even took it a step further and probably never even gave him the opportunity to set out any boundaries (contractual or not).
- Elena just did what she always wanted. I don't think he had a say, even if it was a torture for him.
- Elena was probably more about the give-and-take of pleasure/pain and the threat of punishment.
- I think she used touching as a threat. She knew about his Haphephobia but used it against him. I took what he meant as her touching him like slapping, groping, etc.
- Never gentle?
- I'm not sure. Probably not. Elena isn't known for gentleness!
- I also think she was the first to touch his "junk" - which was the first step...
- I think she used the threat of punishment if he didn't let her touch him, which would've probably been so much worse than tolerating touch.
- She was his Domme. He had no chance when she touched him and he said he had his goal in mind where she was concerned.

- I guess the point I was making is that she wasn't a traditional Domme or dominatrix. She probably did not allow him to choose the hard and soft limits. She probably said to him, "if you want sex you have to follow my rules."
- Don't forget she knew Christian's past from Grace, and he told Ana she only touched my face at first. Christian, like Ana, knew absolutely nothing about BDSM but he was a 15-year-old kid with raging hormones. He would've done anything for her and he said that he was her submissive for six years and wouldn't have changed anything if he could. She had to teach him from the beginning and that included soft and hard limits.

(Un)conditional Love?

One of the most confusing topics about relationships is the discussion of conditional vs. unconditional love. Are there limits to love? Or must it be absolute and forever? This chapter delves into the dynamics of unconditional love and how it was explored – and challenged – in the *Fifty Shades of Grey* series.

Let's talk "unconditional love." What does it mean to you? How and where might it apply to FSOG?

- It means no matter what... Who ... Why... How... When... You love them. You accept them.
- You love that someone no matter what. Nothing can take you from them. They are your heart and soul almost as if you were one. As Ana and Christian. Like they were made for each other and grew to know that.
- E L James Author - For me, this is what these books are about. What happens when, as a child, you don't receive unconditional love - which for me - for all children should be a right. And then what happens when you decide to give it freely... Unconditional love is what we all need. Always. Every single child. Every single adult. It makes me sad posting about this today...
- To give love to everyone without restrictions, without conditions; young, old, kids, teens. All people matter and are worth love.
- Unconditional love: The "no matter what, no matter why, I will be the one that will choose to see the best of you, accept you, cherish who you are, forgive you, champion you, choose you and allow the depth of our love to wash us, embrace us, encompass us in the best of times and the worst of situations, you will forever have my love, my heart and my faith."
- This was Anastasia's love for Christian. I absolutely loved the part in *Darker* where she was struck "like a thunderbolt - that's what he needs from me, what he's entitled to - unconditional love. When she was recalling his walls coming down from the night before, even as

she questioned herself as to whether, or not, she was capable of such love, she knew that it was something he desperately needed and her resolution to do just that when she decided to buy the little Seattle key ring the next day before they went to see Flynn. I think that sometimes we don't always realize our capacity to love and the depths of our love until you face it squarely in the worst of situations and then you recognize it, irrevocably, that "Yes, I cannot live a moment without this person and would traverse the depths of hell" to be with the one who has become your very soulmate. And, in turn, it was Christian's love for Ana.

And I-I-I Will Always...

"Christian, I will always love you. No matter what you do to me." What is your reaction when someone says this?

* I have a mixed reaction, because although I love my husband very very much, I can never say I'll love him no matter what he does to me. To me, I think people take that as a pass to do whatever and they still expect you to love and be there. For me, there's always a breaking point. I might still love you, but that doesn't mean I'm going put up with whatever you do to me. Maybe it was just bad wording or I took that statement too literally but I hope this made sense.
* It totally makes sense - and I agree with you. It's similar to someone saying "I'll never die." We all die. We shouldn't make promises that, in the end, we can't control.
* Okay good. I was hoping it didn't sound like rambling. I completely agree. I've always been very open and honest about what I want from my husband as far as being treated or whatever. I wouldn't expect him to stay with me if I treated regardless of how I treat him.
* This wasn't a promise in my opinion; it was a reassurance.
* I didn't think of it that way. I guess I could see that, especially since Christian needed reassurance often.

- I think it can be a true statement. She said she will always love him, doesn't mean she'd tolerate it or stay with him. But when it comes down to it he's been her first everything and they've been through so much together. She'll always love him and he, her. At least that's how I interpreted it.
- That she loves him a thousand percent! Christian is like a magnet and Ana is bonded to him (pun intended)!
- It's called unconditional love; the purest form of love.
- To think that no matter what someone does to you, that you'll have to "always love them" terrifies me! What if he physically hurts her? What if he hurts her kid? What if he steals from her? Cheats? Becomes an addict?
- But see she didn't say she'd stay with him no matter what. She said she'd always love him. There's a difference. It didn't sound like a promise to me.
- I think it's the "no matter what you do to me" part of the comment that's a bit disturbing. On a soul level, there's unconditional love. But on this "human" level, it's difficult to make or keep this promise.
- I don't think Christian can distinguish one kind of love from another. He's like a child in matters of the heart.
- He certainly heard it - and would use it - as an unbreakable promise.
- He did use it – when she was telling him she was leaving. Unfortunately, she had no idea what the heck he was talking about when he said "you said you'd never leave" because she said it in her sleep. She only found this out at the dinner after Jose's show. I think even after they got back together he was always nervous that she'd leave again. That's why anytime they have a tiff he asks her "Are you running? Please don't leave again."
- You're right. In this case - in *Freed* - with the part "no matter what you do to me" is a bit loaded, don't you think?
- Absolutely. But I also think he was so insecure that he needed to be reassured that she loved him, no matter what. Personally, for me, that's a really *huge* ask. I'm not sure I could ever say "no matter what you do to me."

- For me, those words might mean "I will love you - want the best for you." But it does NOT mean I'll stay "no matter what."
- I'm torn between how to take this statement. She does love him, yet she left when he hit her with the belt. To say you love someone no matter what they do to you it's kind of a scary promise, even with lots of love.

Happy Not Happy

Personally, I LOVE that the first FSOG book/movie didn't have a "happy ending."
What about you?

- It was sad and my heart broke for the two of them, but true love never runs smooth. Especially for someone like Christian who doesn't believe he deserves to be loved.
- Only because I knew there were two other books. Otherwise no. I think I told you way back when I read the first, the ending tore me up then I found out there were two more books, I was elated and downloaded those puppies so fast.
- I kind of envy the people who thought the story ended with the first book. Yes, heart-wrenching. But also extremely powerful. What a message!
- Why do you envy them?
- It's what made me want MORE.
- Yes!
- I watched the movie with three friends. None of them had seen it. One had read the books twice. The other two had not read them at all. So I enjoyed seeing them see it for the first time. I played only the alternate ending for them. One friend yelled at the end, "I'm glad she didn't sign that f*cking contract!" It was fun seeing them looking forward to seeing what happens next!
- I loved all three books! I was hooked after the first three words! The end of the first book tore me up. These books are truly the best I've ever read!
- I'm willing to bet that if the first book hadn't ended so dramatically, none of us would be here talking about it.

The power in the story (in my opinion) was that she LEFT. She knew her limits and walked away from "everything" because she wouldn't allow herself to be hurt/treated that way - physically and emotionally.

- If only the haters could see that.
- When the first movie came out, some people were online calling it "abuse." They obviously hadn't read the books or seen the movie and had pre-judgment about it. So, finally I couldn't take it and I spoiled it for them by yelling (in all capital letters), "SHE DOESN'T TAKE IT! SHE LEAVES IN THE END!" That shut them up!
- Ana had to leave, I was angry with such an ending, but I'd be angrier if she didn't.
- Isn't it more impactful that way?
- As in real life, stories are usually about the journey not the ending.
- It left us wanting just what Ana wanted... MORE.
- As author Orson Welles said, "If you want a happy ending that depends, of course, on where you stop your story."

Christian and Ana Growing Up

Early childhood events can impact the rest of your life, and that was certainly true with both Ana and Christian. From the death of Ana's father right after she was born to the overdose of Christian's "crack whore" mother, both characters faced challenges as young children that affected them for many years to come.

Impact of Early Childhood Abuse

The psychiatrist in *The Fall* said this about Paul Spector, "When young children are abused they experience fear and anxiety they then attempt to contain those feelings by acting out sadistically. If a person is able to do to others what he fears may be done to him, he may no longer be afraid."

Do you think this is true in general? Is it true about Christian too?

- I think Christian liked BDSM because it gave him a way to unleash his anxiety. He wasn't just hurting everyone. It was more about a willing participant.
- Certainly not all abused children grow up to be sadists.
- I take umbrage with this. Because that's saying that Christian's abuse turned him into an abuser. That he was taking that abuse out on Ana, and I don't want to believe, or do I believe, that that is what this book was trying to convey. That being said there are posers in the BDSM Community who will search out for weak or not informed people to do just that: exact their abuse under the guise of dominance and submission and that is not what BDSM is about.
- I'm going to flip this around and give you another side. There is such a thing as therapy spankings, floggings canings. For the specific reason of release and comfort. Aftercare is as important as the spankings. And it's not done for sexual reasons.

- It does seem like at the end of the first book Christian was using the punishment with the belt as a way of reducing tension.
- Yes there is so much more that someone not in the lifestyle that E.L. James doesn't know.
- Now I understand his reaction better; why he was sweating, etc. It never seemed like a sexual moment to me.
- I think Ana did it to please him. There are reasons people are Doms and subs respectively. And it has nothing to do with abuse.
- Maybe he didn't see it as abuse if it was consensual. A lot of people don't see it as abuse if the other person agrees to it.
- Sometimes abuse has nothing to do with it, and sometimes it has everything to do with it. I know people who were abused physically emotionally sexually who are in the lifestyle and have not used that as their reasoning behind it. And I also know the same kinds of people who found acceptance and love and equality in the lifestyle. It's a very broad culture.
- If is consensual, it's not abuse. Both are getting something out of it.
- I was abused all three ways and that keeps me away from that lifestyle. We do soft stuff like a flogger and nothing heavy or hard. I think the pain would just take me back to that time. Much like the celebrities in the media and their sexual assaults have taken me back to a time I don't want to remember.
- First of all - Just to clarify: I wasn't implying anything about Christian or the lifestyle. I have a lot of respect for the people I know in it! Also, one of the things that I find most intriguing and incredible is the way BDSM has healed so many former "victims" of abuse. The power of the limits and the safe-word.
- I think the reason Christian was the way he was is that he equated punishment with love.
- I got the impression he didn't believe in love. Elena drilled that into him. If he didn't believe in love or wasn't

deserving or capable of it, how would he equate love and punishment?

- Maybe I should have said "caring" then. I'm thinking about children who act out to get attention. Most of the attention Little Christian got was negative/punishment. As he got older he felt he deserved it, so he therefore thought the person giving it "cared" enough to give him what he needed/deserved. Am I making sense? It's complicated.
- I think he knows his parents, especially Grace, loved him. He doesn't understand why, though. I think it was romantic love he really didn't believe in. That is my impression anyhow.
- I think he thought they loved him, but since he didn't think he was lovable, he thought they were disillusioned or misinformed/misdirected.
- I'm enjoying this conversation and how you all think and how you go off in different ways. It gives me pause, and I appreciate that.
- I can see how triggers happen. I am sorry for other people cruelty at your expense. Yes, BDSM does and has healed SO many people.
- Some do equate punishment as love. Battered woman syndrome, and children, sadly.
- I just don't understand, except that we are all different.
- Oh yes; different. And that's not always a bad thing
- I LIKE different!
- Definitely not a bad thing. I like all the different views I get from people.
- I agree 100%. Following my abuse as a child and domestic violence as an adult, I use BDSM to control everything in the bedroom. I can't have touching in any way shape or form and it helps me control that. I also express myself through Domination.
- That makes sense, being the dominant. I probably could handle that. I just don't think I could handle being the submissive as a victim of abuse. Do you ever take the submissive role or just stick with Dominant?

- I've never been the sub; I really wouldn't be able to deal with it mentally.

Parental Control

"My folks, they kept me on a tight leash; they didn't understand."

Do you think it was the best solution for Grace and Carrick to keep Christian "on a tight leash" at 15? Do you generally believe in stricter parenting - or do you have a looser approach?

- As I see it, they did it because the way he was always angry, brawling, not acting like his brother. They thought he'd learn to control himself instead of trying to defy his parents. I'm a bit strict. Having teenagers is a bit of challenge somedays, but I also believe they need some freedom. They need to learn on their own that life is hard and not easy. They need to enjoy been young, but they also need to know I'll be watching and that they'd be in trouble if they break the rules.
- Christian had a lot of problems. He fought a lot and got kicked out of three schools, so they had no choice.
- It depends on the child. I lean more toward strict parenting because I want to keep my kids from the kinds of harm people like Elena could inflict on them. But they can negotiate with me on some things. Honestly, my parenting style can change from day to day. I think they were doing the best they knew. Like one of my favorite quotes from Maya Angelou says, "When you know better, you do better." They probably followed what the therapist told them was best for Christian.
- I think the key is to bring them up right from the beginning, so they know right from wrong and they'll stay in line. Sure, they'll make mistakes and get into trouble, to test the limits. That's part of growing up. You have to give them enough freedom to learn from those mistakes.

Ana's Childhood

We know a lot of Christian's childhood. What are your thoughts about what Ana's childhood was like – at any age?

- She seems to have been a responsible, if not slightly withdrawn child. She probably felt secure with Ray, but when Carla started fooling around with Stephen (my impression), it probably made Ana feel insecure about her future.
- I've always had the feeling that Ana's moving back with her second father, Ray, was because Stephen had done sexual things to her. It's called "covert molestation:" touching, invading privacy, taking nude photos, that kind of thing. I'm not saying those were the specific things done, merely defining the term. But it seems like something inappropriate happened with him.
- You just know that something traumatizing happened to young Ana (in her teens). She's just too quiet and too much of a loner, and her confidence was completely shaken. I really wish her past was examined in more depth, so we'd have an idea of what made Ana who she was by the time she met Christian; who in so many ways, "fixed" her, the same way she fixed him.
- I always thought that that third husband probably made inappropriate remarks and touches, but maybe didn't go further than that. He just said and did things to make her uncomfortable. And she probably also didn't approve of his relationship with her mother. Whereas Ray was a ray of sunshine and stability for her, someone who really loved her, even more than her own mother.
- Maybe it's just me, but I didn't sense any self-confidence issues with Ana. What were they? Anybody recognize anything?
- She didn't recognize Jose's attraction to her. Her mother's dismissal of her had to have had an impact.
- Also, she couldn't take a compliment from Christian. When he kept telling her how beautiful she was, she refused to believe it. Or at the very least was quite skeptical.

99

- She thought herself as being plain; I don't think she thought herself attractive. How old was Ana when her mother married the third time, I'm thinking maybe she was old enough that she would remember inappropriate touching, and would have let it be known especially when she was trying to get Christian to open up. She loved Ray, I wonder if Carla and the third husband thought her to be in their way, maybe he convinced Carla that Ana would be better off with Ray, she was a little, um, dingy. Just speculation.
- She also didn't believe Kate's compliments about her. And Flynn called her out about her self-esteem issue during their therapy session. I didn't feel that she had really low self-esteem. I felt like she was probably a typical girl who didn't think she was pretty enough to be sought after. A lot of girls feel that way even without having been abused. It's still uncomfortable for me to have my hubby compliment me sometimes.
- Ana was an introvert, which explains a lot. But I think it goes further than that. As attractive as she was, she had extremely limited interactions with boys growing up and through college. It's a red flag that there was something else going on in her past that made her withdraw like that.
- I don't think Carla was good for Ana's confidence. (Remember when she kept telling her daughter she regretted having her?) I feel like Carla was more the attention-hog and might've even felt competitive with Ana. I also feel like she dismissed Ana's needs and prioritized her own interests (projects, husbands, etc.) over her daughter's.

Motherly Instincts

Do you think Ana was one of those girls who always wanted to be a mom? Who played with baby dolls and did some babysitting?

- She was naturally nurturing, which makes her seem motherly. But she was also so withdrawn from men and had fanciful, romantic notions about relationships, not to mention a mother that wasn't much of a role model, it seems like she wouldn't have had ambitions to be a mother.

- She didn't seem like her primary goal in life was to have children. She probably thought "maybe, someday," but didn't give it much thought.
- Many girls grow up with the notion that it's expected that they become mothers. I don't think Ana necessarily grew up with that idea because of her interest in literature and wanting a career. However, I think parenting would be second nature to her.
- I think she probably played with dolls growing up. She would've been a good, responsible babysitter. I think she knew she wanted to have kids one day. But I don't think it was something she thought about every day.
- I think motherhood crossed her mind often. However, she also felt that at this particular point in her life, she wasn't ready. She kept thinking that she should be "at least 30." I think the fact that Carla was a mother so young influenced her (she thought Carla was pretty flighty). We know next to nothing about Ana as a child (I wonder if that's deliberate). I do think she played with dolls, but I don't think she did any babysitting since she was rarely anywhere long enough to really get to know families who needed a babysitter. I think her maternal feelings are strictly instinctual.
- Ana did have that side to her. We know how she felt being an only child. My guess is that deep down she had those thoughts for her future. Besides, she acted more like a mother to Ray.
- She definitely was a motherly type.

Ella

I'm curious how many of us give Ella a bit of slack due to her addiction issues. Does it in some way excuse her bad decisions? If you don't mind, with your comments let us know if you have someone close to you struggling with addiction and how that influences your thoughts.

- It's difficult to say, because like everything there is many shades of gray in addiction and addicts. Some can be cured, while others are forever lost. Ella had some love for Christian. Maybe if someone had come to take her away from drugs and prostitution, she might have had the chance to be a good mother.
- Let me say this first, I had 4 brothers. Two of them died from natural causes. One is healthy and happy, but my middle brother is a drug addict. The one who I thought would be dead already, last I heard, was still alive. The last time we saw him was the day before our oldest brother's funeral. He was trying to borrow money from my sister-in-law. He got mad because she didn't give it to him. He wouldn't come in the house to see anyone and left. Last we heard he was in jail. We don't even know if he knows that our younger brother passed away. He was my world and he made me feel like I could take on the world - like I could become the dancer/ choreographer I wanted to be. But, I had to let go because you can't help someone who is not ready to be helped. I keep him in my prayers and hope that he's okay.
- I feel that Ella loved Christian. He was the one person in her life who truly loved her. But she had her demons. Her pimp kept her high, beat her and Christian regularly. She didn't know how to protect him because she couldn't protect herself. I always felt that she didn't commit suicide but overdosed. A four-year-old is not going to know the difference; to him, she fell asleep.
- I can't imagine the torture of addiction. Nor can I imagine the despair she must have felt. I do think she had to have moments of lucidity where she could have done what's "right" by her son, and by not using those moments for his best interest, I can't excuse her behavior.
- I give her a lot of slack. She was a sh*tty mother, but addiction can be a crippling thing. However, I did lose a lot of sympathy for her when she called him "Maggot" in *Grey*. But, I never saw her as a villain. She was a

f*cked up mess who could not even take care of herself, let alone a little boy like Christian. The only true villain I saw in his childhood is the f*cking pimp that tortured him. That guy should have been castrated.

- Yeah, I forgot about the "Maggot" quote. I can't forgive that for any reason. No excuse for that.
- It does make me wonder how Christian survived his infancy. Can you imagine Ella breast feeding, or warming up a bottle? What about changing diapers? To me, it's nearly a miracle that he lived to be four years old with her.
- It does make you wonder, especially if you have children and see how much care they need. No wonder he couldn't talk.
- I can honestly understand and forgive Elena a lot easier than I can Ella.
- According to the Fifty Shades Widia, Ella killed herself? I know she overdosed, but that doesn't necessarily mean she killed herself. It could have been an accidental overdose. Do we know for sure that she committed suicide?
- I tend to think that there's a level of suicide in (most) every overdose. Even if it's just not caring if you live or not, choosing the addiction over life.
- I see your point, but to me a suicide is intentionally taking something with the sole purpose of ending your life, not just to get high. I never got the feeling that she deliberately overdosed to kill herself. I think she just took too much of something one day, maybe it was stronger than she was used to, but that she never intended to actually end her own life.
- But by taking the drugs, she didn't care if she lived or died. She wanted to escape - in whatever form it took (IMO).
- I'm not sure if that's really true. I've never been an addict, but I don't think they are all suicidal. I don't think most of them don't care if they live or die. I think they are just chasing that high. Wanting to zone out for a while, but not necessarily actually die.

- But by taking the drugs they know the risks - and don't care.
- I give her some slack. Addiction is terrible. I've seen many friends addicted to drugs and alcohol. I had a friend and neighbor who was a responsible person. She had a job, apartment, etc. She got hooked on speed, snorted it. Lost everything. She lost weight, had sores on her face and picked at them. She was a mess. I had moved away, but one time she came to my place and I let her stay a few days. She stole a lot of money from us. I never saw her again. That was in the 80's. I had another friend who was an alcoholic - really bad. When he was 13, his dad told him "I'm going to kill myself." He went and shot himself. I guess it had an effect on him. Anyways, he lived on the street and turned tricks sometimes. We would let him come over and stay so he could clean up and eat. One time, he came over beyond drunk. He went into the fridge found a watermelon, cut some of it, then put the rest back, but smashed it and shoved in a drawer. Another time, when I was asleep, he took my car in the middle of the night. I woke up to hear him driving into the driveway. He ended up blind and paralyzed from falling off the top of a van when he was visiting his family. They gave up on him. I kept in contact with him. He was in a place that took care of him. He tried to kill himself more than once. He got a razor blade, cut up his legs because he couldn't feel. Another time, he tried to cut his penis off. It was terrible. He did get better and was moving into his own apartment, through the state. This was in the late 80's early 90's. We would talk on the phone. I moved again, sadly I don't know what happened to him. He's probably dead. Another friend who was my roommate became addicted to speed, also. Sold it, and she also was an alcoholic. Short story, she ended up in jail. After she got out, I let her stay with me – this was in the mid 90's. Happily, she is in a good place has a good job, and owns her own condo. I keep in touch with her. So I know what addiction can do to people. Terrible demons. Guess that's why I give Ella some slack.

104

- I think I'd have a lot more compassion if she hadn't had Christian. Once she did, she should have at least given him up for adoption.
- In my opinion, being an addict is not only hurting yourself, but everyone around you. Ella didn't care how much she took as long as she got her fix. Addiction to anything and overdose is intentional, I know from some family members.
- I have a granddaughter who wanted to stay with us to help herself get clean. My grandson said "sure, I'll help you out." It's his sister from another mother - half-sister, I guess. This was just recently. She was addicted to heroin. She was high when my grandson picked her up, and she seemed to get a little better. She knew no one in this area. She wanted to borrow the car, but didn't say that to my husband. She said she wanted to visit a friend, and asked if that was that okay. He said "yes" and she took the car; he was so mad; she didn't say anything about the car. One strike. She wanted to borrow the car to go see her kids. My grandson took her, brought the two kids back for a few days. The way she talked to those kids, if I were her mother I would have choked her. The kids went home, and my grandson told her she had to go too. She stole so much from him and his real sister. It's a big mess. He went to the police, filed a report on her. She stole my son and daughter-in-law's wedding bands, her engagement ring, a charm a few other things. I know drugs destroy the best people. I felt sorrier for my grandson, trying to help her and she sh*t on him; he's too good-hearted.
- I had a brother addicted to cocaine and alcohol. He hurt his back and I took him to the ER. He was high and drunk. I took the doctor aside and explained the addiction. He gave me two weeks' worth of pain killers and sleeping pills to knock him out with. My brother slept through his DTs. He always thought he beat the cocaine addiction by himself without drugs. I let him think that. Unfortunately, he stuck to the alcohol. He developed cancer and the doctor told him to quit drinking, and he would probably beat the cancer.

Unfortunately, he kept drinking. Went to bars with no immune system and a caught blood infection. We lost him two years ago. I wouldn't stay mad at Ella. She couldn't help it. It is truly a disease. I think I would forgive Ella before Elena. Elena was a pedophile. I don't forgive pedophiles. My cousin was married to one. Of course, she didn't know that. He molested her daughter for 6 years. Manipulated and scared the daughter to keep her quiet. I say castrate the male bastards. I wish we could do that to females. We found out after my cousin left him. We locked the bastard up for 13 years. Wish it could have been for life. My little cousin was given a life sentence of hell when he abused her. She will never be a normal person with a normal life.

- Terrible. I say castrate them, too. I forgot, my ex-sis-in-law was an alcoholic. She went through withdrawal. She had to be admitted because she saw bugs crawling the walls. My ex-hubby became addicted to gambling. He moved to Las Vegas with his wife. He had to go to Gam-Anon. He's always been kind of a loser. Never kept a job. He's retired now. My daughters keep in touch with him. I see him once in a while at family stuff. All kinds of addiction.

- Do you put Elena in the same category as your cousin's ex?

- Yes, I do. My cousin's daughter was molested from the age of 11-17, so she was a little younger at the beginning. He used alcoholism as an excuse to judge. I think he just pissed the judge off more when he said that.

- So you think Elena was as guilty as your cousin's ex who molested his own daughter, or step-daughter, who was much younger? (I guess I'm asking for three reasons. One, the double-standard of an older woman vs. an older man. Two, the distinction of a family member vs. a family friend. And, three, Christian was just a year under age - could have been only a month. Still illegal... just feels different to me).

- I think our experiences influence our perceptions. I was telling another Deeper member that she might feel different about Carrick mentioning a prenup if she had children. Maybe they aren't the same, but because I've experienced the pain in my family, and have seen the effect it has on my little cousin. I see it as the same.

- I can't see Elena as a pedophile. She didn't do anything Christian didn't want to, I guess. He was 15, a teenager and at this age, young boys get crazy about sex. The lifestyle she led was wrong to me, but I guess he even liked that.
- To me, Elena's biggest offenses came to light the way she continued to try to control him after the relationship ended, especially when Ana came into the picture.
- We need to find out from E.L. James if, in her mind, Ella overdosed or whether it was suicide. I wish I had thought of this when she was answering our questions.
- I don't cut her any slack because I've seen stuff like this. There's no excuse for not taking care of your child.
- Addiction or not, if she had one single moment of lucidity she should have found another home for him.
- And we know she did (have moments of lucidity). He has memories that are good ones. Not many, but still enough.
- I always have compassion for individuals who have addiction problems; however, having said that, I believe Ella was selfish to not give up Christian so he could be adopted. I also believe that those who have addiction issues need psychological help and should not keep acting out their addictions.
- My ex-husband was a drug abuser - marijuana, cocaine when he could afford it and mushrooms, pills; he was an alcoholic, but a functioning one who didn't drink during the day; he was a sex addict who was into BDSM (when I didn't know it). He didn't make love; he just f*cked for the sake of feeling power and release. I don't know if he was capable of love. He also didn't get help with a therapist on a continual basis. I could no longer handle it after being his enabler for 25 years. I finally had to let go.
- Damn, how did you stand it for 25 years?
- I was crazy.

- I think it's peculiar how we make excuses for people we love that we wouldn't tolerate from people we don't know. Addiction is a disease, and it's far more difficult to heal than people realize.
- I went to a lecture on addiction a few years ago. Fascinating - and terrifying - what drugs do to the brain, especially heroin.
- I'm not sure I cut her slack, but I just wish she had the strength to seek out the help she so desperately needed. What shocks me more than anything is the fact that no one in the neighborhood called Child Protection Services (CPS) about the fact that there was a little boy in the home who was severely neglected. I think if CPS had intervened, Ella would likely have been forced to seek help and clean up her act enough to properly take care of her little boy.
- Yes! Why didn't someone intervene?
- I really think her pimp had more to do with her not seeking help. I think he would have liked her to get rid of Christian. She didn't see a lot of sh*t he did to that poor child.
- I wonder about that, too. Why he didn't find another home for Christian. I guess we'll never know.
- Addiction isn't just an attachment to something. According to several sources, "Addiction is a brain disease that is characterized by compulsive engagement in rewarding stimuli, despite adverse consequences."
- How old was she when she became addicted and a hooker, and how old was she when she had Christian? She was obviously a victim from beginning to end. Was it her fault? Yes. Was it her family's fault? Yes. Was it her pimp's fault? Yes.
- Addiction is hard to break, more for some than others. I believe that you need to hit rock bottom before you can pick yourself up. Unfortunately, In Ella's case, she had a pimp who wouldn't let her pick herself up, and unfortunately, ended worse for her and terrible for her 4-year-old son. You have to look at what drove her into drugs and prostitution in the first place, and whether this

108

was her only way of coping. She needed money to take care of her son, but put it back into drugs and her pimp. She was weak, and didn't see any way out. She was so young she couldn't protect her son or herself. Maybe there is a book in there about Ella's life.

- If our beloved E.L. James reads this post, I would love her to see how the characters she created have led to such rich discussion and insights. For many people, this group has offered not only friendship and bonding, it has also provided a form of analysis that has led to greater self-development. What could be more beautiful - and important - than that?

- I've been thinking about this. About how our reactions may be affected by our experiences with addiction. It's not only a cruel disease for the person addicted, it also wreaks havoc on the people around them. Do we identify more with the person addicted? Or the people hurt by addicts? Hmmm.

- I can't judge her. She was heavily addicted to drugs, left alone without any help, abused by the pimp. Nevertheless, she gave birth to Christian, didn't give up on him. In the moments of lucidity, she baked cakes for him. It's difficult to answer. A friend of mine, who, at the time was 11 years old, had an alcoholic mother. I guess there was also child abuse, because she slept in the shed many times. One day, she found some courage and went to a judge and asked to be sent to an orphanage.

- I have read many of your posts before I decided to respond. Addiction is a disease not a choice. I have complete sympathy for Ella. When you witness it daily, you see another side of it. She was completely helpless, and that is how an addict feels. They don't want to do it, but they feel like it is their only option. Trust me, it is not so black and white, and it is an epidemic in this country. I'm surprised that Christian didn't become an addict himself, just because of the pain he was feeling. In some ways, I guess he did, and that is why he thought Elena helped him. She taught him to harness his pain and release it through BDSM. Addicts will drain you and everyone they love, and you really can't help them unless they want to help themselves first. But giving up on them is just as destructive to their psychological state. They already feel unworthy of love and when you shut them out, I don't think it is helping the situation at all. They will hurt you and you will want to just quit on them, but you can't. They need you more than ever, especially when they hit rock bottom. It's really hard, and it hurts a lot.

- I'm not sure about this. I have a friend who was struggling with an addicted stepson. I advised her to go to a family support group. She was advised by them to let go/give up. There was nothing more she could do, and by always giving in, she was just enabling him. She finally realized this, and it has healed her immensely.

- Well, I have someone who is very very close to me, who is an addict. It is ultimately their decision to seek help and get it, but that doesn't mean giving up on them. There is a difference between supporting them, and enabling them. So, I will have to disagree with what the person in family support told that lady.

- My friend was destroying herself. Destroying. Again - it was undeniably the right thing for her to do. The best advice she could have gotten. I'm so thankful she sought help and got the best advice.

- I feel truly blessed knowing there are people I can share with, and know that they are not going to stone me to death for the things I know or do. I really appreciate this group

- Interestingly, my friend called me this morning. She said she went to Al-Anon and there was a son who spoke who really got through to her. She also said that by not enabling her stepson, he has improved his life.

- While I agree that addiction is an illness, I honestly don't think it's the same as other illnesses. Why? Because of the behavior of so many addicts. The way they lie, cheat and steal to get their next fix. The disregard so many of them have for anyone around them. The attitude of entitlement they have, treating others like they "owe" them something that they don't. I had a friend who was going through a very difficult time and offered her a place to live - for free. At first she was fine - going to AA meetings a couple of times a day. But, then she started drinking. As soon as she did, her behavior changed. She started lying to me, taking things, etc. Here I was, trying to help her, and she was using me. I gave her a final ultimatum, and she finally left. I have no idea what happened to her. And, while I still pray for her, I couldn't do any more. Correction: I wouldn't. No way would I let her destroy my sanity. By the way, I did go to an AA meeting with her - while she was drinking. It blew me away. I think everyone should experience an open meeting, to learn more about how it is. I have enormous compassion for them and what they go through. I really do.

- But who gave Ella the drugs? Who started her on the drugs, and at what age? Was she abused as a child? Was she groomed by an adult and used as a commodity? Interesting how it all came full circle when it came to Christian, groomed and abused by an adult. If it was all she knew from an early/teen age, then what chance did she have? I cannot remember how old she was when she died.

- I think she was an addict who put her needs above her child's. I don't hate her as a person, but rather how she was raising her son. Plus, I don't think we get any sense of her until *Grey*, and it just seems like she was going down a hole that was going to only lead in two places: death or rehab. Yes, I have a family member that is an addict, and I have been raised around addictions.

- I'm not sure if addicts can see anything past their own needs. After a while the physical addiction is even stronger than the psychological addiction. I met my youngest three children when they were first brought into my clinic. Their biological mother had abandoned them left them with strangers she met with the circus (can't even make this sh*t up) when she was so wrapped up in drugs. I had to admit two of them, aged 10 months and 3 years to the hospital, due to illness and neglect. I wasn't a foster parent at the time, so they had to go into the system. I watched them get bounced through four different foster homes before their biological mom opted to terminate her own rights, rather than stay clean. I was doing volunteer respite care for some of the fosters who were my patients and had gotten to know the boys by this time. I saw my 2 and 3-year-old hold hands, and pray for God to send them a mommy and a daddy. My husband and I called DHHR the next day. I am laying here, holding my baby, and I can't imagine anything being more powerful than how much I love my children. Addiction is beyond my medical understanding and personal understanding. (Side comment: The little parts from Christian as a child makes me bawl like a baby. I can't help it.)

- Wow. What a story.
- Amazing. You are quite a woman!
- The small peeks into Christian's childhood devastated me the first time I read them. I work with children, and witness the destructive things they live through, and it breaks my heart.
- My dad was a doctor who was recently and publicly suspended for an ongoing alcohol and opiate addiction. I'm from a small town in North Dakota, and was embarrassed for him when it made the news in an ongoing story about impaired doctors. He has been through long-term rehab and refuses to go again. His addiction has cost him everything, and he can't, or won't stop. I'm a public defender and deal with addicts all day long. I'll admit to being frustrated and perplexed about how to fix the problem of addiction. Sometimes, I get angry with my dad and my clients for continuing to destroy their lives, and I'm not always fair about it.
- I believe addiction is a disease. So, in my opinion you can't really blame them for their actions. But, I do

understand why people who have been affected by growing up with addicted parents, feel abandoned and let down. Even anger. It's a tricky one.

Breaking Up is Hard to Do

Many fans were both shocked and devastated when they read the ending of the first book in the FSOG series. "What?" they asked. "She... left?"

Yes. She did. E.L. James took a risk with this ending. It most certainly wasn't the "happily ever after" of traditional romances. Whether she knew all along that there would be subsequent books in the series or not, we'll never know. But even when readers were aware of the sequels, indicating their story wasn't over when it was "over," it was still heart wrenching. And significant, as you'll see.

When It's Over, It's Over

Christian made this clear to Ana - if she left, it was over-over-over. How do you think this fact influenced the plot of the book? If he'd left it more open-ended, how might that have changed the story?

- I don't know that she would've come back. She knew she wanted more and couldn't accept his offer to be his submissive and that lifestyle. She liked the pleasure, but not the punishment aspect.
- He was too in love to lock those doors.
- I don't think it would've changed the story one bit. While Christian was the one who said it, I don't think he really believed or felt what he said, especially when Ana kept hesitating about giving him her decision. In *Grey*, he kept thinking to himself that he didn't know what he'd do if she said "no" because he absolutely had to have her, and couldn't really face moving forward without her. Let's face it, she walked out on him, and HE was the one who initiated contact to get her back. These are not the actions of someone who says "once you go, that's it."
- That's so true - from his POV. But what about Ana's POV?

- It made her a bit nervous and she was conflicted. She really did want him, so I think it was in the back of her mind, especially until she ultimately made her decision.
- I think that his saying that to her was a big deal. I really don't think she thought there was any way they would reconcile. Of course, we don't really know what was going through her mind over the weekend, after they split because the story does not tell us. I know she was in pain and probably stayed in bed the whole time and cried, but what was she thinking? Did she fantasize that they would get back together? I don't think so, because even though some of his actions showed that he had feelings for her, his words said something different. I think if he had not said that, it would have changed the reconciliation. He even told Flynn that he had not even considered a relationship her way. As much as he wanted Ana, I don't think in the beginning, he thought there was any way she would take him back as he was. I do think that statement set into motion the whole setup for *Darker*. Without it, I don't think the reconciliation would have been as miraculous.
- I think, because of his statement, she knew that if she left, there was no turning back. That's why she gave back the computer and phone. She might have mourned the loss, but she wasn't going to go back - for any reason. I'm also SO thankful for this - because we know she didn't leave as a "ploy" to get him back. She left because she had to end it before it got even darker.
- Yes! Absolutely! She was genuine from the start.
- Brownell I thought it was harsh (and ultra-controlling) of him to give this ultimatum. And in a contract, no less! It was, in a word, heartless. That being said, I'm glad that the ending was definitive. She knew that her decision was final; not only for herself, but to him, too. Too often we leave relationships open-ended, which often doesn't allow for healing and moving on. For the reader, it made the ending that much more wrenching.

When She Left

We all know Christian's journey to seduce Ana into becoming his submissive. In the end, he also realized he wanted a different relationship with her. He was left bereft when she left him. What advice would you have given to Christian (before you knew what happened to their relationship) as you saw things start to unravel for himself and Ana?

- I think Flynn's advice is good here - "walk before you run."
- I felt panicky at times and wanted to become a little elfin-like creature and run and sit on Ana's or Christian's shoulder and give advice. It was almost overwhelming for me, at times because, obviously, through my own life experiences, I saw the writing on the wall. Do you mean that Christian and Ana moved too quickly in their relationship?
- Not per se, although it was rather speedy. But, we know things worked out in the end. For both of them, it was their very first relationship, and they had no idea how to navigate within it. In a way, at least they could learn together as they went along. I'm thinking mainly about the belting. Christian was showing Ana the worst. He did it per Elena's advice, who was hoping and praying it was too much and too soon - and she was right!
- So, what advice would you have given Christian regarding the belting?
- Oh, it's a difficult one, but he should've introduced Ana to harsher aspects very slowly. She knew nothing about BDSM except what she looked up online, and got some pointers from Christian. And, he definitely shouldn't have belted her! He got lost in the moment, which was very wrong.
- I would've told him that he was obviously pushing Ana away - and asked him if that's what he really wanted.
- I think I would've told Christian to talk to her, and open up to her, because deep down inside that is what she wanted. In terms of Ana, I would've told him to not

show her the harsher elements of the lifestyle. It will only alienate her and drive her away. I would've said to Ana that he isn't ready to open up yet, and pushing him will only backfire.

- So, if Christian was reticent to talk, how would you have encouraged him to do so? Pretend you have Christian in a room by yourself and he asked for your advice. If you could keep your hands off him, how would you have begun the conversation?

- You are good. Do you have a therapeutic a background? Here's what I would say, "I saw that girl you were with yesterday, and you looked really happy. She also looks very vanilla to the lifestyle. Have you told her about your sadist tendencies? My mother used to put cigarettes out on me when she got mad." I think that's how I would try to get him to talk.

- No, I don't have a therapeutic background professionally. I do have an interest in communication, am intuitive, somewhat skeptical, and genuinely want to help people. At one point, I worked for Planned Parenthood as a sex education counselor under Title IX, of the Public Health Services Act. The goal of the program was to work with teenagers to lower the incidence of teen pregnancy. We dealt with communicating, self-esteem issues, and just one thing that led to another. I also taught art to high school and junior high school students.

- Damn, don't you wish we could have been elves on Christian's shoulder? I guess part of me just wants to save Christian and Ana from so many tears.

- I know the feeling, (wanting to save someone). Though, I do think they needed to feel the palpable pain in order to really change. One of the most important parts of the story!

- He should not have given Ana the ultimate punishment, even if he thought she should know. Maybe she shouldn't know at all. After all, it is a brutal punishment. But, I think Christian couldn't resist because, as we saw, he so loved every whip of that belt. You could see the pleasure all over his face. I would've told Christian that whatever has happened between you both, I see you are in pain as never before. If she has left or she isn't talking to you, then you must go to her and explain yourself, and tell her how sorry you are. If she needs distance, then give it to her, and if she loves you, she will come back to you, as long as you communicate with her. If you don't hear from her after a while, then go after her.

Transformation

Relationships, especially important relationships, change us forever. This is as true with real life as it is with fiction. And it's especially profound with Anastasia Rose Steele and Christian Trevelyan Grey.

Pygmalion

"Hmm. The jacket is worn and cheap. Miss Anastasia Steele should be better dressed."

Why do you think Christian was saying this? Was he judging her? Or, wanting to take care of her?

- I don't think he meant this as condescending. He was being observant and already thinking that he wanted to provide a better "life" for her.
- Christian was immediately drawn to Ana. Right from the get-go, he wanted her, and with that came the thought that she could look so much better with nicer clothes. He was quite willing to do that for her, providing she would agree to be his sub. I don't think he was judging her, he was merely making an observation, and really did want to take care of her - I think it's ingrained in his nature. Also, he never commented out loud about what he thought of her clothes. It was his internal dialogue. If he said it out loud, Ana would've sassed him right back and that would've been the last time he would ever see her. I'd be the same way.
- I agree. If he had said that to her she would've never seen him again. There is a time, place, and a way to tell someone they should be better dressed. He had couth.
- I think he was implying she was far too beautiful to be wearing cheap clothes.
- He was attracted to her from the beginning and wanted her so bad that he thought about caring for her from the start.
- I think he thinks she deserves better quality things, the finer things that life has to offer.

- He was fighting the urge to treat her like a sub.
- He wanted her to have nice things.
- He was picturing, in his mind, what she would look like in some beautiful clothes!
- His observation really bugged me. I thought he was being very condescending and judgmental.

Which Hurt More?

Which hurt Ana more?
- The six hits with the belt?
- Not being able to touch Christian?
- Not being able to sleep with him?
- Christian telling her that it was wrong for her to love him?
- Something else?

- Realizing that they were no longer together.
- The belt, and his telling her she can't love him. It is a toss-up between those two for me.
- I'd go for not being able to touch. It's such an important part of a relationship. Christian loved touching Ana, yet she was not able to (when on many occasions she was dying to). That must have been very hard.
- I think that as much as the belt hurt, it hurt her even more that Christian wouldn't let her touch him.
- I would say it's a toss-up between not being able to touch and not being able to love him. The last one, I think, hurt her more than the hits from the belt.
- Christian telling her it was wrong to love him.
- The physical pain from the belt went away somewhat quickly (a day or two). I believe the emotional pain/hurt from not being able to being able to touch Christian hurt Ana more.
- The belt, not being able to touch, not sleeping in the same bed, not being able to love him the way he needs. So, I guess, all of it.
- Not being able to be what Christian wanted, "a true submissive."

120

- I think it was the gap between not being what he wanted/needed and what she was able to tolerate for herself. Making that decision to leave, that she could never be "enough" was excruciating – far more than the hits of the belt.

Who Needed Who?

Do you think Christian needed Ana more, or do you think Ana needed Christian more? Did they need each other equally? Why do you think Ana was THE ONE and not the others? What made her special?

- As much as Ana was in so much pain about the breakup, I think Christian was in much, much worse shape. He had horrible nightmares and it seemed that whenever they ended with Ana, he seemed to feel much better. He was more determined to "win her back." She was "special" because she challenged Christian like no other woman ever had. I think he really admired that, and it made her stand out way ahead of the others.
- They were meant to be!
- They needed each other, maybe not equally, but she was so different than the others. She wasn't into that lifestyle and she didn't care about his money. The others wanted the money and hoped to be Mrs. Grey. (Well, some of them did.) Ana was very different, and they were meant to be together.
- I definitely think he needed her more.
- They needed each other but Christian needed Ana more. He never got close to his subs. If they said they wanted "more," he would end their contract. The others wanted his name and money. Ana just wanted him, and he could see that she was different from the others.
- What made Ana special is that she touched his heart (unbeknownst to him), and somehow he touched hers (unbeknownst to her). In this respect, they were equally innocent. Neither had experienced love. So, they were evenly matched.

121

- He needed her more. As much as Ana was hurting, she was still strong. If Christian had insisted on the BDSM relationship, I don't think she would've come back. He was in much worse shape.
- I agree. She would have ultimately been okay. Yes, he's a tough act to follow, so it would take a while, but she'd be okay.
- I think they needed each other equally.
- I think he needed her more. He NEEDED her. She was falling in love with him, but I don't think she needed him. She was young and strong, and discovering the world for the first time truly on her own. I think she would've been heartbroken, but she would have eventually picked up the pieces and moved on. Christian had everything else. He was the master of his universe, but the one thing he had never experienced or encountered was the innocence of true love. Once that box was opened, he could never go back. He couldn't undo those feelings. For him, this chance at feeling alive… whole… was something he never knew he even wanted, but once he experienced it, nothing else would ever do.

Who's Changing Who?

Christian claims it's Ana who's changing him. What do you think? Would you change for someone just to be with them?

- Would it be changing yourself or uncovering what you really need?
- I'm already 100 shades of weird. Why change?
- We are all Fifty Shades f*cked up. Just saying. LOL!
- Yes, I had a life before and after *Fifty Shades of Grey*. What was I doing before then?
- I don't think you really "change." You can just improve who you are. I think Ana strengthened and put forward a part of him that was hiding deep in his heart and soul. Elena fed his anger and need for control, while Ana has nurtured his kindness and love. These are feelings he already had inside himself. Elena brought out his dark side, while Ana brought out his light side.

- I think most people don't change that much, especially men. I think people do change a little for someone. If you have to change a lot, then maybe you aren't right for that person.
- I think Ana and who she was: challenging him, her intelligence, independence, beauty, innocence, sweetness, that which exuded the need for protection brought out Christian's well-hidden nurturing side. He didn't recognize that part of himself. Christian changed himself because of his need for Ana.
- It's a relief to be accepted for who you are. Compromise is a good thing and does require a modicum of change in us.
- Ana and Christian changed each other - most definitely for the better. They made each other better people! Can't be upset about that.
- I think that when you find the person that you simply cannot live without, it awakens parts of you that you were not aware existed, until that moment. I believe that's why you feel that you are finally alive, and wonder how you existed until then.
- Brownell - Here's a quote from one of my books that encapsulates what I think: *There's a fine line between trying to be everything your mate wants you to be and wanting to be loved for who you are. - from DUET stories Volume III: A Chorus of Voices by Brownell Landrum.*
- Also - I think, as several of you have suggested, is to find someone who "brings out the best" in you. Someone who really believes in you, someone who is your champion.
- I think they were both changing each other because she had no relationship before this. Together, they were learning how to be in a relationship. He had never been straightforward with a woman, nor had he ever been with a woman that had never just signed his contract automatically. Christian gave her confidence and made her feel sexy, and made her feel like a beautiful woman. I feel like Ana made him feel loved for the first time in

his life. He eventually accepted that he was able to be loved.

- My life changed when I met my husband. He helped me, and he saved my life. I was going in a really bad direction and hanging out with the wrong people, and doing the wrong things. My husband took me away to live on a base. He told me that he loved me, and that he wanted to be with me. He wanted to save me because I used to be anorexic and bulimic. I weighed under a hundred pounds, so I was slowly killing myself. I did change for the better, and he made me feel beautiful for a change, after being with a man who beat me for four years.
- We are all brought into each other's lives for a reason. Some for a brief moment, and others for a lifetime. Your husband is your lifetime. You are blessed, my sweet friend.
- I'd be willing to compromise.

Change is Inevitable

Who do you think changed the most during their relationship? Did Christian change more to accommodate Ana's needs, or did Ana change more to accommodate Christian's needs? How important is change in a relationship? People often say that you should not try to change the other person, but people can and do change. I know my wife has certainly changed me in ways that I could have never imagined back when we first met. And I'm sure I'm responsible for change in her as well. Discuss.

- I think they both changed, but Christian changed the most. I don't think most people make major changes. I believe most people make small changes for the one they fall in love, but they don't change in major ways. Christian changed in major ways that I find is unusual. I've taught my daughter and her friends not to expect that kind of change in a man. Now if they meet a man and he changes, that will be a sweet surprise for them. I just don't want them to expect it and count on it.

124

- But why would that be a "sweet surprise?" Shouldn't a person fall in love with them the way they are now? Why would you want them to change, unless there is something about them that you don't like? In that case, perhaps you should question whether you should really be with them in the first place?
- I think you took that wrong. I'm talking about the little changes that we make when we compromise with our spouse. I assumed that is what you were referring to when you said your wife changed you. Wanting a spouse to change something small doesn't mean you don't love them or shouldn't be with them. I wanted my husband to stop smoking, but I sure didn't make it an ultimatum. I loved everything about him but that one thing. Should I have turned down a life of happiness with my soulmate because of one thing? Of course not. I didn't expect him to quit, but it sure was a sweet surprise when he did.
- I get that. My wife is always late to everything and it drives me nuts. I'd love it if that changed, but I've learned to live with it. I still love her, no matter how many times she's late for something.
- My husband had that same issue with me. I wasn't late for work but pretty much anything else that wasn't of major importance. I have changed that over the years. Now I'm on time or early. It has been a sweet surprise for him.
- I don't think my husband changed at all. Nor did I. He has his weaknesses and I have mine. Nothing disturbing though, thankfully!
- I think maybe Christian changed the most, but Ana became the most "entrenched." What I mean by that is that she was suppressed so much by him that it was a more difficult situation for her to get through. He forced her into silence and submission. (Even though it wasn't sexual submission, she was still his "submissive" in many ways, i.e. not being allowed to go out with her friends, not allowed to ride the jet ski, etc.) It might have been her tendency to be quiet and not share a lot, but when you're told you "can't" do something, it has an effect. She could have become more suppressed - but

thankfully, she broke free. (Maybe not completely but she did to a significant degree).

- Christian definitely changed the most. Ana was so inexperienced that it wasn't so much of a "change" for her. Christian had to learn how to love and be loved; Ana was already capable of that emotion. Watching him change and evolve and learn to accept the love from her was really why I love him so much.
- Christian. He was rigid in his life manners and styles. He had a system; almost robotic. Ana was more fluid and flexible to start. Of course both changed. However, he had to revamp his whole system to accommodate loving someone.
- I believe people change just being in a relationship; they mature together to fit their needs, completing each other. The so called "change" should always be done voluntarily. Otherwise, it is living with the restraints and constraints of trying to be what the other person wants. I hope Christian's change wasn't imposed on him, because if it was, sooner or later he'd be back to his old habits.
- Brownell Landrum - I think it depends on the motivation to change (or change someone). Spoiler Alert! In my book, *Five Reasons Why Bad Things Happen*, change is a key component of the "why" things happen. If a behavior is creating a negative outcome, it needs to change; pure and simple. There are degrees, of course. Anyone would have to acknowledge that drug addictions, for example, are likely to lead to negative consequences.
- Christian changed the most I think
- I think they both changed. Ana matured fast, from girl to woman, under the influence of Christian, and Christian developed his softer side. They say opposites attract, but during a relationship partners tend to look alike each other more and more.
- But don't you think this change was imposed on her? That she was forced to behave in a certain way until one day she might rebel?

126

- They both changed. Ana did mature more with Christian. And with Ana his life, Christian changed in good ways.
- Christian is the one who went through the most profound change. Without Ana, he would've continued his relatively solitary existence, living with demons and depression as his only constant companions. He never knew there was good in him or the world until she persistently showed him there was.
- I think Christian changed the most. But there's a difference between women trying to change their man (make him something he's not), and men changing themselves. In this case, he changes his life dramatically. But he chose to do so. No one is changing him. Ana changed too, but she wasn't very experienced, so I would say she developed her own way or matured.
- He had to change, or she wouldn't have come back. I see it as a forced change. It worked for the book, but in reality it doesn't usually work out.
- A drastic change like his is not very realistic in real life. But, to compare it with real life, some people spend years living really bad lives. Criminals, gang members, selling drugs etc. and can suddenly make a decision to completely change their life. I have a friend who did after many bad years and suddenly went into charity, meditation and helping people after years with criminal stuff and a quick time in jail while his sweet wife was pregnant. It's kind of the same, so it does happen.
- That is why I used the word "usually." It does happen but not often.
- It seems to me that when people make major, dramatic changes like that (kicking drugs, etc.), they've often "hit bottom" and saw the fork in the road ahead of them: continue and they'd destroy themselves, or make the change and start a new life.
- As I've been thinking about this question, I think Ana changed more, at least externally. She went from innocent, shy, insecure college student to wife, mother and business executive in one fell swoop. Christian's

transformation was also profound - perhaps even more profound - but it was more internal than external. He didn't change location, jobs or his daily routine nearly as much as she did.

- I believe that Christian and Ana changed in equal measure. They both needed each other. Christian needed Ana to show him that he is not the unlovable monster he thought he was. Yes, he was deeply flawed, but she accepted those flaws but also looked past them and saw a beautiful, com(passionate) man. Ana changed in that she went from being a sheltered young woman who hid behind her classic British novels. Christian showed her that she was beautiful and brought out he confident and sexy woman he knew she could be. In short, Ana taught Christian to love, and Christian taught Ana to live.

Christian's Dilemma

Chrisian seemed to be conflicted at the end *Grey*. What was he so tormented about, and how did that affect his decisions?

- After the break-up, Christian was going through a major dilemma. He'd never experienced these painful feelings before. He was so lucky that Ana understood more than he could imagine, and they both learned so much from each other's worlds, and were therefore able to meet each other halfway.
- Brownell Landrum - I think his pain was a gift. Without it, he could not have transformed. I wrote a book called *Five Reasons Why Bad Things Happen: How to Turn Tragedies into Triumph*. I had a section about the benefits of pain. Really fascinating research on the topic. Christian is a prime example.
- Acknowledgement of pain and allowing it to run its course can be one of the most magnificent lessons ever experienced.
- He had deep feelings that he then knew he couldn't hide. They were real, and all because he was in love.

- It was good for Christian to feel pain. It made him realize how important Ana was to him! It's so true. You must not be afraid to allow yourself to feel the pain. Sometimes, it is needed to heal.
- The thing, in this case, was that Christian grew up at a young age, and was only able to identify with physical pain. But, when confronted with Ana, the feelings were alarmingly new from the beginning. That was a shock in itself. As I was reading *Grey*, I noticed after the doctor's visit, when they had their time in the RROP, his thoughts were those of severe joy and pleasure. I thought back to how he described his first encounter with Mia. There was that care, love, and protective innocence. He was encountering all of these feelings with Ana; in a different context, of course. That set the stage for how Ana had become a part of his "soul." To have that awakening, and then have it snatched away, had to feel like a sledgehammer to his being.
- It was so sad that Christian lived in all this pain for so many years. He didn't know how to deal with it, and get Ana back.

Has He Changed?

When Ana and Christian reconciled at the beginning of *Darker*, in the restaurant, Christian threatens to take her over his knee if she doesn't eat. To me that doesn't sound like he's changed at all. What would you think if you were Ana?

- Maybe he feels guilty for being the reason she lost all that weight and that's the only way he can convey his feelings? He doesn't care what he has to do. He only cares about the fact that she has to eat!
- I think he was still confused and wasn't watching what he said. Maybe he says it out of habit. He has lots of guilt about being the reason she lost weight.
- I think he said it playfully, staying true to who he is. But, secretly he's hoping it still had enough effect on her. He didn't have any intentions whatsoever of carrying out the action.

- You're probably right. It still made her uneasy, I think.
- I'm sure it did. Especially because it was the first time a spanking had been mentioned since the incident. The first mentioning of something after a traumatic event is always the worst, no matter how delicately approached.
- I think he was grandstanding.
- It's not about whether he's changed or not. It's about the fact that he's really worried about her not having eaten. He has issues about hunger and that's ingrained from when he was a child, and will never change. You combine that with Ana "defying" him to the point where he feels the urge to punish, and you have someone who will say things like that.

Christian's Rebellion against Elena

Why did Christian (eventually) rebel against Elena? What must have happened? Did he realize she was manipulative or kept him under control? If yes, what made him realize that? I guess it isn't so easy to get free. Leila is another example. After 2-3 years of being separated from Christian, she still obeyed his commands - she just knelt obediently in Ana's apartment. Thoughts?

- Maybe because once he experienced feelings - deep feelings of love (for Ana), I think he saw Elena in a different light. He says to her in a wounded way "you never once said you loved me." I think he finally realized what love was, and thought about their whole relationship differently.
- I think the difference came when he discovered what love is - with Ana. I'm not sure he thinks of Dom/sub relationships as being wrong. But I think he misunderstood his relationship with Elena. He thought she always meant well. I'm not sure Leila has anything to do with it. Can't wait to read his thoughts in *Darker Grey*.
- I just think Christian began to recognize that he was not a natural submissive. He needed that at one time, but as he grew older, he realized that he needed to be the one in

control, so he left her and began searching for his own submissives. I don't think Elena fought him on this either, in fact she probably encouraged him to move on. Of course, she continued to have a lot of influence with him, until he met Ana, at least.

- Wasn't Ana the first submissive he found on his own? And all the others, Elena's protégées?
- Yes, which is one reason why I think Elena didn't like her. She saw her as a threat to her influence over him. Ultimately, that turned out to be true.
- I agree with that. I also think Elena was concerned about Christian finding someone outside the lifestyle who wouldn't understand the lifestyle.
- I think she brainwashed Christian into the rules. And I also think Elena's rules and influence were important in his rise to success.
- Oh, certainly she manipulated him, and she expected everything to be reported at the salon for sure. So cunning. And, Ana was too intelligent for her.
- I thought the reason Christian and Elena split up was because she got caught by her husband. I thought that was the trigger. I agree that Christian was not a natural submissive. At some point, Elena had to give him some freedom. As his confidence grew, which, frankly, we have her to thank for some of it, he knew that he couldn't stay forever. She was probably losing control over him, which she didn't like either.
- I agree, that was probably the trigger, but I suspect he had been wanting to take more control, even before that.
- Concerned or scared to lose him. Hmm.
- He was at a vulnerable and very influential age when she sank her fangs into him. She had him convinced that her way was always the right one. Although, she mentored him to become a successful business man, it took someone else to open his eyes, someone who authentically loved him, like Ana. This helped him realize everything she made him believe wasn't true. He had strong feelings for Elena at some point, whether or not it was love, I'm not sure.

- I got the same impression that he felt something for Elena and since it hadn't been reciprocated, he let it go (his words in *Fifty Shades Darker*, "You never said you loved me").
- As far as their splitting up, I agree with the previous posters. He outgrew his submissive phase. He began to come into his own, and began to crave control over her, and Elena doesn't seem to be one to be dominated. Although, it makes me wonder. In the books, we see her as such a confident, strong willed, powerful woman. Yet, in her marriage, she was a battered woman.
- I think it was probably her lack of control in her marriage that led her to dominate an impressionable young boy in the first place.
- I have always felt like Elena was the submissive in her relationship with Linc. I am also convinced that she was abused before that, probably even as a young girl. I think she's a tragic figure.
- I don't hate her as much as most. I also see her as a tragic figure more than a villain. She is not even in the same league as Hyde.
- And yet, Hyde was also a tragic figure, or at least he had a tragic upbringing. I think, in some ways, his story is to demonstrate the contrast to Christian, where one got adopted by a loving family and the other didn't.
- But do we really know his history? Sure he wasn't adopted by a wealthy family, but how do we know he was adopted by an abusive family? He managed to go to college and make something of himself, so it must not have been too horrible.
- I think his photographic memory and intelligence got him through everything. I think he did it all on his own with no help from anyone.
- Too bad his envy destroyed it all.
- Imagine having your sexuality heavily programmed and influenced at 15. I think Christian's personality was always dominant, and he expressed it sexually. The fly in the ointment is that 15 is obviously way too young to be exposed to BDSM because there is a lack of maturity,

in terms of fully grasping consent, responsibility, bodily integrity and boundaries. BDSM is not inherently unhealthy - it's just not for everyone, and is a complex arrangement that no 15-year-old can fully comprehend. I think Ana opened his eyes to real love and thus, opened both their eyes to all the possibilities two people in love can experience sexually.

- Elena "raised" Christian to be a dominant, to be controlled and driven to succeed. I think she kind of saw him as king to her queen, and they would both have submissives.

Back to the Red Room?

Wasn't it a bit shocking that Ana's wager for the game of pool was going back to the playroom should she win? Considering what happened last time they were there, and Christian's obvious reluctance. What do you think?

- Nope - no shock there. She was attempting to meet Christian halfway by at least telling him that she was open to going back there, as long as he wasn't going to use the canes, whips, and belts. He just wasn't ready to go in there because of what happened, and couldn't risk it happening again, only to lose Ana again. Even after they were married, he did punish her (for Cocktailgate), and he was so remorseful about that. He seemed reluctant to go in there again, even though she wanted to go in there.
- She liked all the things but the belt. She even wanted to try some other hard limit tools. I guess Christian was a bit reluctant to take her into the RROP, even though she liked all that kinky stuff.
- Oh, I think she liked spanking, especially with these naughty silver balls.
- She liked the kinky f*ckery, so I wasn't surprised. She trusted him.
- At first, I was surprised. Then I thought, what is she trying to do? Please Christian against what she really

wants? Then, I switched to...ah, she's willing to meet him half-way knowing what she doesn't want.

- What struck me in this part was how afraid he was to go back there. Of course, he says it was because she left him afterwards, but what concerned me more than that was how he was afraid he'd lose control. Like an addict being tempted. That was very scary to me.

Winning Her Back

What do you think about his approach when Christian decided to try to win Ana back?

- I absolutely love the moment at the beginning of *Darker* when Christian begins to share his emotions and feelings. I also hated his first words in the car, and being angry because she didn't eat. But, I also hated his note with the flowers and his email to Ana at work, because he reveals nothing. But, that's the mysterious part of him. I'm obsessed again.
- Yeah, he actually behaves really arrogant. But, fortunately he makes up for it with "we've chased the dawn, now the dusk" and "I've been trying my whole adult life to avoid extreme emotions, yet you, you bring out emotions in me that a completely alien." The next chapter is even better with "the thought of anyone else having you is like a knife twisting in my dark soul."
- His complexities are what keep us hooked. We vacillate between our attraction and our revulsion of him - but somewhere inside we sense there's a wounded boy with a heart - and that's what we are searching for.
- That's what Ana and all of us fell in love with. The complexity of him is exactly why he's so lovable and interesting.
- LOL, we are all pretty much in that boat with you.
- Thanks, E.L. James! We are addicted to the *FSOG* books!
- Thank you, E.L. James, for this amazing story!

What if She Hadn't Left?

What are your thoughts about this dialogue?

"'If I hadn't gone, would you be standing here, like this, now?'
His eyes melt, the color of a storm cloud, and he smiles his shy smile, my favorite smile. 'No,' he says and steps into the elevator still holding me. He leans down and kisses me gently. 'No, Mrs. Grey, I wouldn't. But I would know I could keep you safe, because you wouldn't defy me.'
He sounds vaguely regretful... Sh*t.
'I   like   defying   you.'   I   test   the   waters.
'I know. And it's made me so... happy.' He smiles down at me through his bemusement."

- He regrets that she didn't sign the contract, but he's also grateful that even after she was scared and left, she still wanted him with all his fifty f*ked up shades.
- It's his realizing, as the conversation goes on, that the life he once loved isn't his life anymore, and he's okay talking about it with Ana. He realizes that he can be truly happy without it.
- I think there is a small part of Christian that still wishes she had signed the contract but at the same time is very happy that she settled for another type of contract...a deeper and more meaningful one that would last a lifetime.
- I think Ana is flirting with him by saying that she likes defying him!
- I love this part - so many interpretations!

Before and After

On a scale of 1 to 10, how dark is/was Christian to you...
- before Ana?
- after Ana?

- Before Ana, an 8. After Ana, a 7. After their breakup, a 2 or 3.

135

- I don't think he was ever as dark as he thought he was. I don't think he'd ever really hurt anyone, before or after Ana. All of his efforts to feed the world, the care he showed for his submissives were examples of this. Sure, he didn't love his subs, but he cared deeply for them. I don't know how to number it, but in my opinion, he was never really all that dark.
- I agree - he thought he was all bad, unworthy and undeserving, so he built those walls up and appeared cold and dark. But he wasn't. He was afraid of loving and being loved, damaged, vulnerable and deeply hurt. He just needed someone's love, patience and understanding to get through.
- I agree. I don't think he was as dark as he claimed to be. Yeah, he had a rough start and his past with Elena, but he had a good heart that was buried and never had that one person in his life to help him unbury it. Until Ana.
- I think the term "dark" should reference the lifestyle and the misconception many have of it. That subject matter would be dark, taboo, and forbidden. Christian wasn't dark. He just didn't understand himself. All the therapy in world wouldn't help anyone until they hit rock bottom. It took Ana for Christian to get there; to help him see there is "more." He wasn't the monster he thought he was. He wasn't broken, just bent.
- Before Ana a 9, after Ana a 7.
- If I had to put numbers to it, I would say before Ana, a 4, and after Ana, a 2. He was really a soft, kind-hearted man in wolf's clothing. I don't see the BDSM lifestyle as particularly dark in and of itself. I follow a Tumblr blog called Happy BDSM, and they feature photos of happy smiling people participating in BDSM. It is not always dark and dangerous.
- Agree, it's how others perceive BDSM. It's misunderstood.
- It's really hard to quantify his darkness. I imagine that being a billionaire he has to be somewhat ruthless in business, and while E.L. James gives a better understanding of his work ethic in *Grey*, the description

wasn't all that cutthroat. We do get a hint of what Christian is capable of when he sets out to dismantle Elena's ex-husband's company for his duplicity in the chain of events of *Darker/Freed*. I think of Christian as cold, rather than dark, and there is a bit of a difference. He was withdrawn, not yet capable of a real connection with anyone until Ana. Now, if I quantify that, I would say about a 9, and after Ana, maybe an 8. After his son was born, probably a 7. If he does indeed suffer from PTSD, that doesn't just go away. You can't love those types of problems away, but you can change using coping mechanisms. With Ana, he has a more emotionally healthy coping technique. Who Christian is will not change. He is still a control freak (obviously), and he will probably still have issues with other people touching him (outside of maybe his family). Now, with all that said, if the *FSOG* series had ended another way, with Ana leaving him, I do believe Christian would've embraced the darkness that he'd been trying to hide in all this time, but fortunately the story didn't end that way.

- Before Ana, I'd say 6. After Ana, I'd say 0. She took his edge away!
- How do you think Christian's "lost edge" affected his life - positively and negatively?
- I think he was stuck inside his own darkness, no way out, forged by his past and locked in. He has an inner anger which I feel is his "darkness" - an explosive temper (the guy who danced with Ana, Jack Hyde when he bribed her (although Ana prevented Christian from going into SIP to hurt him) and Jack again in *Freed*) and the need to beat brunette women - to punish his mother for not protecting him. I think the darkness and the BDSM are linked, but are two parts of him. BDSM is about control and release, his inner hatred and loathing for himself and the anger it produces is something else. He will always have that darkness, as you cannot remove the pain of his childhood. But, Ana is his shining light that brings him out of it, and to something new... something more. He is a 10 to start with (the worst he feels about himself, all the knowledge, uncertainty and experience he has) but

Ana starts to break this down. At the end of the first book an 8, in *Darker* a 5, and in *Freed* a 3, but it will always be hiding in the shadows.

- I just don't think I can agree with that. Really, a 10 to start with? To me that would make him a psychopathic murderer. On a scale of 1 to 10 in terms of darkness, you'd start him off as a 10? Then, where would you put Jeffrey Dahmer or Ted Bundy on this scale? I just don't think he was ever all that dark. He thought he was. He thought he was worthless scum, but that doesn't mean he really was. Just my opinion.

- I agree; I think he was "darkest" after Ana came in to his life. Only because she always asked questions she began forcing and encouraging him to deal with his feelings. In *Darker* they broke ground and he allowed himself to be more at ease because Ana constantly reassured him that she would never leave. At first, about an 8, ending at about a 4.

- Everyone's scale can be different for this question. It's more about Christian's darkness than his being compared to anyone else.

- A previous poster mentioned PTSD. That would be the root for his "darkness." But is it really darkness? Is it really Fifty Shades of f*cked up? Many people have it and it can vary to the extreme. And, I would agree, you never get over it, but you use tools to learn to cope with it. Ana was his coping mechanism, which brought him out of the darkness. Are we not all Fifty Shades of f*cked up to some degree?

- EXACTLY! LOL

- I certainly am!

- Raising hand here.

- Not me. I'm 100% normal.

- I love these threads... reading others' thoughts is just as exciting as reading the books.

- I don't believe he was "extremely dark." Just in the dark, with a lot of misguided anger (misdirected also by Elena). His thoughts were dark because of confusion; his actions were dark because misdirection at such a young age. I believe he was a "6" before Ana. Like it was said, he wasn't a serial killer, but definitely a"1" afterwards.

- 6 to start, and 2 after Ana. She was the day to his night, but she liked some dark too. So between them, he will never be 1, as she will keep him a little in the dark. He was giving all that stuff up for her, and she was disappointed slightly. She took him back in the Red Room.
- Well, if he ended up happy, I guess it worked out for him. But he still lost the edge, which made him interesting to begin with.
- At the beginning, I'd say he's a 5. He was a lot harder on himself than he should've been (again, he does hate himself). But he had more of a heart than he realized. By the end, I'd knock the number down to 2 or 3.

Forgiveness

I have a question, which could be Fifty related. Where is the line for forgiveness? We all know holding a grudge is not healthy. What is/isn't forgivable? Does the background of the abuser make a difference to whether it's a forgivable action? I'm very interested to find out where that line is.

- I think nearly everything is forgivable, if there is true remorse. But, I would have a very hard time forgiving cheating or outright attempts to lie or deceive me.
- Totally agree, but what if they don't show remorse - if you know it's there but that person isn't in the place to admit wrongs? I guess I'm talking about nature/nurture. How can one forgive wrongs made, if the person doesn't see it?
- Some would say forgiveness is not for the person being forgiven, but for the person doing the forgiving. I'm not sure I always buy that, but I do wonder about people who can forgive someone who murdered a love one. They don't do it for the murderer, they do it for their own peace of mind.

- You nailed it. That's exactly what I mean, but with that, forgiveness brings peace and understanding, to maybe build the bridge with the other person involved. Forgive, but don't forget.
- My brother has stolen from me many times over the years. I love him and forgive him, but I would still not leave my wallet alone in the room with him.
- So learn and make changes, if possible?
- The older I get, the more I realize it's not me, it's them. Can't change the past, but can make a positive impact by forgiving the wrong-doer.
- It depends on how you see the relationship going forward. That depends on the person who caused the offense. As you may have heard me say, there are four steps to forgiveness: 1: Admit wrongdoing - shows you know what you did was wrong. 2: Apologize. 3: Make amends. Preferably by doing something the other person suggests. 4: Never do it again. Unless someone is willing to go through those four steps, you can't rebuild trust and should walk away.
- It's possible to walk away and forgive in another way - which is the release of resentment. Send them prayers - from afar.
- I have tried to walk away but then I have nothing. What about Ana when Christian hit her with the belt? She walked but went back. She forgave him, because she loved him, sins and all.
- She wouldn't take him back unless he changed. She was very clear about that.
- I think forgive for me depends on if I think the person seeking it is generally sorry. But there some things that I cannot forgive, like hurting my mom or my cat or endangering me in some way.
- Forgiveness? It is not meant for the offender, but for the injured person. One must choose to forgive, for it is a matter of making sure you're in the best position to heal and move forward. Now, when it comes to abuse, you have to use more than simply your heart to know what is the right thing to do. In the case of Christian and

Anastasia, what he did was not abuse, not in my eyes. Anastasia crossed her own line, desperate to know if she could handle the worst that Christian had to deal out to her. He asked her more than once if she really wanted to go through with it (if I remember correctly) and she did not safe-word. One must use their common sense to decipher if the relationship is healthy, or not, and take it from there. I'd also venture to say that if you are in an abusive situation and you are asking yourself, "Where is the line that I should draw?" you might be in an abusive situation, already.

- Good question! You can forgive but decide a situation is too unhealthy or forgive and try again. It's highly individualized and depends on the other party, too.
- I think there is a big difference between forgiveness and accepting what someone has done. Forgiveness is for you. So that you can heal. But acceptance means that what the other person did is ok. I would forgive most things but it doesn't mean I would trust that person again, or that I wouldn't prosecute them to the full extent of the law if they committed a crime against me.

Absolute – or Conditional – Trust?

I have a Sir. I am what is referred to as an alpha sub. You've all heard the arguments I'm sure from the BDSM community. The number one law in BDSM, as I believe it is or SHOULD be in EVERY relationship, is TRUST. I pose this: Do you think Christian trusted Ana? Everyone puts the emphasis on her perspective. He intrigued me more because he was so tortured.

- To answer your question, "Did Christian trust Ana?" I would have to say that I think trust is not absolute. It's conditional. You can trust someone to be there for you, but maybe not to babysit your kids or have your ATM PIN code. As far as Christian: He trusted her to keep silent. He trusted her to be kind and understanding. He did not trust her with all the security information. And it took him a long time for him to trust her not to leave him again.

- See...this is where I struggle. My conundrum. Trust for me is synonymous with love and yet I KNOW it is entirely possible to love someone I cannot trust. I think it's the basis for failure...in most relationships. You might be onto something with it being conditional...

- Yes. Thanks. I think it can be dangerous to think trust is unconditional. You just have to learn what you can live with - and what you can't.

- I think you quite simply and eloquently answered my dilemma that I've been debating in my mind for years.

- As to me I wouldn't stay with somebody I couldn't trust completely. It would be so destructive, exhaustive for my mind, my well- being. I wouldn't be committed to such a person. It would subject me to too much hurt, so why even try...

- I think early on his trust in her was conditional. Once he admitted to loving her, he wanted to love her unconditionally. But he still had the issue with being touched and he still didn't trust her enough to be completely truthful with her. He lied or withheld the truth to keep her safe. I think it all came down to after she sacrificed herself for his sister. He loved Mia as much as he loved Ana, and for Ana to willingly give herself to save his sister, she proved that he could trust her with his own life. She broke promises to him and it's difficult to rebuild trust after that. He also broke promises to her. They both had a lot to learn. They both had trust issues with their parents and needed to know that their spouse would always be the one person they could fully, unconditionally trust. Being in such a new relationship they had to take time to build trust.

- I don't think Christian trusted Ana at all in the beginning because he has trust issues. I don't think it had anything to do with her. It was his own inability to trust (which is understandable).

Religion

"Religion?" you may ask. "In Fifty Shades of Grey?" Our answer is – yes. The books may be a "love story with kink," as the author has stated, but if you did deeper (and we did!) there are several references to faith and religion, from symbolism to church to marriage vows.

Madonna

"I've never really looked at them before: all figurative paintings, all religious - the Madonna and child, all 16 of them. How odd. Christian isn't religious, is he?"

Why 16? Why Madonna and child? Did it have to do with his Catholic background? (E.L. James confirmed via Twitter that he was raised Catholic) Thoughts?

- I think he bought them in honor of Grace. She saved him.
- I thought it was more about the mother and child ideal - in contrast to Ella.
- Maybe it was also his sarcasm, as well as his ideal.
- Maybe the Madonna paintings are a symbol of how his mother, Ella, should have been with him. Being Catholic myself, after the virgin of Guadalupe, we pray to these saints for love, guidance and protection from all harm, so maybe he has these paintings to feel safe.
- I wonder if he had them because he wanted to be reminded of his Catholic upbringing. Like he really hadn't turned his back on God.

Names and Symbolism

Here are all the meanings of the names in the books:
Christian = (obvious)
Grace = God's favor
Elliot = A form of Elijah, meaning Jehovah is God
Anastasia = Resurrection
Kate = Pure (is the name of many saints)
Weird coincidence or Deeper?

Do you think Christian was the name he was born with? Or did Grace and Carrick change it? Either way - is there a meaning behind choosing that name, do you think?

- I think that may have been his birth name, but I don't think he had much education before the Greys.
- If that was his birth name, I don't think his birth mother used it much. I'm not sure she talked much to him. There were probably lots of hours of silence for little Christian. This scene in the book (before his questioning his real name in *Grey*) was the only time I thought that E.L. might have been hinting that Christian might not be his birth name. If his mom didn't use it much, it would be easy to change it once the Greys adopted him.
- Oh man. I just had an epiphany about his name. Got chills. Christians believe in being saved by Grace. God's Grace.   *mind   blown* Ephesians 2:8-9 - "For by grace you have been saved through faith; and that not of yourselves, it is the gift of God; not as a result of works, that no one should boast." I'm not sure who else has had that thought, but I'm in awe at E.L.'s thoughts and creation of these books.
- I don't think Christian is the name he was born with. A few things that stick in my mind are things that are referred to in *Grey*. Firstly, his birth mom called him Maggot (how horrible!) So, I'm thinking that possibly his real name was Michael. He even questions in his mind that Christian may not even be his birth name. I'm thinking that Grace and Carrick changed the boy's name so that he could have a clean start in life with no ties to the past. Also, we find out that Grace is a devout church-going Christian, so she and Carrick decided that should be the boy's new name. Then there's the legal requirement for adoptees to have their name changed as well.
- I always wondered if it was his birth name. Love Christian though.

144

- His name, Christian, has always intrigued me with its double-meaning.

Ana and Christian's Faith

We don't know much about Ana's religious background other than her praying for Christian when he was missing after the Charlie Tango crash. How important was faith in both of their lives? Do you think it changed over time?

- Faith was much, much more important to Ana than to Christian. We saw that when Charlie Tango went down and Christian went missing. For Christian, from a very young age, he felt that God had turned his back on him, and therefore turned his back on God. I wonder if, in time, Ana had restored his faith.
- I thought from reading *Grey* that they seemed to be Catholic. Thoughts?
- I thought so too, but I'm not Catholic so wouldn't really know the subtle differences.
- Yes I thought that too. Talking about Catechism and a couple of words seems like Catholic.
- I grew up Episcopalian. It's very similar to Catholicism. They have priests, etc. I was pretty sure he was Anglican - which makes sense, given E.L. James' being British.
- Just reading about the differences: Differences relate to recognition of the jurisdiction of the Bishop of Rome (the Pope) as holding an authoritative teaching office for the whole church; the ordination of women as deacons, priests, and bishops; the use of contraception, divorce, and remarriage. We are Orthodox Christians, which goes back to before the great schism when the Roman Catholic Church was one with the Orthodox Church. With what Grace said and with all the pictures of Mary in his apartment, it made me think they were probably raised as Catholics. I recall Grace saying something about services at night or maybe midnight. And I recall them mentioning a priest I think. I'll have to find the passage.

145

- I thought the pictures of Mary and the Baby were what his idea of a Mom should be like with the Baby. Which his own Mom wasn't. He had so many of those pictures.
- Episcopalians have priests.
- I don't remember it stating which faith he was.
- I don't recall it stating it specifically either. Just a few clues.
- In *Grey*, he does talk about learning about catechism and guilt (when Ana says that she didn't recall reading about nipple clamps in the Bible), and when responding, he's thinking to himself that the Bible taught him about many things, like catechism and guilt. So, it might be a hint that the Greys were Catholic.
- I forgot that part. Yes, that points more to Catholicism.
- I just read the catechism is not specifically tied to the Catholic church. We also have this in the Orthodox Church as well as other religions, including Episcopalian and Presbyterian. It just means "to instruct verbally."
- So Orthodox, Catholic, Anglican/Episcopalians all observe "Mass" though it may have a different name. Orthodox Christians call theirs "Divine Liturgy." While from what I read, the other three call it "Mass" It is also called "Holy Communion," "Holy Eucharist," and "Lord's Supper." It's the service of the Eucharist, which is when we take communion. So, I guess they could be any of the three, besides Orthodox.
- This took place on a Sunday. Lutherans also call it Mass.
- Ana wanted to go to church after Christian didn't die. I figured both were Christians, but didn't go to church.
- I got the feeling Christian has retained much of the faith he was taught at a young age. He is just a cynical man. He likes to pretend otherwise. I think of the pictures in his apartment.
- If anything, I think Ana had the least faith, but she was compelled to pray for Christian, and ask God to watch over and let Christian be alright. Didn't she say to herself she'd go to church or something, if he came back alright?

146

- Yes, she did. I think Ana had less religious structure in her background. But I do think she had an innate faith/spirituality, even if it was under-developed.
- Gillian Griffin - When I wrote "Meet Fifty Shades," I made the assumption that they weren't Catholic, as E.L. James has Christian and Ana married by Reverend Walsh, rather than Father Walsh, and they weren't married in a Catholic church, nor is there any mention of a wedding mass. I have Reverend Walsh discussing the interpretation of "obey," with them and the origins of the wedding vows in Anglican services, as Ana refuses to include that in her vows. Just my interpretation, I could be totally wrong.
- You were/are very insightful!
- My husband's family is very much Catholic (his uncle is a missionary priest). I chickened out of doing the "classes" in order for us to get married in their beautiful Catholic church. We were married in a tiny Baptist church. With Christian wanting to move everything so quickly, she wouldn't have been allowed to marry in the Catholic church, without the somewhat lengthy "training" classes, I'm pretty sure. This is probably why they opted for the reverend. They could figure out all the particulars and decide on a religion together eventually.
- Our priest is also called "the Reverend John Smith," in the Orthodox Church. But I agree, that unless the priest rushed them through the classes, they would not have had time to complete them before the wedding.
- I thought Christian said somewhere in one the books that he gave up on God.
- I think he was lying to himself. He makes too many references. Just my opinion.
- I think what he said was that God gave up on him a long time ago.
- I asked E.L. James on Twitter. She said Christian was a "lapsed Catholic." I have no idea about Ana, but I suspect she was Protestant and not especially religious or much of a church-goer.

Take Me to Church

In *Darker*, after the helicopter crash and reunion, Ana said she wanted to go to church because she owed at least that much to God for bringing Christian back to her.
Do you think she went that Sunday? Do you think Christian went with her?

- Yes, and yes. I think he went with her.
- Do you think they went to church with the Greys, or some place of Ana's choosing?
- Good question. I think they went alone. I don't know why. Just a hunch.
- Hmmm... they called him Reverend, right? Although our priest is titled "Reverend" we call him "Father." So, I don't know if they had a Catholic wedding or not. I hope we will see in the movies. But that's a good thought!
- Good point. We know E.L. James said Christian was a "lapsed Catholic." I wonder if Carrick and Grace went to church. I also suspect Ana would not have been Catholic, so she might have been more comfortable calling the priest a reverend.
- In *Grey*, didn't Grace ask Christian if he wanted to go to church with her? That she was going to, or went to midnight, or evening service. It was when Mia was out of town and so was Carrick. I think.
- After that lovely post-birthday breakfast the following morning, where Christian gets into a heated argument with Carrick about writing up a pre-nup, it's quite possible that they did go to church...together. I think Christian needed to prove to Ana that he loves her unconditionally, and would do anything she wanted to make her happy.
- Let's hope we find out in *Darker Grey*!
- Good point! I could see that happening.
- Yes! Christian would fly to the moon if Ana said she wanted to go.

148

Use of Psychology and Psychotherapy

Read FSOG and you'll be able to "read into" quite a few references to psychology, from Jung and his "multiple selves" theory to Wittgenstein and SFBT. Even some of Christian's business philosophies had a foundation in classic psychology. And then, of course, there's Dr. John Flynn, Christian's most trusted advisor and support system.

Anger Management

From what we learned through reading the trilogy and *Grey*, Christian received psychotherapy for many years. Even though he didn't always accept the various methodologies, he was more willing to listen and contemplate suggestions from his current therapist, John Flynn. Some thoughts why? And how Flynn helped Christian with his anger issues?

- Christian realized he had problems stemming from neglect and physical abuse as a child - fifty shades of f*cked up. His anger made him like a keg of dynamite ready to explode.
- The good thing about Ana is that instead of focusing his efforts on punishing her with pain, he can punish with pleasure. But if he gets really angry he can he will resort to going sailing, or flying, or driving.
- There is no one cure fits all plan. How does any good man handle his anger? They direct it toward something else. Sports, driving, exercise, food, hobbies. There are all kinds of ways to handle anger, besides BDSM.
- Childhood trauma can result in all kinds of physical and emotional disabilities, including those you mentioned, but I think there is hope. With proper care by a qualified counselor, one can begin to heal and move on with their life.
- I don't think Christian would've been that way, if not for Elena. So that, to me, is how he dealt with his anger. Pleasure in pain. He might have handled it another way, if that did not happen. So, I think she has, somewhat, to do with his becoming a Dom with subs. And he had a

therapist which is good for him. At least he could talk to him, which helped a lot, I would think.

- I agree about the need for exercise - like kickboxing with Claude.

Seeking Flynn's Input

Ana called Flynn the "expensive charlatan," yet she wanted to meet with him before she said "yes" to Christian's proposal. What are your thoughts about therapy in general? How about pre-marital counseling? Do you think people who seek therapy are more emotionally healthy or less than those who don't?

- I think it is helpful. I wouldn't equate it with being emotionally healthy.
- I think the difference in getting advice from a best friend vs a licensed therapist is that the latter is a professional who has education and experience in helping individuals or couples or groups work through and understand problems.
- Best friends can't give objective opinions. They are emotionally involved in your life, like family. Also, you run the risk of people repeating your biggest secrets. Therapists can't. The most important factor is the knowledge and therapies they can use with you to help you. Best friends and family don't have that kind of training, unless they are therapists too.
- I don't know if it helps or not. I wouldn't like it. I don't let people know my feelings. I keep that to myself.
- It can be helpful. Sometimes, a therapist can give you ideas or options you didn't consider, i.e., "try it her way."
- I've had my share of therapists. One was just like you see in the movies or on TV - just sitting there listening. A total waste of time. Another was actively getting to the bottom of the issues and helping me change. (As I envision Flynn). I thank God every day that I met her. On another note, I have wished forever that my parents would have gotten therapy. Instead, I was my mother's "therapist" since I was 5 years old. Talk about screwed-

up! If they had cared enough about their relationship to try to fix it, everything might be different!

- I'm really biased about this issue. First, I have a sibling who's a psychiatrist, and from all accounts a really good one. Also, the sibling's son is currently in residency to become a psychiatrist too. I work in a mental health and addictions facility, and have for the past 29 years. I've seen the good that therapy does, but I also hear about the bad side too. Really, in order for it be beneficial, a patient needs to be open to it, or it won't work, no matter how good or bad the psychiatrist is. I'm all for pre-marital counselling in so far as it would highlight some of the challenges a marriage can face, and how, as a couple you'd handle those issues.
- I agree. Patients have to be open to it.

Ana's Subconscious

"Yes, you're a lucky bitch, my subconscious snaps. But you have your work cut out with him. He's not going to want this vanilla crap forever… you're going to have to compromise. I glare mentally at her snarky, insolent face…"

What do you think about Ana's subconscious - especially in this scene? Where does this voice come from?

- I never really liked her subconscious in the story, especially with all the gymnastics phrases. In this instance, it seemed so mean and unnecessary. Why was she always beating herself up?
- I agree - it felt venomous to me. And showed some deep, psychological self-abhorrence.
- Do you think in a way she was just as self-deprecating as Christian was?
- I wanted to throw her subconscious into the Sound! It still gets on my nerves to this day. Ana's lack of self-esteem was wearing on me, as well. The richest and sexiest man in the world loves her just the way she is, yet she continues to beat herself up. No pun intended!
- Elena was the voice speaking through her subconscious.

151

- Hmmm... That's an interesting point. Elena was trying to make Ana question herself, I guess. This wasn't long after the masquerade ball. That's a good point.
- I believe that Ana's subconscious is her voice of reason, and she listens to her very often - sometimes much to her chagrin. But, that voice has also served her well. Ana's very smart and she knows deep down that she needs to compromise in order for the relationship to work between the two of them.
- I can't say I agree. A lot of the time, her subconscious was downright nasty to her. Overly critical.
- But she did listen to it. Even though it was frustrating that she did. Yes, her subconscious was nasty, but I think that's where much of her self-doubt comes from.
- I agree with you there! I think her subconscious is the negative, cautious, worrisome part of her personality. Sometimes, however, her subconscious is the voice of reason.
- Her inner thoughts, how she really wants to react to things but she thinks before she speaks.
- Ana's ability to recognize, identify and separate these different parts of herself, the subconscious and the inner goddess, (plus the occasional use of her full formal name, Anastasia, versus the more casual Ana), helps us understand and relate to the character from multiple points of view. And it helps her through her voyage of self-discovery.

The Expensive Charlatan

Am I the only one who didn't like Ana referring to Flynn as "the expensive charlatan?" Why did she do this? Why did E.L. James have her do this?

- Sadly, psychiatrists are subject to negative stereotypes. As someone who works in a mental health facility, I can tell you that those stereotypes are grossly unfair. Psychiatrists help people in ways you can't even imagine. Having said that, Ana didn't know Flynn, and also didn't know the extent of the therapy that Christian had been through when she said it. Interestingly, when she said the same thing to Flynn, he wasn't the slightest bit offended. I think her opinion of him changed after she had her appointment with him. Once she knew how much he helped Christian, she stopped calling him the "Expensive Charlatan."

- I think she called him that just to be funny. I agree that once she saw how he helped Christian and her, she stopped making fun. It is an unfair opinion that people seem to have. They don't understand how beneficial therapists can be.
- I can understand her thinking this. When you are not used to the luxuries of life, you sometimes feel that folks that have plenty are above you. She probably thought he was taking Christian's money, and not helping him.
- Prejudice like this bothers me. I thought it was mean of her to say it to Christian. Especially since she had no idea how much it cost, or how much he helped Christian. What if he had listened and stopped going? Flynn's response showed both maturity and class.
- In all fairness to Ana, she had never met anyone like Christian before. We also don't know her experience in the mental health system. We know next to nothing of her formative years (I wish we did). It's very possible that she had been to a child psychiatrist that wasn't helpful to her, which could explain her comment. Again, we just don't know.
- I hear you. I just think it was shallow and judgmental of her, and actually seemed out of character.
- Shows she's human and not perfect, and she has much to learn about people.
- It does sound like something she might have heard from Ray. I can't see him being open to it.
- Possibly.
- I agree, it was mean of Ana to say that to Christian, especially since she didn't know how much it cost and that Flynn was actually helping him.
- I really didn't think much of it. I thought she was joking and it wasn't a big deal. Christian didn't seem insulted or

bothered by it. If he had, I would've gone back and read it again and rethought it. Maybe I missed something here.

- I felt the same way as you did.
- Ever since Freud stupidly analyzed women's sexuality, psychiatrists have been getting a lot of negativity. Maybe E.L. James was contrasting Freud with the way women's sexuality really is, through Ana.
- I didn't like this either, wouldn't say it to anyone just out of respect. I guess she was very anxious about this (like a fish out of water). That's why she made these blunders.
- Perhaps she thought he was overpaid and his services were not equivalent to his prices. Christian mentioned he paid him a pretty penny for his services. I don't think it was fair, but I think she was naive.
- Yes! It really bothered me, especially the way she said it. She could have gotten her point across another way. I didn't take it as her joking either.
- I think that started out to be a joke to Christian. She is educated, she wouldn't say "shrink" or your "head doctor." It didn't bother me.
- Not only was her saying this a slam to Flynn, it was an affront to Christian as well. Even delivered in jest (I believe she was specifically relating to Christian's stalker tendencies), it was not a nice thing to say once, much less repeatedly.

SFBT

Flynn advocated Solution Focused Brief Therapy (SFBT) with Christian. Had you ever heard about Solution Focused Brief Therapy before *FSOG*? What do you think about it? How do you think it might have helped Christian? How might it be good advice to you?

- I never heard of it before. It sounds like great advice. It did help Christian so much that he got Ana back. I think it would work for everyone who would listen. It got Christian away from his darker moods and ways. As he said, they were still there but he learned to control them.

154

- No, I hadn't heard of the term before reading the book. At first, it seemed a little simplistic. I'd have to think about it before I buy into it. For Christian, it seemed his desperation made him change. Maybe that's what the theory is all about. I know for myself, right now, I'm in an artistic void/vacuum that I don't seem inclined to get out of. Do I just "do it" and make art or do I try to figure out the "why?" If you know the answer, let me know!
- I think it seems like good advice, to look forward instead of backward. But, you can't be in denial either. What happened to Christian in his formative years can impact a person for a long time. The thing I like about SFBT is its focus on what you want and how to get it. For Christian, it really seemed like the right therapy at the right time. With all his previous psychological treatment, he had probably done the work on his past. Now was the time to move onward and upward - with Ana! If anyone wants more information, I'd recommend Googling it. Quite interesting.
- I love this because it shows that you have a choice to be one way or not.
- I had not heard specifically of SFBT, but do recall a therapist wanting my ex-husband to just move forward and go with the goals he wanted and forget his past. I don't know if she had that theory in mind or not.
- I looked it up, and found out it was real.
- Never, and I deal, to some extent, with psychologists, therapists, and psychiatrists.
- I have been through this. It was part of a program I was in. To go into detail about it would be hard for me to explain, but it entailed getting deeper into your inner self, finding the root of what may have brought you to be how you are. It was a bit tough for me... They did exercises that made you address your inner being and your past, bringing together the root of the matter. I don't know if any of this make sense, but it was pretty intense for me emotionally. But when we realized what the source of

the problem was, I felt a weight lifted. This may/may not apply to Christian's situation, but that's as much as I can tell you.

Arrested Development

Now here's a controversial question. First the quote:

"Dr. Flynn's words come back to me... Emotionally, Christian is an adolescent, Ana. He bypassed that phase in his life totally. He's channeled all his energies into succeeding in the business world, and he has beyond all expectations. His emotional world has to play catch-up."

Do you think men are less mature emotionally than women? All, or most, or some? If so, what makes them that way?

- I honestly think it depends on the man and how he was raised in life. Not all men are adolescent but in Christian's life, it is totally understandable that he is the way he is.
- I think a good portion of men are conditioned not to be emotional. If they are too emotional, it is seen as a weakness. In Christian's life, it is understandable, and I think what Flynn said is true.
- I think it depends on the man. Most men I've met lack maturity until about 25. My husband totally changed once he hit 25. He saw things from a different perspective that I saw back at 21 (but I am also an old soul). I also don't blame him for being a bit immature, his parents were teenagers when he was born.
- My hubby is incredibly emotional, especially with my kids. He has a very stressful job, so at work, he's very macho. Once he is back home he's a different person.
- This is such a loaded question! I really do think that men are adolescents in adult bodies. I love my husband dearly (we've been together for over 34 years!), but he's impulsive and childlike in so many ways. He does things without thinking of the consequences, but knows how to turn on the charm like no one I've ever known. When it

156

comes to taking care of household chores, I feel like I'm his mother, having to constantly ask him to pick up after himself - he never takes initiative around the house. For this, I blame his mother. She coddled all of her sons this way. On an emotional level, my husband is constantly seeking reassurance that he's done good. Without it, he becomes extremely self-doubting (sound familiar?). So, I really do think that men really are adolescents in big boy bodies.

- Women are naturally emotionally more mature. They are also wired to handle more pain and stress than men. It's biological. Then you add societal expectations into the mix, and men's lack of maturity is reinforced. That being said, there are a lot of men who "step up" and become good role models and fathers. It's partially how they're raised and partially what they're allowed to get away with.

- I do believe too that there's much truth in what Dr. Flynn said. I have known some men that do need to catch up with their adulthood and stop acting the way do. Many men work hard to achieve success and forget to leave time for family and fun. There needs to be a balance.

- I think Flynn was right on. In my own family, not so much. My father-in-law died when my husband and I were 23 and he had to take over the family business. Not only did he have a young family to support, but he had his mother and mentally challenged brother - he learned to grow up very fast.

Support System

"He hasn't seen Flynn in nearly three weeks. Is that it? Is that the reason he's unraveling? Sh*t, should I call Flynn?"

How often do you think Christian saw - or talked with - Flynn? In what ways did Flynn help Christian?

- Once Ana was in the picture, I'm sure Flynn did a lot of explaining of Ana's POV, to help Christian see things from her perspective, too.

157

- Let's hope so! I agree that he probably saw Flynn weekly. I hope he helped him talk through his control issues with regard to Ana.
- I'm not sure how much Dr. Flynn helped Christian. I think he was just an outlet for Christian to vent his problems, rather than offering real suggestions for improvement.
- Oooh! I LOVED Flynn! I think he was enormously beneficial to Christian. He got him to focus on the future and the changes he wanted to make. And, most importantly, he earned Christian's respect. (Not an easy feat to accomplish).
- It seems to me that Christian saw Flynn for every doubt he had. He was always looking for reassurance of his decisions especially regarding Ana.
- I can't pinpoint how often he saw him, but I think Flynn was like Christian's conscience. He was the one who pulled Christian back on track when he veered off of it. He reminded him of his good and worthiness.
- It says he didn't usually go longer than two weeks without seeing him. Other than that, I can't decipher the frequency either. I'm guessing he had Flynn on speed-dial though.
- For sure.
- Up until Ana came into Christian's life, he probably saw Flynn on an as-needed basis. Then, of course, Flynn went on holidays and knew nothing about Christian having met Ana, in that short time between appointments. Christian then went completely off the rails when Ana left, and he told Flynn all about her. Until Christian won her back, I think they spoke daily because the nightmares were getting worse by the day, and he was even having horrid thoughts in the daytime, and he needed to get through those without completely losing his mind. Flynn just being available to Christian was the biggest help in getting him through his crisis.
- I think a lot of what others have said are true. He probably saw Flynn on a weekly basis. I've had a therapist for a long time and it's mostly you talking and

them listening. Though, when they do talk, it's usually to say, "Why do you think that way?" or, "Why did you do that?" They will tell you that they think it's because of something that has happened or you believe, that makes you do these things. They ask a lot of questions, but I think it's more for you, so they can draw things out. It's actually very therapeutic.

- I'm thinking he would see Flynn weekly. Flynn helped Christian realize that he does Love Ana more than he thought he did!

Soothing the Savage Beast

What do you think about the iPad Christian gave to Ana?

- If this wasn't Christian's attempt at hearts and flowers, I don't know what was. He had lots to learn in this department, but he gave Ana an iPad with his "mixed tape" of songs that "say it all" for him, and the British Library app which contained all the possible books Ana would love to read. The screen picture of the model glider, and the main screen wallpaper of them two together after the graduation, was such a thoughtful gesture. He must have spent a great deal of time creating it for her.
- It was an incredibly thoughtful gift; especially from Christian, who is an extremely busy man.
- I wish every man was able to change the way Christian did. And, he did it in only five days.
- I love love love envisioning his doing that, putting together the songs and books. Ahhh!
- He really did put a lot of thought into the gift. Once he decided to do everything he could to win her back, he focused big time, to the point where he told Andrea to clear his entire social calendar for the week. Once Ana agreed to go to Portland with him, he worked hard at creating the perfect gift which said it all for him. He made it impossible for her to be angry with him. This was his version of hearts and flowers, and most assuredly, "I love you."

- He was in love with her. He wanted to show her how much, with the iPad, the music and the British library on it.
- I know! He had all that time away from Ana; searching his soul to give Ana a part of himself!!
- I picture him getting frustrated, then putting so much effort into it. I love regretful, apologetic, hearts and flowers Christian!
- Absolutely loved this gift. To me, that beats flowers and stuff hands down. This was so much more thoughtful and romantic, with real thought behind it!! Loved it.
- I love that *"Every Breath You Take"* was included!!
- Has anyone ever made a mixed tape? Received a mixed tape? What were you (or they) trying to convey?
- That "all over the body" feeling. Butterflies. All happy, can't sleep. All you can do is equate everything you do, eat, play, think and hear, to that person.
- I absolutely love that Christian made a mix tape for Ana. Before then, he was unable to express his true feelings. hopes or desires for Ana. As his note said, the mix tape "says it all." The songs really told a story of the happy memories they made together (*Witchcraft, Spem in Alium*), the regret he felt (*The Scientist*, by Coldplay), and promise for the future (*Try*, by Nelly Furtado). Until reading the books, I never thought of putting together a mix tape to convey how I felt about my husband, but then again, neither has he. I know I'd really love to get this as a gift, and he'd probably love one from me too. This is a project to think about.
- I made one for a friend of mine when we were probably 13. She lived far away from me and we only got to see each other in the summer. I did the whole DJ thing and introduced the songs. That was a great memory. I wish I could get the cassette from her and listen to it. I'm sure it would embarrass me, but the kids would love it. I loved that Christian made her the mixed tape, only updated. It made him more human, and showed her that he was serious about her, and their future.

- Yes; I did receive a mix tape from my first boyfriend. Unfortunately, the relationship was short lived. We broke up after a few months. It was a nice gesture from him.
- Yes; my husband made one for me when we were going out; that was 28 years ago, and I still have it.
- My hubby made me a digital playlist about six years ago, after we had been going out for about six months. I'm very into my music, so he knew I'd read into the songs he was putting on there for me - some beautiful, and some cheeky. Hehe!

Soul Connections

"I love thee to the depth and breadth and height my soul can reach."

Elizabeth Barrett Browning knew that it doesn't get much "deeper" than the soul, and the Deeper Group knows that a soul connection between two people is the most powerful and meaningful kind of love there is.

First Time Ever I Saw Your Face

When he looks into Ana's eyes for the first time he seems mesmerized. Do you think he ever felt like that about anyone before? Maybe he dismissed it before?

- We know next to nothing about his other subs except that they all shared similar physical traits. I believe Ana was the first brunette that caught his attention because of her blue eyes (among other things, like her full bottom lip).
- I think Ana was different because his soul recognized hers. They knew each other "before" and were destined to meet.
- No, he never felt like that. Otherwise, it wouldn't have affected him. I think his fear of her seeing right through him was a huge factor - Ana's innocence -"cutting through the crap," as he states later.
- I think he was shocked how she was able to pull off the veil of his disguise. I think it was in Darker where she says something about "stop hiding from me." I think he was always hiding on some level.
- I think that is why he is so mesmerized by her. If you think back to the interview, he totally doesn't want to be there, but when she starts to crack through that armor, he wants her to stay longer.
- I don't think he realized the deeper connection with Ana at first. He was just feeling the attraction and thinking about getting a new submissive. Christian wasn't open enough to his higher self to recognize a soul connection.

It took him time to discover their relationship, their bond was "more."

Fate or Free Will?

Let's talk about Fate and Destiny. Do you believe people are "born to be together?" Do you think Ana and Christian were destined to meet? Have you ever felt that kind of "soul connection" or destiny with someone else, romantic or otherwise? How do you perceive "destiny" or "fate?" How does "free will" come into play? How about Divine Intervention?

- I believe there is someone for everyone. That one day, either at the beginning life or while you're living your life, you'll meet the one that is just for you. Everyone that is in your life is in it for a reason. Love, for instance; there's no going wrong with it. It's a powerful, intense fire; burning and all consuming. It can bring you to your knees. But when you find that someone that was designed for you, it'll be perfect.
- You'll have your chance, and it's up to you to take it. I believe in an interconnection that's only for one other person and that other person is just for you.
- I'm not so sure that even when people are destined to be together, that it's always easy and effortless and perfect. Even Ana and Christian, who were born to be together, they went through some very rocky times. And I believe that it's possible to make some decisions that can affect your destiny. It's the old paradox between free will and fate.
- He must be hiding because I've never seen him. Makes me think I'll never meet him. I've been waiting a very long time. Not sure I can wait much longer.
- I'm one that doesn't believe in love at first sight. Maybe because I've never experienced it. I don't use the words fate or destiny either. I do have family that says, "Oh it's fate." If things are meant to be, then it'll happen.
- Brownell Landrum - I believe we are here for a reason/purpose, which (to me) confirms my belief in

fate/destiny. I also believe in free will; that our decisions affect our path. It's like we have a road map before we're born, but it's up to us to decide which paths to take and how quickly. Some paths might lead to the same destination. Some might not.

Here's a passage from my children's book that explains my views:
We decide on our lessons
The paths we will take
Awards we might go for
And mistakes we might make

For life isn't easy
And not always fun
But easy is boring
Like games always won

So we set up our challenges
With mountains so high
To test our endurance
And reach for the sky

It doesn't much matter
If we get to the top
What matters much more
Is what we do when we stop
© Brownell Landrum

(There's more, but you get the gist).

- I believe that soulmates are "someone you were destined to meet." I don't think there is just a one-and-only "mate." We all have many people in our lives who we're destined to meet. Some for love, some for lessons, some to fulfill a common purpose.
- I've given the whole concept of fate/destiny and free will a *lot* of thought. The "why" things happen. It's a key message all of my books.

- I think everything happens for a reason. At times, I'll question if it is for good or bad. I'll ask, "Is it meant for me?" Many times I've wanted to achieve a goal in life, but while on that road something else happens and my life was turned around.
- I think of free will and destiny like we are in the middle of a snowstorm and have more than one road to choose.
- I believe in love at first sight, destiny, fate, and soulmates. I believe we get more than one soulmate if we lose the one we are meant to be with. I think that only certain people get soulmates.
- I think we all have soulmates. And they're not always in the form of a romantic partner.
- Is love destined for everyone? Would it also apply to marriage? I know people who claimed to be in love but never ending up married. In my beliefs, you fall in love, get married, and live happily ever after. Do you think, if you lost your first love, there can be anyone destined for you again?
- I've been in love a few times, but I've had my heart broken many times. I just don't see a soulmate for me. Maybe the ones who don't ever get married are the back-ups. They aren't necessarily destined for one until something happens. Who knows?
- I've never been married, though I've been asked more than once. I don't think it was supposed to happen for me. I've had too many other lessons and things to accomplish first. Though I do think it's still a possibility for me in the future. Either way, I have to learn how to appreciate what I have.
- Maybe I was too young to recognize it; or too stupid and wild to keep it. Marriage is not always a dream come true, but for some of them out there it is. Mine is pure karma. Maybe someday I'll find another "one" soulmate and connect on a whole new level. Who knows? I can't lose hope.
- I haven't found my soul mate and feel it's highly unlikely now at my age. It's kind of depressing me. I've been single now for 18 years with no dating at all. Imagine if

I finally meet some 70-year-old and then asked him to tie me to the headboard!

- We are all destined for the paths we cross. Some souls have a deeper connection. Souls that are meant to unite will know it when they meet. Christian could've screwed up, but their intense connection was beyond what they could control. Two true souls uniting.

- I think they were aware they could've messed it up, but the deep love anchored in their souls was much stronger than that. They would eventually get together.

- My husband wasn't supposed to be born. His mother had her tubes tied before he was born. We grew up in the same community and never met until college. He swears that as soon as he saw me he knew he was going to marry me. Had I known him when we were younger, we'd never have been interested in each other. Timing is everything.

- I had a brief affair in the early 80's. I was shocked at the strong attraction we had for each other. This person took me to a new life that I'd never dreamt. Also I have to say that with my younger daughter, the connection we have is almost like we are the same on so many levels. We have this psychic connection.

- I believe in the confluence of fate and free will. I believe that we have a destiny, lessons, and relationships we plan for this lifetime in advance. However, I also believe we have free will which can cause problems or can help us along our path. Look at Ana and Christian. If he had not come back to her, then they could have not moved forward together.

- Sometimes, I think it might be a coincidence, but in my heart, the hopeless romantic in me, believes in fate all the way. Christian and Ana? To me that's fate. Kate got sick, she asked Ana to go for her. It was fate; they were meant to happen. Just think: when they woke up that morning they had no idea their lives were about to change forever. Both were not looking forward to that interview. And then... that fateful look and touch of hands when he helped her up!

- I definitely believe in fate.

- I had dreamt of my husband before I met him. My second year of university I won a grant to Naples, Italy, and he lived there.
- Before I knew my husband, he was at a party at my brother's house next door to my parents. I dreamed of his face when I was in high school, and I painted a portrait of him in college. All before I met him. We were definitely destined to meet.
- I'm not sure about fate, but I did meet someone in my past who I still know. I know we were meant to be together, even though we aren't at the present moment.
- I do believe that they were meant to meet. Was it fate? Possibly. If Kate didn't meet Ana, become faithful friends, Ana wouldn't have met Christian. If you take their destiny a bit deeper into their possible past life connection, were they lovers then? I feel souls are never parted from their mates in the afterlife. I think they are eternally bonded; it just took a while for Christian to find his lost soulmate in Ana.
- Soulmates are the ones we are born for and to. Twin flames when one soul splits into two. All of these souls are connected. We have lessons together. At the base level or string level there are connections that keep us tethered to certain souls. With Christian and Ana, it's obvious by the way they were both bothered by each other. Bothered to the point where Christian couldn't get her out of his head, and Ana couldn't get him out of her heart. Theirs was an immediate chemistry that's unbreakable. Of course, there is the choice of free will. They could've been bothered to the point of aggravation and stayed away. Souls aren't made that way. In science when something causes an action by aggravating, it creates a series of reactions. Stardust reacts differently, and yet the exact same way hydrogen becomes helium. Once the course is in action, Christian and Ana had nothing else to do but collide. Souls are tethered to a force stronger than supernovas.
- I've walked this earth many many many times. I believe we each have our own and collective destinies and fates. They're tied together. Some lifetimes I work on me;

others I am here to help you work on you. I have many connections here in this lifetime that I know, to the core of my being, I am tethered to. This will never change.

- I think we are born in love. We're here to love. This is the unifying factor. So of course we look for something; for someone to connect with. So, yes, I believe that people are meant to be together. I believe that it comes when we aren't looking, but we have to realize what feels right before we can understand what was wrong before.
- I believe that my husband and I were meant to be together. I think Ana and Christian were meant to be also.
- I think it was Divine Intervention. A Higher Power brought them together.

Divine Providence?

Do you believe Fate would've brought Ana and Christian together if Kate had not gotten sick and went to the interview?

- This is a real mind-breaker. Perhaps Christian would've met Ana through Kate, but it's hard to figure out how their paths would cross.
- I'm thinking the same...that's a good question. I think they would have, eventually. It's just a matter of how else it could've happened...
- If it's meant to be, fate will find a way and don't forget he was giving a speech at the graduation, Kate could've introduced them to each other.
- Remember he was giving a speech at the graduation so Kate could've quite easily introduced Ana to Christian and the rest, as they say, is history.
- Yes; I think they were meant to be.
- Absolutely! The Traffic Angels would've made it happen one way or another. Maybe graduation?

Weathering the Storm

Do you think that the couples that are "meant to be" are the ones who go through everything to tear them apart? If so, how does that apply to Ana and Christian? How does that apply to you?

- I really love this. It's so real and true. So many people have fantasized that relationships are supposed to be easy, and smooth, and perfect all the time. As you know, I talk a lot about the confluence of destiny and free will, and how both play a crucial part of what happens in life.
- This couldn't be more true. When going through things and making it through to the end, it shows how much one wants to be with the other. One learns the lesson at hand and builds a stronger bond. When going through the hard times of a relationship, one is reminded of what they have in the other. Because, let's be realistic: we do forget and take things for granted. Sometimes, taking the other for granted is what puts our relationship in the rough, to begin with.
- When I first read *FSOG*, I felt that it was the right time for Ana to find someone (finishing college and starting out into the world). Christian was also ready, even if he didn't know it.
- If they hadn't have met when they did, they would have still gotten together. Fate always finds a way, and their destiny was to travel life's highway together.
- It had to be fate. The circumstances of their meeting was just too overwhelming. When Ana fell into the office, they knew it, even if they didn't understand it right away.
- I think it was divine intervention.
- Soul calling to soul. True love always finds a way.

This Stops Right Here

Ana wasn't sure she wanted to step into this kind of relationship. Christian told her it was the only way because that's the way he was. I felt he panicked when he said that, and maybe he thought, "I will lose her if I stay this way."

The thought of a hearts and flowers relationship frightened him. I wonder what might have happened if Ana would've said, "Ok then it stops here and now."

What would be his reaction?

- How would the story have turned? They weren't that far into the relationship, yet he felt he needed to have her. I can't wait to see some of the responses.
- If she would've said okay, then their relationship would've been just like the others. She wouldn't have stood out as being different. Which probably would've ended fairly quickly because he seemed bored of the "same old, same old" and seemed to be looking for something different...she would've been Sub #16 in a continuing long line of subs.
- Good point. What was it about Ana, I wonder, that set her apart from "the others," that he had a different interest in her?
- Yes, I think he felt really puzzled and alive for the first time in his life, meeting this lovely creature.
- I think he somehow felt, from the first moment that she was innocent and this in itself was novel to him. So, therefore, she was already different.
- I think eventually they would've worked things out, though the path might have been slower and rockier.
- I think Ana still would have stood out and he would've fought to keep her. There was something between the two of them that sparked she fell into his office that day. To be honest, I think Christian started changing the minute he met Ana.
- Yes; from that minute on...
- All I have to say is thank heavens Ana was different from the others. Her differences are what set him on a path to healing and happiness!
- He said he fell in love with her from the minute she fell into his office.
- If she said yes right from the beginning she would've been #16. Laws of attraction prevailed here. There was

a deeper connection whether Christian realized, recognized or felt it. I believe that when you are attracted to someone on a higher level there is a deeper connection.

- That's beautiful! The heart being a wild creature and yet so vulnerable.
- I think he was bored with his life. I think Ana was the first person to tell him no, and didn't sign the contract right away. She was exotic, forbidden fruit.
- I think he was sick of all the "Yes-Sirs" in his life.
- I think it was love at first sight and he just didn't know it.
- That is so true. They say forbidden fruit tastes the best, and indeed Ana's not giving in straightaway must have made him wild with desire.
- I think he realized when she left him that he fell in love with her when she fell into his office. If she'd said yes to a relationship his way I still think it would've changed him. She was different. He would've done anything to stay with her. She'd never have been just #16 to him. She was his forever love.
- His thoughts and actions were not in sync until he had a huge existential crisis, whereby he dissociated in time on the floor in front of the lift. Although he kept questioning his motives from the moment he met Ana. A process he was not aware of until Dr. Flynn confronted him with in therapy!
- We often need a trigger in our lives and also being at a point when we're no longer happy with how things are. I'd say meeting Ana happened just at the right time.
- You have to remove yourself slowly sometimes in your own time from a Toxic person (Elena) to see the real dynamics (truth). This helped in Christian's process toward recovery, seeing less and less of her increased his wellbeing. If Ana walked in 18 months prior it's another story! Dr. Flynn would also have been working on other stuff in therapy. And Christian would not see Ana as he did on the gray morning of 9th May 2011.
- Ana's being innocent, which Christian didn't know, was that "trigger," that sent Christian's less than complex

world into another realm that he was unfamiliar with. It was that time for him to get a "grip" on life, thus the timing was in alignment to meet Ana...his destiny!

- Ana never signed the contract. He even did away with the rules and punishments. He just wanted her back. I think it was a great love story.

Christian Grey's Strengths and Weaknesses

Gorgeous. Tortured. Brilliant. Complicated. Wealthy. Deprived (if not depraved). Competent. Insecure. Generous. Selfish. Talented. Guarded.

All of these words comprise the sum total that describes Christian Trevelyan Grey. Contrary to what outsiders might think, it wasn't just Christian's strengths that attracted us, but his weaknesses as well.

Dark or Damaged?

Christian often referred to himself as "dark" and "damaged." What do you think?

- I keep on hearing Christian being called "dark" and that is absolutely fine, but for me, personally, I have never seen him as "dark." What I see is a lost soul whose start in life was horrendous, then at a vulnerable age, was molested by a pedophile who taught him how to "f*ck hard" (using his own words). Then, one day, this beautiful ray of sunshine literally falls through his office door - his beautiful Ana, with her self-esteem issues and lack of confidence. Two sad and lonely souls had found each other; soul mate had found soul mate, and what ensued is a beautiful love story. Christian taught Ana to value herself, he taught her to look deeply into herself and see the beautiful, sensual, strong and smart woman that she is. On the flipside, Ana shows Christian what an honest, normal, and loving relationship is like, and how rewarding that can be. I'm not going to say she taught him how to love, he already knew how but didn't recognize the fact. He says that he doesn't do romance but almost from the very beginning he romances her.. No, Christian isn't dark, just misunderstood. He's human, and has his faults - who doesn't? No one is perfect, but we love every single one of those faults.

- I'm not sure I would call Christian "dark" as much as I would say that he had demons he battled with. He was a sadist, yet I believe he did it because he equated punishment with love. It's kind of like a child who is bad just to get attention. He learned that through his birth mother and it was reinforced with Elena. In some ways he had trouble trusting Grace's love because she didn't punish him. To him, punishment was his way of saying he cared, so he could keep Ana under his control, to keep her "his" and also to keep her safe.
- I just feel sometimes he's misunderstood, and since reading *Grey*, I feel I'm starting to understand him, and why he is the way he is.
- He didn't realize he was doing the "hearts and flowers" for Ana almost right from the very beginning. He just never recognized the emotion. It was there the whole time, and she helped him understand it.
- He's not what I consider "dark." When I think of "dark," I see someone that is like a serial killer or murderer who soul is beyond repair, that has no regard for humans, animals, or any living thing. Christian, by far, is not any of these things. "Misunderstood" is the most appropriate word to describe him.
- Christian's self-abhorrence is what made him dark. To himself.
- *"Give your heart, and say come take it. And she will see you're a good man."* Sia
- Oh...that one just made my heart take a leap!
- *Heart Leaps R Us*
- That's another thing these *FSOG* haters don't understand. There is also humor in the books and film.
- As we all know, there are a lot - of deeper messages and insights in the books!
- I think it's a matter of perception and opinion. To me, a lot of the description you gave is dark. I don't believe his sexuality has anything to do with his being a dark person. He isolated himself, was closed off, and had a rough early start. He wasn't completely damaged to the point of no return, but there was definitely some darkness to

him. Maybe not to the extent as some claim, but certainly some darkness and mysteriousness there.

- I do agree that people, especially non-fans have jumped to extreme and unjust conclusions about the character that is Christian Grey. I personally love him, and I am drawn to him in so many ways. But I think, as fans, we have grown our own understandings of who he is, and became, as the story developed. We watched him evolve and recognize his own issues. We are very protective of our man because we've taken the time to get to know him and when you know someone's story an understanding is made, not judgment.

- He is not dark. From the beginning, Christian stole my heart because I thought he was very romantic and caring towards Ana. Who wouldn't want such a man? So totally caring about the needs of a woman. It seemed to me he never got tired of pleasing Ana, and himself, of course.

- Even though he didn't recognize it or acknowledge it, he was more of a "boyfriend" than a Dom to her from the very beginning. All the "firsts" and the fact that he broke all his rules for her were clues.

- She changed him from the start.

Sexpertise

I love a sensual man who is willing to explore a woman's body. In what ways do you think Christian explored his women's bodies in ways that were pleasurable to them?

- I think he was ultra-attentive to the physiological responses from his subs. Elena taught him well. However, he was sorely lacking in understanding emotional responses. Even in, and especially in, the Dom/sub world, emotional response should be keenly understood.

- But what would've happened if he had understood the emotional responses of his submissives, and had never met Ana?

- He would've at least had more compassion when he let them go.
- I think he had some compassion, but was never open to exploring it before. At least he realized that there were a few who wanted more. He wasn't willing to give it, so he let them go. Also, he might have secretly thought he wasn't a good Dom because he couldn't get them to obey and understand he didn't want more and what he was offering should've been enough for them. Poor tortured soul. All those feelings he never felt, he thought he was losing himself, but he was really finding himself.
- I think he had compassion but never showed it outside of aftercare. Even then, he didn't want to give his subs the wrong idea - associating compassion with feelings.
- I think he knew there were certain areas that women like to be touched and kissed. He must have observed it in having sex with his subs, and with Elena because what we learned in reading the trilogy was that Ana was able to have an orgasm through breast manipulation, and liked to have the back of her knees kissed. What other areas did Christian explore that were spot on for Ana?
- Raking his thumb nail across the bottom of her foot. Then following it with his teeth... swoon! Also, the way he rubbed his thumb against the front of a certain part of her anatomy.
- Each experience should be unique unto itself. Like you said, Ana liked being kissed behind her knees. A very sensual man would explore, but not all men are sensual. They can be sweet and loving, but a true sensual man who knows a woman's body and knows what stimulates, and what reactions are rare.
- That is so sad and too bad. It makes me wish *Fifty Shades of Grey* was required reading for young men and women. I mean that for mature people interested in a loving relationship.
- So true, but not everyone would get this story either. Part of the problem, is that many do not even express themselves in a loving manner in front of their children. I may get an eye roll, but I am a very affectionate person.

176

I saw my parents hug, snuggle and kiss often, and very appropriately. My husband never saw his parents show affection like that. So, with that said, he pushes me away if I go overboard with affection and the kids are nearby. He doesn't think it "right" to show affection in front of them. I tell him it is very healthy to show them how much we love each other. It's never over the top, but if you are not exposed to affection, how do you know how to be affectionate?

- I understand what you are saying. Maybe you could ensure that your children know that (about your husband) so they don't come away with the wrong impressions. Of course, you would say it in a loving way.
- Oh, they do know. And it's all good, but we do learn from our parents. My kids have a lot of me in them.
- I was raised like your husband, with very little affection from my parents. My husband was raised like you. It has been a learning experience with him and our kids. I have had to remind myself to be affectionate with all three of them. It's not natural to me because I didn't experience that as a child. It has become easier recently and hubby and I have started being affectionate with each other in front of the kids. I think it is healthy for kids to see that their parents are in love. It is something I wanted to feel comfortable doing in general (showing affection), but until reading this set of books I didn't. These books have changed me, and all for the better. I didn't realize that this was another thing these books have done to improve my relationships until just now.
- I am glad these books have helped! It is a challenge for sure, but it is very healthy to show affection. I may be over the top sometimes, but we have been married 26 years. A marriage doesn't last if you aren't doing the right thing. Since *FSOG* came out, my husband is trying to keep up. Being empty nesters now is even better! Keep trying hard - it's worth it!
- I always tell men, "you want to know what women want? Read what women read."
- My hubby is trying to keep up with me too since reading *FSOG*! He says after his race in November, he will take

177

the time to read the books so we can discuss them. We will see. We cannot wait to be empty nesters! But our youngest is 6. We will be married 20 years next June, and have never been happier. You are right. It takes a lot of work to keep a marriage together. But failure was never an option for us going into it. I'm glad to hear that you guys are doing well too!

- Very beautiful testimony from all of you. I hardly ever saw my parents cuddle, and I think I missed affection when I was young, probably one of the reasons I'm so complex now, and why I hate myself.
- Oh, I pray that you will come to love yourself one day. You are worthy of love. *hugs*
- Yes, you're worthy! Never doubt you are. We have to find the one thing we love about ourselves and build on that. You have it inside - don't think you don't. We all have something we don't like about ourselves but we have to look beyond those faults and strive to make ourselves happy. You can do it too!
- Thank you, I'm trying, but don't really succeed for now. I wonder if it will ever happen.

Handsome Devil

Do you think looks help or hurt a person in their bedroom techniques? It's often been said that the really gorgeous people don't have to work so hard (pun partially intended) in bed, while those with a little insecurity are more inclined to "hone" their skills. Relating to Christian, do you think his insecurities helped - or hurt - him in the bedroom (or RROP, as it was)?

- I think it made no difference to Christian Grey. He was the Master...and Supremely Confident.
- Do you think that was a basic inner part of his being? Or because he was so well trained?
- I think Ana being that certain kind of beautiful, and inexperienced made it really great in Christian's point of view. A hooker can be beautiful, but a lot of guys would be turned off.

178

- I think that in a lot of cases looks tend to make a person a little lazier in bed. They seem to have learned that they can get by with just that. A little bit of insecurity in that area is a good thing. I do believe it makes them willing to be a little more skillful. I believe that was a big part of Christian's makeup, as he tended to go overboard with things. He worked hard to be highly skilled in everything.
- I don't think looks made a difference for Christian in the bedroom. He had been well trained and he had confidence in his abilities with sex. He gave his all when he was in there because he knew he was good at it. If he was good at nothing else, he knew without a doubt that that he was good at pleasing a woman sexually. I think his insecurities made him want to excel in certain areas of his life. He'd strive to be the best of the best. I wonder if his abilities that Elena honed, were one of the reasons Elena did not want to let him go.

Setting The Bar

Do you think Christian set the bar so far beyond Ana's sexual comprehension that she not only fell in love with the way he conquered her, but made her feel so that no other man would ever come close?

- I think he did. I know my husband did that to me.
- Certainly he set it up so that no other man could come close to him. Though I will say that although he did desire her, he also gave mixed signals. He left her without having sex with her; he pushed her away many times, and sometimes (at first) he treated her a little like "I want you but if it's not you then it'll be someone else." As we know, he did this to help him maintain control, over himself and his emotions and over her. However, once she left him, he was confronted with the realization that there was only one woman who he desired - for the rest of his life.
- Well, I doubt any man could have come close to Christian for Ana, no matter what they did! It was her

first, last and only, and she was very lucky with what they had sexually. She wanted to ask Kate for a comparison! Kate would've laughed at her if Ana had been explicit. Although, I now recall Kate asking Ana (in the book) if he brought her to a climax.

- I agree, he did set her up, but who doesn't remember her "first?" I do, and if you are lucky, you had a very gentle caring experience. No, I didn't marry my first, but I am very close to my "first." We chat often and, yes, it was hard not to compare others to him. I think most men like to "conquer" their women, on any level, whether in a Dom/sub relationship, or pure male ego.
- I think it's the testosterone!
- Haha. Yes!
- Said exactly correct. She had what she wanted, and with Christian she didn't desire any other man. He could do it all. I would sure feel that way, but I'm not Ana. I don't think any man could compare to Christian.

Confidence and Self-Esteem

Confidence vs. Low-self-esteem. Christian doesn't think highly about himself. In fact, he almost resents himself on many levels. He's really unsure of himself, and always fears that Ana will leave him. But he always exudes control, elegance, and grace. His sexual self-esteem is HUGE. Is it really possible be both self-hating and that confident at the same time? Thoughts?

- I'm not sure he was as self-hating as much as he felt undeserving of love. A lot of "givers" can feel that way - which is why they keep giving. Does that make sense?
- I suppose it does when I think of it that way. It's mostly the feeling of not deserving to be loved that puts him down.
- In *Grey*, he seems to hate himself. He also seems to be resentful that he is handsome. But then he uses those looks to his advantage when he needs to. He's good at many things, including sex, and I think that gives him confidence. I was good at softball when I was a kid/teen

and, although I wasn't the prettiest girl, I had confidence in myself because I knew there was at least one thing I was really good at. I think that's kind of how Christian feels about himself.

- It seems possible. It resembles my ex. He had an over the top idea of himself sexually, and very low self-esteem.
- He did hate the fact that he was so handsome.
- It's a mask that Elena taught him to put on when she taught him how to be a Dom. Inside, he didn't even respect himself, so his Dom persona worked in business too.
- I think it's interesting when someone's exterior vision of themselves is in conflict with their inner self. On some visceral level we expect attractive people to also be attractive on the inside as well, when it's often not true. In Christian's case, he had a good soul; it was just tortured. I suspect he got even better looking the more and longer he loved (and was loved by) Ana.

Temper Temper

I was really pissed at Christian for being so brash with Ana, especially after she ran away from Jack. He seriously was cussing at her and was mad, yelling at her, "Get in the car!" I would've screamed back at him, and it wouldn't have been pretty. Even back at the apartment he was still fuming.

- I HATE how women are expected to need protecting. Not all women are like that!
- It fits his personality, his anger management issues, and need for control. I didn't like it, but it does fit him. If he'd been different, it wouldn't have been Christian.
- Also, she has just fallen to the ground and he's being so mean to her. Let Taylor handle Jack! That's part of what he pays him for.
- I just took it as him being so mad at Jack, and excited. I didn't take it as his being mean to Ana.
- Ana lacked good sense at times, and Christian learned quickly that he had to be emphatic with her in order for

181

her to listen (so he could protect her). It fit Christian's personality and didn't bother me.

- I think he was very unfair, he was mad that he was right about Jack, and that he wasn't in control of the situation to protect Ana as much as he felt he should. Sometimes trying to match the power at the moment in time, escalates the problem, removing the focus from the situation at hand. In this case, I wouldn't have spoken up right then and there, but he would have gotten a "talking to" once the situation was dealt with.
- I don't think Christian knew how Ana fought back against Jack until he went inside the building and Jack told him what she did! So, I could see Christian being upset with Ana at first!

Analysis Paralysis

In *Grey*, Christian said he was "paralyzed by her anger." I suppose he didn't experience it before with any of his subs. Why doesn't he want to go to the center of all his pain and hurt?

- It becomes too real for him. He's unable to face what he has done for so long; it's the only way he's known.
- In the movie, it looked like her anger snapped him out of his anger.
- In a way, he's like a bully who finally has someone stand up to him. He doesn't know how to handle it. And, as we know, it is *exactly* what he needed!
- Yes, Ana awakened him. Not so boring for him anymore! His heavy sweating scared me. He also looked like he was in a trance. It was hard to watch. I also remember the audience's mad and shocked reactions in the movie theatre. As we walked out, all those women were saying "what a beast," and "poor girl."
- Do you think Elena showed real anger towards the teenage Christian, the very first time she kissed him and slapped him, then acted like nothing happened? Outside of their Dom/sub relationship, you think she got mad at

him? If I recall, when he was a teen, she would scold him to get his crap together, right?

- I'm sure she dominated him and exercised the requisite S&M stuff with him, but I doubt she ever showed the vulnerability that comes with real anger.
- Christian prides himself of "knowing what makes people tick." He thought he knew Ana, but he did not count on her reaction to the belting. He was shocked that he totally misread the situation and was completely horrified by Ana's reaction and the ultimate outcome.
- He was in real shock!
- His subs wouldn't dare get mad at him.
- I thought he was paralyzed because of all the things you guys mentioned, but also because he had become the thing he feared/hated the most. He had become the pimp that beat him. He remembered the rage he felt as a child who got beaten and was tortured. He normally only felt that in his nightmares, and now he was feeling it when he was awake. Also, he was upset because of something he did to someone else.
- I agree with that analysis!
- So true! You could feel his despair already, before Ana asked him to "show me how bad it can get." He was really struggling with himself.
- Very sad.
- For both of them.
- He didn't want to go "there" because that would mean he would have to face the fact that he hurt the woman he loves. He hasn't realized that just yet. He does realize it when he starts having the nightmares where all the women in his life eventually morph into Ana. He only admits to himself that he loves her after a dream he has the morning of the day he "wins her back." He says it out loud for the first time ever, albeit a few days later.

Christian's Coping Mechanisms

"Christian blinks at me in disbelief. 'So all yesterday evening, when I was begging you for an answer, I had it already?' He's dismayed. I nod again, trying desperately to gauge his reaction. He gazes at me in stupefied wonder, but then narrows his eyes and his mouth twists with amused irony.

"'All that worry,' he whispers ominously. I grin at him and shrug once more. 'Oh, don't try and get cute with me, Miss Steele. Right now, I want...' He runs his hand through his hair, then shakes his head and changes tack. 'I can't believe you left me hanging.' His whisper is laced with disbelief. His expression alters subtly, his eyes gleaming wickedly, his mouth twitching into a carnal smile.'"

When I re-read this, it occurred to me that Christian had two responses when he faced emotions he couldn't handle: either violence/sadism or sex. What do you think?

- Yes, that occurred to me too. He didn't know how to react to the emotions he felt, he'd kept people at arm's length for so long.
- I agree with your assessment. I wondered when he'd tell Ana that his initial response would be to "beat it out of you." When the other subs would disobey, would he only do punishments in the RROP? Or, would he do it right there on the spot?
- Ana did say that he used sex as a weapon and he didn't play fair. He didn't know any better at that stage of their relationship, but she soon shows him (excuse the pun) the ropes.
- Love the pun! Hehe.
- Definitely sex, and when he can't spank he denies her orgasms.
- Yeah he was trying to punish her in the only way he could handle. RROP, orgasms denied and thoroughly well f*cked.

All Over the Place

I was just thinking about how on the night Christian took Ana's virginity, he wanted her to be his sub. In fact, he told her, "this is the only kind of relationship I know."

184

But by the next morning, he is good with her cooking breakfast, and snuggling in the bath tub, etc. Then, an hour or so, later he is educating her on what her being his sub will be like (sub room, etc...). I'm pretty sure Christian had multiple personalities.

- No, I don't think so. He wanted her for a sub right from the start. He was thinking he needed a new sub while she interviewed him. After her took her virginity, he just did what he normally does, I guess. She made breakfast and (all subs made breakfast) and they continued her training. She knew he had a one-track mind!
- He clearly bathed his subs (I doubt it was the first time with Leila). And they cooked for him. Plus, he did say it would be a negotiation. In his mind, he was going about business as usual.
- She was making herself at home.
- I don't think they'd discussed that aspect at that point in the relationship.
- As I recall, one of the things that hurt Ana was when she saw Christian bathe Leila.
-
- She didn't actually "see" Christian bathe Leila. She was across the street at the bar with Ethan and saw Christian carrying Leila out to the hospital vehicle (I don't think it wasn't an actual ambulance).
- Part of being a sub included cooking. And the bath comes in the form of aftercare. There's nothing better, except the sex that came before.
- But the thing that separated her from the others, in the early part of their relationship, was that she slept in his bed with him. They made love, then he left her sleeping in his bed, went out played the piano. She came and got him, he took her back to his bed, and they made love again, and then they slept together in his bed all night.
- He acted by emotion when he was being kind to her. He acted like a Dom when on the subject of the contract.
- I believe, his mind was saying this is to be a sub/Dom relationship, but his heart was making him act differently

185

before he realized what was happening, and it's not his usual relationship. That's why there's always a first.

- I think he was just mixed up in his feelings and what he wanted.
- He wanted Ana, and she was a virgin, so things went a little differently. He had to take her to bed and she talked more freely with him than any of the others. She was trying to understand him. He said he had many firsts with her. Yet, in his mind he still wanted her as his sub. He was waiting for her answer, even though she wanted a normal relationship. He even offered to take her out once a week. So he was changing a little even though she never signed.

Bossy Boss

Do you think Ana was attracted by Christian's bossiness? Would she have preferred if Christian permitted her to do and say whatever she wanted? Or did she prefer for him to be in charge? How about you? Do your men know when to say STOP and ENOUGH?

- Mine sure does. But I am a pushy woman so he needs to.
- I wouldn't like it in just any circumstance during the day, but when it comes to sex, I like it.
- Interestingly, I could more easily answer a question about what Christian likes about Ana than the other way around. I think she liked it when he was bossy with confidence. When he knew what he wanted and what was best and made decisions. He was clearly the expert in bed and she gladly relinquished control to him and liked it when he was bossy when they were having sex. I think she didn't like it when he was bossy out of insecurity, though. When he tried to tell her what to do but it was because he was afraid. Does that make sense?
- Yes of course I think he liked when she challenged him and it might have been a decisive factor on her favor. I love my husband and chose him because he knew how to stop me when I was freaking out. I actually left my ex

because he had no power to "control" me (you know what I mean). I could tell him off and do whatever I wanted and he was powerless. I think I got bored in the end and moved on.

- It reminds me of the book, "Why Men Love Bitches." It's pretty interesting. I don't think any of us want a doormat, men or women.

- For me, I don't ever wish to disrespect my hubby and regrettably my tongue can be sharper than I like at times. I have asked my husband to hold me accountable and call me on my shit when I don't always recognize it in myself, when I've had a bad day and what I say is not how it should have come out. I choose to hold myself to this higher standard; but, sadly, I'm not perfect in that pursuit. He is great at drawing the line and in turn (when I have had a really bad day), I have become quite adept at letting him know (beforehand) that it may take me a minute to de-stress and nothing is directed at him. Now, as for Christian and Ana, it took her a bit to stop feeling like an "errant child" when Christian would go into his bossy mode. However, it grew on her, he was her "Fifty, in all of his bossiness" and she didn't want him to change. All that she asked was that he would be more open with her with the things that affected their relationship, their family and their lives, and he, out of love and trust in her, learned to do just that.

- We can sometimes push the men to the limits but they must know when to say enough. I think if Ana had accepted José he would have been her "doormat."

- Trust and respect is the basis of communication. However, the men of the world today would rather be selfish. I think Christian wanted to hide his sensitivity. And Ana liked to feel safe.

"It's What I Do"

"'Thank you for ordering my favorite breakfast.' "'It's your birthday,' Christian says softly. 'And you have to stop thanking me.' He rolls his eyes in exasperation, but fondly, I think."

"'I just want you to know that I appreciate it.'
"'Anastasia, it's what I do.'"

When Christian says this - it makes me think he's saying that he's done this with others. Do you think Ana took it this way? What would you think?

- I thought it hinted at that too. But, then I just want to think that he meant that it's what he wants to do for her – to take care of her.
- He pretty much takes care of everyone in his life.
- It's his mission to take care of Ana.
- I think he likes to do things for Ana!
- This is his way of taking care of her. He may have done it for others, but I'm sure it has a deeper significance when he does it for the woman he's madly in love with.
- He was also brought up to have manners and thoughtfulness. I'm guessing this caused a push-and-pull between him and his girls, wanting to treat them right but also maintaining a distance. And, of course, Elena gave him mixed signals, setting that stage as well.
- Totally agree!
- As much as he took care of others, I don't think he went all the way, like he does for Ana. This was a special day for her and he wants to show he cares more for her. This was a way to show a different side of him - the more lovable and caring Christian.
- He never took care of the others like he did Ana. He wanted to make all her dreams come true, and that includes making her his priority.

Make-Up Sex

Did you notice that it seemed like Christian always got lovey-dovey and opened up more after they had a big fight? Why do you think that is? Does it happen with you? Share your stories!

- Love that observation. I think he was lovey-dovey out of remorse. He often felt guilty for letting his anger get the best of him. He opened up because I think he felt he owed Ana something in return for her tolerance of his craziness and extremism.

- I guess it has to do with his being more relaxed after sex.
- Making up after a fight is the best sex ever.
- He was so afraid of losing her, he opens up a little at a time. Not so with us.
- Oooh. I'm so familiar with Christian's behavior. When hubby and I have fights (and we have doozies!), I shut him out (much like when Ana did when she was super-angry after she told Christian she was pregnant, and he went and got drunk with Mrs. Robinson). Then when he wants to make nice, he's quite the suck-up. He's so nice and so sweet, and so incredibly affectionate (he always says "time to make up, I wanna play"). My hubby is a real charmer and knows that I have a ton of trouble resisting his charms. So, again, I can totally relate.
- Christian feels more vulnerable so he opens up.

You've Gotta Have Friends

I always wondered about the fact that Christian didn't seem to have friends. He had acquaintances or employees, yet, no true friends, especially male ones. There's Elliot (who I'm glad he's closer with than I thought - thanks to *Grey*) or Dr. Flynn, or even Taylor, but surprisingly it was women he was mostly surrounded with. Those who he loved (like Ana, Grace and Mia), relied on (like Ros or Andrea). There were those who seemed to be unfazed, and actually disliked him (like Kate or Dr. Greene). And, of course, there was Elena. I suppose what I'm trying to say is, that whether they love him or not, Christian seems to be more comfortable amongst women. Perhaps it's because he thinks it'd be easier to charm them?

- Wow - interesting perspective!
- That's interesting... I never really gave that a thought.
- Do you think maybe he felt like he could "control" or influence women better than he could men? Whether, as

you suggest, it's because he could charm them with his looks or whatever, or for some other reason?

- Not sure if I agree with him, (that it's easier to charm women) but it's an interesting thought.
- Yes, that's what I'm thinking. He's aware of his extreme good looks and although he's not vain, I'd say he wouldn't hesitate to use them whether it's in business or just everyday life to influence and/or control. There was this time, for example, when he went to Ana's apartment ("nice knowing you" scene) when his charms worked even on Kate, who we know wasn't his biggest fan.
- I do think he had male friends. There was Elliot of course, and Claude Bastille. Even though Taylor worked for him, I think their relationship went well above that. Remember, male friends prefer to do things together. They don't usually just sit around and talk. They play golf together, or watch a game together. They shoot baskets together, or go running together, etc.
- Your comment sounds like the assertion in the movie "When Harry Met Sally" that suggested men and women can't be friends.
- I agree; I think it is control issue. He needs to have control and it is easier for him with women.
- My ex didn't have many male friends...preferred women as friends. I thought it was odd. I didn't know he was a Dom at the time I had these thoughts. Don't really know what to make of it except that he liked women. When we lived in SF, he didn't like going to the Castro district (predominately gay neighborhood) because he feared being hit on by men. He was handsome, wasn't homophobic, just fearful.
- Christian also had Mac who he seemed comfortable with. There were a few male "friends" invited to his birthday party. Flynn, Mac, and maybe Claude. But I think he may have just been more comfortable around women. His mother never beat him, her pimp did. It may stem from that.
- Good point! About the pimp. Hmmm. Also, I think Christian wouldn't have called Taylor his "friend,"

190

though in many ways they were friends. Remember how he told Ana not to get too close to the "help?"

- I think it's because he is a sensitive soul, attuned more to women than to men, who often lack sensitivity, softness, and compassion.

Picking A Fight

When Christian punched the "Blonde Giant," it obviously wasn't the first time Christian has gotten physical with Ana's admirers. Has anyone else experienced this in relationships, how does this make you feel?

- Any kind of violence is abhorrent to me, so this would've made me physically sick. And it would probably have made me shy away from Christian.
- My husband has almost fought a few times, but usually his sh*t talking and stare diffuse the situation. I push him away and beg him not to do anything and thankfully that has worked. He actually showed up to my work place once and started yelling for the guy to come out. So embarrassing!
- I've had the domineering guy who wanted to fight. The first one was so big and tough. It scared me he would really hurt someone. We broke up a few times, and I dated others. When I went out on dates, I wouldn't go where I knew he would be. I knew he would start something. Once I was in a car for a date, and we were going to a bar I didn't think he would be at. We were looking for a parking spot, and he came out of the bar. The guy even yelled "duck," and I ducked down in the seat. He went after one guy I dated and hurt him, so I didn't take any chances. I didn't like it. It made me mad, but yet made me feel good all at once. I knew he still cared, and I was still madly in love with him. I know; That's a little psycho.
- More than a little, I think.
- Yeah it was. I didn't see it that way when I was younger though. If he would've expressed his feelings for me, I wouldn't have liked it even a little. It was the only way

191

that I knew he cared. I avoided him though, because I sure didn't want anyone hurt on my account.

- It's interesting what we "accept" in someone when we're young that we can look back and ask "what was I thinking?"
- Exactly.
- Violence is not something that I can handle. My body starts shaking and my heart starts to beat so fast. I'd be really angry at him. Once my brother was dropping me off at my school bus stand. A guy came and started to flirt and saying stupid things that my brother slapped him so hard. I was completely shaken by that. I was angry at him but I also had to hold him back. This is something which doesn't sit well with me.
- I'm the same way. Makes me physically sick.
- I know. And I can't stop thinking about these kind of incidents.
- I think it would make me uncomfortable to see my husband be physical with anyone. In high school I took care of myself physically a couple of times. Bullies suck! And I made sure they didn't bully me again. But someone else hurting someone on my behalf wouldn't sit well with me. Honestly, I'd prefer to handle it myself either verbally or physically, if need be. My hubby is a lover not a fighter.
- The best kind!
- Even though I hate violence, I wrote a movie screenplay that featured a man rescuing his woman when she got kidnapped. I DO think men should be prepared to ACT if something like that happened. It wouldn't have to be violent - just action-oriented and not sit around.
- No one has ever gotten inappropriate with me so none of my dates had to deck anyone.
- When I was dating my ex in high school we went to a movie theater and the guys behind us were making lewd comments. I have never seen him get so mad that he actually turned around to punch the guy. That, right then and there, should have given me an inkling to his temper, and I would never have married him.

192

Ana's Strengths and Weaknesses

When we first enter Ana and Christian's story, we see everything from Anastasia's eyes. Her insecurities and fears, her excitement and apprehension. Sometimes confident and other times self-effacing, Ana is simultaneously simple and complicated. We cheer her on as often as we question her decisions. And yet even if we wouldn't want to trade places with Ana, we still enjoy living vicariously through her.

Opening Up

"He stifles a smile. 'What is bothering you specifically, Miss Steele? Spit it out.'
"Okay.
"'What's bothering me? Well, there's your gross invasion of my privacy, the fact that you took me to some place where your ex-mistress works and you used to take all your lovers to have their bits waxed, you manhandled me in the street like I was six years old—and to cap it all, you let your Mrs. Robinson touch you!' My voice has risen to a crescendo."

Do you think Ana would've been as open with Christian if he hadn't told her how important she was to him?

- Yes, I do.
- Probably not. I think it gave her confidence to be herself and let him know.
- I think I would've said the same thing, if I was Ana!
- Speaking for myself, I would have to feel really secure in the relationship before I would express myself so freely! (Or I'd be out the door...)
- I don't think she would have. Compare *FSOG* with *Darker* and you'll see that once she knew he had feelings for her, she opened up, and so did he. Before, she was intimidated, and even told him that was partly why she didn't express herself more and tell him want she wanted.
- I think she opened up because she was no longer fearful of punishment.

193

- I agree.
- No I don't think so, she was a self-confident (not about her beauty though) self-opinionated person. She didn't care about his money and position in the world. She wanted to be treated with respect, as she respected herself. Well, maybe self-opinionated is too strong to say about Ana but she knew what she was saying.

Attractiveness

"'You have no idea how attractive you are, do you?'
"I flush. Why's he going on about this?
"'All those boys pursuing you—that isn't enough of a clue?'
"'Boys? What boys?'
"'You want the list?' Christian frowns. 'The photographer, he's crazy about you, that boy in the hardware store, your roommate's older brother. Your boss,' he adds bitterly.
"'Oh, Christian, that's just not true.'
"'Trust me. They want you. They want what's mine.'"

On a scale of 1 to 10 - how attractive do you think Ana (in the books) is? How attractive in Christian's eyes? Do you think Christian is right - that the other "boys" wanted Ana? Was it more because of her looks?

- I think she was probably an 8. He thought she was a 10, and, of course part of that was based on his love for her. Of course, they wanted her. She was sweet, kind, funny, smart, pretty, and unaware of her overall attractiveness.
- I think Ana was more attractive than she knew. In Christian's eyes, she was the most beautiful girl in the world (10+). I think he also loved her smarts and her personality too, which made her even more beautiful to him. I also think Christian was right about the "boys." They liked Ana for sure, she just wasn't interested in them.
- I think Ana was beautiful. She's one of those "late bloomers" who didn't figure out the uses of makeup to really accentuate her looks. On the flipside, Christian saw something in her that really spoke to him about her

194

natural beauty. He wasn't the only man who saw that in her either. All these guys were practically throwing themselves at her, and she was completely oblivious. That's what totally threw Christian off when she told him she was a virgin. He was so sure that since he felt so strongly about her, other guys did too, and she naturally would've given herself to a guy so much sooner. She really didn't understand how alluring she was to men, and that fed into Christian constantly having to tell her that she was "his and only his."

- I agree totally.
- I like imaging her as a "diamond in the rough." Someone who didn't recognize, and perhaps even downplayed her appearance. She liked to fit into the background; not stand out.
- No doubt about that!
- I would see her as a 7-8! To Christian, she was beautiful and perfect. Her innocence and personality is what attracted Christian to her. He saw her pureness. I think she's just an overall pretty, nice, and fun girl, so who wouldn't like her?
- I think one of the magical things about love is that we become more beautiful in our lover's eyes.
- In the book, Ana is about a 7-8 ish and in his eyes a sure 10. I do think he's right; these men wanted Ana. I think it was enough of a combination of her hidden confidence, beauty and demeanor.
- I think Ana was about a 9. Through Christian's eyes, 10+. I believe the other guys did want Ana. A guy that loves you can tell these things. Same as a girl who knows when someone else is hot after her guy. She was beautiful, intelligent and knew how to joke around.

Obedience

Ana was very obedient. And it seems she did it without reservation. Would this make you feel weird? It would me. Not sure why.

- Do you think she was only naturally obedient related to sexual matters, where his sexpertise was clearly superior to hers?
- I think so. It's definitely easy to be obedient when you don't have experience. I'm far from inexperienced, but I'm pretty obedient in the bedroom. It is like I'm shy to take the lead most of the time. Sometimes, I'm not. Probably more when I'm drinking. I don't know why I get shy like that. I'm far from shy.
- I think this was to show she was a submissive.
- A sexual submissive - for sure! Outside the bedroom? Not sure about that.
- I think she was being obedient, and doing exactly what he told her to do turned her on.
- I think that when it came to Christian, she would do ANYTHING for him (as long as it didn't involve pain or punishment). In her mind that's how someone in love behaves.
- It was sexy. I would've done it. She wanted those balls!
- I agree. I would, too.
- I think you hit the hail on the nead. Outside of the bedroom, there was not a submissive bone in her body. And yes, I can do this.
- There is such a thing as a bratty sub. I think Ana can't help but push, but ultimately wants to please.
- Sometimes the punishment is reflective of the crime. Don't tell my master that though! Lol. My Dom can't see these posts, that's why I love this group, I can express without punishment.
- Wow how nice to know a real sub. Hi! Is it teasing that turns your master on?
- Definitely not; its obedience, for sure. But, that could be for my sexual pleasure, not his. It's not a selfish thing, it's a loyalty thing, I think... I'm not sure now. This is making me think.
- I envision Leila like this. Enjoying getting a "rise" out of Christian.
- I'm not sure, my Master is kind, and loyal and forgiving, understanding and demanding. I have said before, I have

196

an online relationship with my Master but it works for us, and has for nearly 9 months now; however, we've known each other for 3 years.

- I think the different ways people make relationships work is fascinating.
- Just knowing I won't orgasm because he said, makes me happy.
- So, you both have Skype encounters right?
- We have contact every day. But, he understands family first, so if something comes up, its ok. His biggest annoyance with me is that I tend to disappear for a couple of days, and he worries.
- I know I have been accused of this before, but do genuinely want to please.
- Ana was all new to this stuff. She felt comfortable with and trusted Christian. I think when you have a relationship as intimate as Christian and Ana's, it just comes naturally. I don't know if it's the whole Dom/sub thing, but Ana really trusted him. The more they did together, she knew he would take care of her, so it just came natural to her.
- Ana loved Christian, and I think she trusted him, especially around anything sexual because she knew he wasn't going to hurt her.
- I think I would've been more challenging than Ana. I think she was more trusting. He definitely did a good job at reassuring her. To this point he hadn't failed her trust sexually, so her trust was understandable.

Naked Self-Image

Christian said to Ana that he wanted her to be unashamed of her nakedness because she had a beautiful body. What life events do you think happened to Ana to make her initially shy or ashamed of her body, and appearance? (Consider how she dressed when she interviewed Christian?)

Christian didn't seem to have any issue with his own nakedness. But, how else could he be "naked" in the sense of who he was? How could he be more authentic, be

197

the real Christian, imperfections included. Do you think he hid behind the images he liked to project: the successful businessman, self-made billionaire, well-dressed in his bespoke suits, expensive cars, penthouse, home in Aspen, jet, catamaran and helicopter in order to protect his other "nudity" or vulnerability? Do you think this was exhausting to him?
At what point in the trilogy do you think Christian could simply be himself?

- You bring up an interesting question. One of the things I could never reconcile about Ana's character was how self-deprecating she was, and she didn't seem to have a reason for it. Clothes can be used as a shield for women, to keep unwanted attention from them, to build walls in order to hide, but E.L. doesn't really suggest that she had some kind of deep seated issues. I assume that she just may be a victim of her environment. Take for instance how she views her best friend Kate. Kate, to her, is the gorgeous, confident, no-holds barred type. I think Ana just suffers from the typical insecurities that can haunt any woman living in this society.
- I think every girl, no matter how positive and secure her home environment is, goes through phases where they believe they're not as "good" as somebody else. Since we don't know anything about Carla's Husband #3, there's the possibility that something could've happened that affected Ana in such a way that would cause her self-doubt. It's evident that was not a good situation all the way around, especially since Carla wasn't with him that long. I also don't think Ana really had a "bad" self-image. I think she just wasn't in any situations where it would come into play, except, of course, with the all-confident, self-possessed Kate.
- I agree with you. What about the unspoken tension around Carla's third husband? I wondered if perhaps he had made inappropriate advances towards Ana that prompted her being shuffled off to live with Ray. Along with that thought, I wondered (let's say the above is true) if perhaps Carla had Ana live with Ray because she felt

that Ana may have done "something" to encourage Husband #3's advances. Often, the mothers of young women who are sexually molested think their daughters are partly to blame. Carla's attitude (mostly in the books) made me think she just wasn't that interested in her daughter - didn't attend high school or college graduations.

- I thought that might be a possibility. Yeah, but there could be something to that. He was a bad egg. I just assume since she was so comfortable in the sexual act with Christian, that sexual abuse wasn't her issue. That somehow, that would have come up in the story somehow.
- What could Christian have done to expose his nakedness to Ana? (Other than the obvious - chuckle!) What steps would he have had to take?
- I think it's interesting how many novels have the female protagonist as being "too thin." It is supposed to be telling us that more women can relate to a heroine that's so thin? I don't know about anyone else, but I can definitely relate better to someone whose insecurities might run the opposite direction.
- I think Ana was a classic introvert; someone who didn't want to call attention to herself, who was more comfortable being in the background. I'm not sure her lack of confidence was related to anything else.

Body Talk

Do you think Ana was scared that once Christian would disapprove of her body? Was she afraid of Christian's reaction to her body? Was Ana ashamed of her body? Would Christian look at her differently by how her body looks? My final question is: Has anyone felt insecure about their body?

- When girls are very young boys start making fun of them, probably because they don't know how to deal with their own feelings about sexuality. If a young girl, at least in my generation, asked her mom about her

199

sexuality, or about boys, her mom would have changed the subject. So a young girl never becomes comfortable with her own sexuality. Add to that, her mom's own discomfort about HER sexuality and a young girl doesn't end up with s lot of comfort in that area. Then there's the whole "good girl" "bad girl" thing. I think it all makes for a very insecure young woman. I held onto my virginity until I was 19 because I felt do inadequate about my body and about sexuality in general. I wish I had not waited that long because when I did have sex, it was with someone who was very selfish. I wish I had my first time with my high school boyfriend who really loved me and was a very kind and generous young man. But I bet among women my age, 65, their life experience is similar. I hope it's different for young women today. I hope that there are no longer "good girls" or "bad girls" unless you are speaking of one's personality.

- I am constantly insecure about my body. But my husband loves my body and we have a great relationship. I think Ana was insecure, simply because she was a virgin.

- Ana didn't have any reason to be self-conscious. She had a nice body. It was her first time, so she was embarrassed and insecure. I feel very self-conscious about my body. I use to be slim like Dakota and now I'm not. I can't stand looking in the mirror or taking pics of myself. I want my old body back so badly. Unfortunately, age and migraine meds are working against what I do.

- I think insecurity comes in a lot of forms. Ana certainly preferred her body to be as thin as possible, which to me is a bit of a red flag. It's one thing if she wanted to be fit, it's another that she wanted to starve herself to be thin.

- Maybe she wasn't trying to starve herself to be thin. Some people just aren't big eaters. Everyone is different.

- I agree with you - but in Ana's case, I do think she was an unhealthy person. She rarely exercised and went long periods of time without eating.

- Well maybe it wasn't because she just didn't eat much; she just didn't want to eat in front of him. I use to be like that, too. I didn't like to eat in front of a guy when I first met him.

- And during their separations she didn't eat, either. And it's not like she ate healthy food, either with Christian or on her own. It wasn't purely junk food, but she had no eye for nutrition or a balanced diet at all.
- Well that was because she was upset. Some people can't eat when they are upset and others eat more. Doesn't mean she was always like that. I guess we just interpreted that part of the story differently.

Brunette Ambition

"'You are still so young, and I know you're quietly ambitious.'
"Ambitious? Me?"

Do you think Ana was ambitious? In what ways, yes? In what ways maybe, no?

-
- That was always the tough one for me. I thought of her as very competent. Ambitious? Not like Christian.
- She grew hungrier and more ambitious as their relationship progressed. She was younger than he was. She obviously had some ambitions, if she went and completed college. Perhaps, if she hadn't met Christian, she would've remained complacent in her life.
- Ambitious to learn, to get her degree, to succeed in her work, not in money.
- I agree. And to do work she enjoys, and finds meaningful.
- I think she was ambitious to do what she loved most. I don't think ambition has to be tied to achieving a higher position. It can just be about being happy doing what you love most.
- I love that answer.
- Thanks. I really think that when she talked to Christian about running a company, I think that was what he was really trying to tell her, when he said that she could be the creative head of the company...again, doing

201

something she loved, leading a team of like-minded people who share her love of books.

- She was ambitious, but I think ambitious in teaching Christian how to feel touch and how to be loved unconditionally.
- Oooh! Good one.
- I didn't really think of her as ambitious. Maybe being the business man he was, he saw something in her that I didn't pick up on.

Catfight!

Ana gets FIERCE with Gia. Have you ever had to fight off a woman making moves on your man? How did you handle it?

- I wouldn't say that I had to fight them off, just establish who's boss. I get rude and I'm not straight forward. They say that you're not supposed to but I'd shove our love in their face. Then, they'd leave on their own. Sometimes, he will get rid of them, if he sees they're making me uncomfortable.
- I was thinking about asking this question for a while, but in a different manner. Thanks for bringing it up. So here is my question. Christian made disgusted face when he realized that Ana was jealous of Gia. It's okay if he gets jealous and uncomfortable, but it doesn't sit well with him when Ana gets jealous. Why? Don't we all get angry and jealous when someone makes a move on our partner? Don't we, even if we know they only love us?
- I don't think it sits well with him when she gets jealous because he doesn't want her to feel inadequate or to doubt herself. He thinks that could lead to her thinking he wants someone else.
- I thought he was just acting that way to show Ana he wasn't attracted to Gia.
- I've never had to fight a woman off my man...but he did tell me that when was working on a film many years ago. There was a girl who kept hitting on him, asking him out for drinks after a long day on set. He kept telling her that

he just wanted to go home to his wife and relax. After numerous rejections, she apparently got the hint that he wasn't interested in her in the slightest.

- There was a woman that made advances towards my husband a few times. The first was when we were just dating. I didn't say anything to her because I wanted to let him handle her. It didn't work, so I told her that she needed to back off or else we were going to have a problem. She got the hint, and it lasted for a few years. About 2 years ago, she tried again and this time I really made it known that she wasn't to contact him at all or else I was going to tell her husband and let him see every message that she sent to my husband. Well, she apparently took me seriously because we haven't heard from her since.
- Go get 'em!
- I actually told her off. I mean, I got in her face and told her off. I'm a pretty calm person, until someone tries to mess with my husband or kids. I can tell the difference between harmless flirting and serious flirting, and this woman wasn't doing harmless flirting.
- Yay!
- In high school a girl made moves on my boyfriend, and slept with him. I beat her ass and threw her in her locker and shut the door.
- Now you're all reminding me about this one girl who was super jealous that I was dating the guy who would become my hubby. She knew we were dating, and she started calling him and trying to fill his head with things that she didn't like about me. He saw right through her and told her where to go!
- The guy I was referring to above was actually my fiancé. We broke up over what they did. We did get back together and then he died. He had a head on collision with a car and he was on a motorcycle. At the funeral, she had the nerve to get mad. His family introduced me as his fiancée and they gave me a rose he was holding in the casket. She felt she should get it. I was steaming mad. She was a one-night stand that threw herself at him. I was his love. I've gotten over it over the years.

When our class reunited on Facebook, I found out she is still pissed after 35 years. She has some nerve.

- Crazy B... she still hasn't gotten it.
- Nope. I forgave her, but she goes around talking behind my back all these years later.
- Some people never learn. How childish.
- No... I let her have the worthless arse!
- I did: right in the middle of Wal Mart! This woman (term used loosely) was following my husband around. She saw me and said, "He sure is cute!" I told her "yes" he was and he's taken. She got mad and stomped off!
- Sort of, yes. I ignored it, just like he did.
- Once, after I caught a woman going to my hubby's work. She didn't know I was behind her. When she turned around, it was so funny seeing her changing colors and looking for a way to get away. I just looked at her - no argument needed.
- Yes, two of my ex fiancés. Women were always chasing them and hanging on them. I hated it. They seemed to love the attention. They both cheated on me too. The first one died. He was on a motorcycle and hit a car. One of my acquaintances, who he cheated with, showed up at the funeral home. She was mad that I was introduced as his girlfriend to everyone and I was given some of his stuff. He was holding a rose in the casket, and they gave it to me. She just about blew a gasket. I told her that we were supposed to get married and she was just a one-night f*ck that meant nothing to him. I was angry she even showed up. The funeral home was full of girls. There was a line out the door and down the street. They set up speakers so people outside could hear service too. After dealing with the two that every girl wanted, I switched to the kind of guy I chose. I'm not usually the jealous type but those two gave me reasons. I just don't care for that jealous feeling.
- I don't either. Feels too hurtful, insecure, and hateful, none of which I like.
- I usually prefer dating men who I think are attractive but don't get noticed so much by women - until, for some

strange reason, they start dating me. Then, the women come out of the woodwork and go after the man I'm dating. Happened to me several times. Ugh. A few of the men went for it, and a few didn't.

- Once my husband was working on a film and one of the women was hitting on him BIG TIME...very Gia-like. She kept asking him out for drinks and he kept telling her no... That he just wanted to finish the day and go home...TO ME!

- Yes I have! And for me, it's more about how he reacts and handles them.

- I have had situations like this before I met my husband. I was just too young and stupid to realize he was making a fool of me. Now, my husband is a country boy and girls/women do look at him, but he doesn't even notice. I do and then I give them the "what the he'll you lookin' at stare." Ha! He would be stupid to lose me and he knows it. I never let my guard down, though, and females around here are not trustworthy on any level.

- We were only 17 and 18 when we married. He walked me to school and back since we were 10, and always told me he was going to marry me. We were each other's first love, first kiss, and first times. I never was worried about him, except once when a girl half his age really had an agenda and then I got him to go to Miami for 14 months. She married an older gentleman while we were gone and divorced him 3 months later, when she found out his ex got all his money. My husband always laughed at me and told me he was flattered but he knew what she was after. My husband became a successful business man, and I always thought he was good looking but of course he was mine. I actually thought he got better with age.

- If they know how to handle it, and send them on their way, not so much. They can look all they want.

Their Strengths and Weaknesses as a Couple

Fire and ice? Or fire and rocket fuel? Hot sex? Or hot mess? Either way, Ana and Christian were a hot couple. And we're not just talking about their smoldering looks and the scorching sex scenes. They pushed each other's buttons as often as they tested each other's limits. Yet Ana and Christian persisted through obstacle after obstacle, ultimately finding their "happily ever after."

Help or Hurt?

As women, we all seem to suffer with low self-esteem, at times; especially, about our looks, age, or weight, or something else. We've all been there. Do you think Christian helped Ana's self-esteem (telling her constantly that she was his firsts, etc.)? Or, do you think he hurt it? (Telling her he couldn't give her "more")? In my opinion, he had her on a roller coaster at all times. One minute, she was enough, the next minute she wasn't. Imagine what that could do to your self-worth.

- Hmmm... I think he was good at complimenting her - her courage, her looks, her body, etc. In that way, he was good for her ego. The challenge was that he made her feel insecure about the relationship. That push-and-pull, the hot-and-cold, the "get away/closer" behavior was maddening. Some people/men might use that behavior to control you, and I think in some ways Christian did. But, the reason we forgive him is that we know (in *Darker*) it was a more profound internal struggle. I think he was sincere in those moments. His own emotions were bouncing all over the place, and she was going dizzy following the bouncing ball. That being said, I'm sure he was quite adept at using emotional manipulation to keep his subs in line. He'd punish bad behavior and reward the good. Yet, I suspect he also kept them on their toes with inconsistency. I'm sure he learned that from Elena.

- How do you think he rewarded his subs, when they behaved the way he wanted them to?
- They might get to choose the scene, or he'd do something they liked, like dancing.
- I would think sex. He didn't seem like he did much else with the subs. I'd guess their reward might orgasms or mouth kissing.
- I think he was very good for Ana's ego. The only thing I'm slightly doubtful about, is how he always reacted to her desire to work. She was ambitious, just graduated and had dreams about being fulfilled in her career choice. Sometimes, I got an impression that as much as he loved her being ambitious, intelligent, etc., he selfishly would have her home with him, then barefoot and pregnant, just so she is always as close to him as possible.
- He was all over the place there, too. One minute he wanted her to stay home or travel with him and the next he wanted her to run the SIP/Grey Publishing!
- Yes! And remember how he said that Linc didn't want Elena to work? He seemed put off by that. Yet, he kind of acted with those feelings now and again. Confusing!
- I think he was just teasing Ana about Linc not letting Elena work. He said "some men were controlling like that." She said "surely a mythical creature."
- Yes, I think he helped her. He told Ana never to be ashamed of her body, as it is beautiful. But, she would be confused as why they couldn't be normal or why she couldn't touch him. But, his being Christian Grey, she had to feel a sense of having that feeling that she was pretty, if he wanted her. Ana being Ana though, it might take her a while to come around and realize that she is very pretty. As everyone that met her thought she was - boys too.
- When they weren't arguing, he encouraged her, told her how beautiful she was, took care of her, believed she could do things that she didn't think she could do, and made her feel beautiful just by how he looked her sometimes. By doing all this over time, he built up her confidence and made her believe in herself.

The Proposal

Why do you think Christian proposed? Was it out of fear? Desperation? Or, had he been thinking about it? If he'd been thinking about it, when had that thought first entered his mind?

- He had been thinking about it.
- I think he'd been thinking about it, and I think all this started after she left him, because that's when he realized that he couldn't be without her.
- That's my thought exactly.
- I think he truly wanted to marry Ana. I think he couldn't see himself being with anyone else. But, in the moment of the proposal, I think it was out of desperation and fear.
- He proposed because, in that moment, after his most feared admission, at his most vulnerable, she was there. She hadn't run, or reacted the way he had expected. To him that was the highest form of love that she had just displayed to him. She had proven everything she promised him, that she would never leave again.
- Maybe that was his way of insuring she would never leave again. He definitely knew he never wanted to be without her again. He may have been conjuring this up since the breakup.
- I agree with all of the above! Christian realized he didn't want to be without her again. So, by proposing, it was his way of saying that he loved her and didn't want to be without her again.
- I think he also saw being married as a way to control her and that she would have to obey.
- I think Christian loved his contracts! It was the only way he knew to keep her from leaving him again. I think during those few days of separation he knew he'd do anything to avoid that separation desperation again. I also think he was a very decisive person. Just because it was quick, didn't mean it was impetuous.

Counting the Minutes

When Ana tells Christian she's pregnant, he yells at her "We've known each other five f*cking minutes" even though they are married. What was your reaction to that?

- I absolutely hated the way he reacted to her pregnancy. Without hearing her out at all, and treating her like that - "save the waterworks" or whatever he said to her crying. He acted really immature, and I was really pissed at him at that point. But, I also got pissed at Ana several times. They both acted really childish and immature, at times. But they were both new in "real relationships'" so I guess it's normal after all.
- Agreed. I would've said, "Well you knew me enough to marry me and f*ck me without a condom. Sometimes the shot fails, you asshole. Oh, but I forgot, you do nothing wrong." Then he went to Elena and got drunk with her after she called HIS WIFE a gold digger. I was like, "Oh hell, no. I wish a motherf*cker would pull that sh*t on me." I think Ana forgave him too fast.
- They had a scary situation. They made her forgive him. I think most would under those conditions. You are just happy to be alive and Christian was just happy she was alive, and the baby was okay.
- Yep.
- His reaction was harsh and insensitive. But she was really immature not to pay more attention and take better care of herself. (Hadn't she already had one scare?) The character of Ana was a lot of contradictions. She was intelligent in some ways and childish in others. I don't blame him at all for the pregnancy. He thought she was protecting herself. But he reacted selfishly and cruelly. What was done was done. I guess these reasons are why I didn't like *Freed* nearly as much.
- What scare?
- In *Darker* when they "broke up" for the week and she did not take her pill; I also feel that with everything that went on with her dad that she was putting stuff on the back

burner, too. I don't think it should have been solely on her.

- Yeah, but they didn't have a close call. He just used condoms. He asked her before they had sex.
- As the old saying goes, it takes two to tango. She should've been more responsible, and he did the plowing. If he'd been a real person, I would've slapped him. He was ruthless, and a complete asshole.
- And, I wanted to slap her for being so irresponsible! Lol.
- Both needed it.
- I truly wanted to reach through the book and smack the hell out of Christian when I read this scene. Even more so when Ana had seen that he had seen Elena. I get that he may not have been thrilled about becoming a father, especially with a lot of the demons within himself that he had to face and was still facing. However, on Ana's side, she had a lot going on as well. Between the car chase, the apartment getting broken into, dealing with ex's, and her dad, it is easy to see with all that stress that she could forget her shot which failed. They both need to take responsibility for the pregnancy. I was so proud of Ana for standing up to him the way she did the morning after.
- I would've gone crazy as hell on him if he was talking to me like that. I wanted to choke his drunk ass out after I found out he was with the bitch troll.
- Their courtship wasn't that long, and to Christian, he would've thought any time was too short for that situation to be popping up in his life. He was just learning to love her and be comfortable with their relationship, let alone bring a baby into it. He said he didn't want to share. Absolutely hated/but loved this part. I cry and freak out each time. But I understand his thoughts. He just didn't need to see Mrs. Robinson!
- He was selfish with her and loved control. This broke all those walls down for him. They were both irresponsible.
- As far as his going to Elena, I can see both sides of it. Yes, he knew it would hurt Ana, but he had no other close friends who really knew him to go to. Plus, he

210

needed that final time to see who she really was. It had to be his decision to end his friendship with Elena - and not do it just because Ana wanted him to.

- I couldn't believe how badly Christian reacted to the news. It made me angry with him. I understand that it was a shock, but the things he said were mean. Ana was irresponsible with not keeping up with her shot but then again dealing with all the crazy situations that surrounded that time it would be easy to forget. I'm glad they worked it out in the end, but that scene was harsh.

- I felt this way too. My feelings were all over the place during this part. It hit me personally because my husband and I got married young and after our first wedding anniversary, I got pregnant (also a birth control fail) but my husband was so happy about it. Although I was happy, I cried when I told him.

- He reacted like an insensitive brat. He knew that they had only known each other for a very short time when they married. But, he also was responding like that out of fear and knowing that he was now going to be responsible for caring/raising another human being. Given his experience with his birth mother, he didn't have any faith that he could possibly be a good father at all. What he didn't realize is that he wasn't going to be alone in raising the child, and that he had an amazing woman who would help him and would make sure he wouldn't screw it up.

- Okay - now I'll weigh in as an author. I can envision E.L. James' challenge writing this. She wanted more drama (they say that it's an author's job to create as many challenges for your protagonist as you can). She wanted the happy ending at the end - which (to her) was a family. So - how to write it? She had to get Christian to finally see Elena for what she was. This scene helped her do that. She also had to keep Christian "in character." If he had been all romance and roses it wouldn't have fit him. He had changed - but not that much, not that soon. Plus, she was setting up the scene with Mia and Jack - to make it more believable for him to think Ana would leave him. Yes, it was a bit contrived - but it also fit the characters.

- I completely agree.
- I was really upset with Christian when he reacted this way. I couldn't excuse him this time for his past or his inhibitions.
- I got another question for y'all. Do you think she forgave him too fast?
- I remember thinking "Well, she's better than I am." I don't think I would've been there when he got home.
- In a way, yes. She forgave him too fast.
- Too fast, especially with the Elena "thing."
- Yeah, he would definitely be in the doghouse for a while with the Elena thing and the abortion comment.
- I was wondering why he chose Elena to talk to. He knew Ana hated her.
- He could've talked to Mia.
- I ached.
- I think once you understand and know what happened was a mistake, there is no sense in holding onto anger. It only hurts in the end. She'd be the only one to really know whether or not Christian deserved to be forgiven that quickly.
- I totally agree with you.
- She also understood where he was coming from with all his issues. I think that made it easier to forgive him, too.
- The key was that he had a true awakening/ realization regarding Elena. THAT was what made her able to forgive -that she knew he wouldn't repeat the mistake. There are 4 steps to forgiveness. #4 is "never do it again."
- I wanted to kick him in the balls and yell, "You're the one who couldn't wait to get married to her five f*ckin' minutes ago."
- I felt sorry for him because I understood it. Of course, he was being an asshole. But he was like a little child throwing a tantrum who I wanted to comfort. By this time, you knew his reaction was based on fear.
- Yeah, maybe a little. Because we understood where he came from and, undeniably, he definitely wanted her on birth control.

212

- I sympathize with men in this arena. They have to depend on us. He went out of his way to do everything he could to avoid it. Now she traps him. Sure, she had reasons and, as we all probably know, no birth control is 100% effective. (Other than abstinence, which we know is unreasonable on most cases, especially this one.)
- But, I also remember the part when he recommends that Ana changes the hours she takes the pills, until she gets on schedule, then she switched methods. It was nobody's fault though. Just glad he came to his senses.
- Yes, definitely unreasonable, in this case.
- If she hadn't missed her shots, then I would agree. But she did.
- Well her assistant caused her to. But yes, she should've been ON that! But with that new fast-paced jet-set life she was living, crammed full of excitement and adventure. I could see it slipping her mind, especially since that was something she never had to worry about before.
- I agree. It fits her personality, and the situation. But, she should have taken responsibility.
- Yes. Life happens.
- The thing is, whatever the right or wrong is, once that sh*t is out your mouth you can never take it back, and women NEVER forget a single thing (which is very important for future arguments.)
- The truth. We will become a lawyer with a law degree from Harvard bringing sh*t from way back in day, in arguments.
- If Ana hadn't saved Mia and risked her life, do you think Christian would've ever still considered that Ana intentionally got pregnant to trap him? You know he is not very trusting, and seemed to second-guess things of a personal nature.
- Okay, I, kind of, was mad over that because he wasn't that upset in *Darker* when Dr. Green put it out there. He was calm, and she was worried about his reaction. But, I do not think that the blame should have only been on her. But, it's how the story was written.

- This confirms what I said in another post: they got married too soon.
- He overreacted, but he was supposed to. But Ana wasn't trying to get pregnant. Sh*t happens. Christian got married out of fear that he would never feel this way ever again. Whereas Ana got married to the man who made her feel things she never felt for anyone. They both thought they would have more time to grow together. Blip was a surprise for both of them - a good surprise.
- I thought he was mimicking her. When he asked her to marry him, she said we've known each other three minutes.
- If he was mocking her, he needs to be kicked in the balls. Jerk.
- How dare you! He rushed the relationship and now he said that. Wow.

Blip or No Blip

Before I pose this question, I want to acknowledge that it could be quite controversial. Let's keep our usual respectful tolerance in mind as we answer.

Ana didn't give Christian any choice whether to keep Blip - or not. Do you think she should have? Would your answer be different if:
- Their wishes were reversed (she wasn't ready but he was)
- They weren't married?

- No. I feel his reaction to the news was all the reaction she needed to make her own decisions, regardless. Secondly, if he did, and she didn't, and they weren't married, it's still her body. That's my take on it.
- Yes, I think she should've given Christian a say in the matter, and it should have been a mutual decision. They were quite lucky to have had things work out as well as they did. Marriages don't often work the way one would hope when the man is forced into a situation that he didn't necessarily want. I think having a baby is best if both plan and want the child. Many people decide not to

214

marry and have children. Personally, I would prefer to be in a committed marriage to have children. I'm not judging those who decided to have children and not be married. I just don't think I would want to do it alone.

- So controversial really. I have no idea how to answer. I'd have to be actually in such a situation to decide. There are so many single moms nowadays raising children and they handle their motherhood so well. He wasn't ready, as we know, but she wanted the baby – a part of Grey inside her body. How could she ever decide not to keep it?

- No, she should not have given him a choice. Not when he acted that way. Sorry. She would have left him. If he'd accepted that, but was a little disappointed, then she could have given him a choice. I think at that time; he would've been okay with it. She wouldn't have gotten rid of the baby, no matter what.

- Hmm, as a man I may have a slightly different view on this. Yes, it's her body, and ultimately her final decision, but I do think the man has a right to be involved in the decision. After all, she didn't get pregnant by herself. However, that said, I suspect if he wanted an abortion and she did not, she would've won that discussion. Plus, if it came right down to it, I don't think Christian would've gone forward with the abortion anyways. I think he only suggested that out of shock and desperation. Upon reflection I think he would have changed his mind.

- I agree with you on both points. I think she should have given him a choice and not an ultimatum. Ultimately it is her body. And I agree; if he'd been given that choice, he would have eventually wanted to keep the baby.

- Remember, at the time he had no idea where Ana stood on the pregnancy. For all he knew, she wanted to get an abortion.

- Interesting. The way I read it, she seemed pretty firm on the fact that she was going to have the baby, with or without him. But it could just be my interpretation.

- Well, it has been a while since I read that section, but my memory is that he halfway blurted that out before he really knew if she wanted to keep it or not, but I could be wrong about that.

- I'm so glad in you're in this group to give us the flip side, but may I remind you, we're dealing with a woman's logic here, and his initial reaction would be the one that would've been stored away for future use.
- I don't think she handled it very well either. She just blurted it out. And, she knew he was going to have a freak out response. But I don't blame her either. I can't imagine all the emotions she was going through, especially after dealing with Ray being in the hospital.
- No. She'd never forgive herself or Christian. She said if he didn't want it, she would raise it alone. That's all the choice he should have been given.
- Yep. She said we can do it together or I'll raise it on my own.
- It's extremely complicated. Here some options:
- Mom wants baby, dad doesn't MOM raises child on her own.
- Dad wants baby, mom doesn't. Then should mother carry full term then turn the baby over to the father.
- Neither parent wants child, puts it up for adoption or terminates pregnancy.
- Both parents want child, co-parent as a couple or apart. Regardless of Christian's reaction to Ana's pregnancy, I never thought he had any intentions of not being a father to this baby. It was never a doubt in my mind. It was just a rash reaction.
- Just to make it even more complicated, what if the woman wants the baby and man doesn't, but the man has to pay child support for 18 years?
- It's true, then what?
- Well, legally the man has to pay, whether he wanted the kid or not. And that's probably the right thing, though I feel sorry for men who get trapped this way, especially when the woman lies about birth control.
- It can get messy in a hurry.
- It's very circumstantial. If there are ways to help those caught up in deceptive situations, there will always be

216

those to take advantage of an out. I think that bottom line, if you are go into have sex with someone regardless of any precautions taken, a person should understand that the action being done is for procreation. A child may result and that is a thought everyone should process with non-permanent birth control. It will just never be a simple thing.

- Blimey, you do dig deep indeed. I've never been in such a situation; in fact, I don't have children at all. But I think if he was so anti-baby at the time (yes, he came to his senses eventually), it was Ana's call either way. I don't think she'd ever go ahead with the abortion. She'd regret it for the rest of her life, and she'd resent Christian. This potentially could've been a relationship breaker.

- Wow...what a question! In Ana and Christian's case, there was no legitimate reason to abort the baby. They were a fairly happily newly married couple, one of whom had issues about what kind of father he could possibly be, simply based on his own memories of his birth mother. Ana's instincts correctly told her that Christian would be a great father. I also think what helped was that she was there raising Teddy with him. I can't even wrap my head around Ana's not wanting the baby. She was panicked but she only entertained the idea in response to Christian leaving her by herself to drown his anger in booze with Elena. If they weren't married, I think she'd still have the baby. Christian would be extremely angry, but he'd come to his senses and at the very least support the baby if they broke up.

- It's her decision, but he has a right to know.

- I got pregnant with my daughter. The father and I are not married. We'd talked of kids, but later down the road. Well when it came back I was pregnant, I told him point blank, "I'm keeping the baby, you don't have to stay if you don't want. I'm not going to trap you. I can do this on my own. If you want to be with me through this, that would make me very happy, the choice is yours. But I know where I stand." He stayed, and our daughter is now 7.

- I agree with everything written. Wish I was good with words I would say the very same thing. You and I think alike on this. I would have said the very same thing. And again well said.
- Ultimately, I think Ana sees it is her choice, as it's her body. But I couldn't imagine Ana ever making that decision without Christian involved in it. As mad as she was, and as badly as he reacted they both knew it was a bad reaction to shocking news. It's a harder position if she wants to abort and he doesn't, one that I can't imagine for Ana. If they weren't married, I think Ana still would have had the baby, and if Christian didn't want to be involved (though I think he would've eventually come around) he still would have financially supported the child and Ana in a nice lifestyle. If nothing else, he was always generous with his money.
- No. He was so shocked as Ana but so angry and cold. So Ana us going to keep her little Blip even if it's on her own. Even if hadn't come around Ana would keep the little blip as her own. Now it was her and someone else to think and care for.
- I think they're both young and I can see Christian point when he says, "I know you are quietly ambitious." I do think they could have waited. He was just getting used to being married to Ana and I can see why he was mad but the way he treats her when she tells him was totally not cool. I guess I am saying abortion should have been on the table.
- Ana should have done just what she did. Except, I'd have left that night and not come home.
- Her body, her decision. But of course she should weigh his feeling into her decision. The final choice is hers. If he didn't want the baby, I'm sure he would have supported it, but I can see that causing problems in their relationship.

Nurturing

In *Darker*, Christian is in the throes of a horrible nightmare, tossing and turning and crying out in anguish. "'You left,

218

you left, you must have left,' he mumbles—his wide-eyed stare becoming accusatory—and he looks so lost, it wrenches at my heart. Poor Fifty."

To me, this scene is something that really pulls me in. If he had really shown this depth of need in the first book, I wonder if Ana would've left - even after the belt. I honestly think if it was me I would have sacrificed myself to be there for him - even if it destroyed me. What do you think?

- It would've made it harder to leave that is for sure. I would never sacrifice myself though.
- I think you're smart.
- Thank you.
- Yes, if he would have shown this deep need, I think Ana would've stayed even after the belt - I think I would've stayed and tried to get through to him about how I felt about the belt, and tried to get him to not do that again.
- I think if she had seen this before the belt, it would have really made it next to impossible for her to leave when he took the belt to her.
- I think it would've been difficult for Ana to leave, if she had had an inkling about Christian's fear of her leaving him. However, I don't know if I could have stayed even after having been beaten with a belt. I would have walked.

Who's Trusting (and Blaming) Who?

While waiting for their dinner and digging into their discussion about why Ana didn't safe-word, Christian responded with this, "'How can I trust you?' His voice is low. 'Ever?'"

When Christian talked about Ana's not using the safe-word, I was so angry at him. How dare he act like this was *her* fault! He did what typical men do, abusers especially: turned it around and made her think *she* did something wrong. Something to deserve all this pain in her heart. She didn't safe-word, so what? What the hell makes him think she'd think of that? She's never done something like that before! BUT HE HAD. He should have known better. He should have reminded her of her safe-words. How could *she* trust *him*?

- I'm with you, though I suspect some of our members won't be. I agree that not only was it wrong for him to chastise her for not using the safe-word, and wrong for her to let him make her feel bad about it! I completely understand why she didn't safe-word. What would've happened if she did? The same outcome. She ultimately couldn't have withstood one hit, much less six.
- The issue wasn't the number of "hits." It was about the fact that he wanted to hurt her to begin with. So if it was one or two or ten, it would've been the same outcome. And it pissed me off for him to blame it all on her.
- She didn't safe-word because she really wanted to see if he'd go through with it. If he was that insensitive to her feelings. Sadly, he was.
- Maybe his tone should have been less accusatory, but it needed to be brought up at some point and discussed.
- I was mad at him. How dare he blame it on her! Even if she used the safe-word it would have been the same outcome!
- He definitely should have reminded her about the safe-words like he did the other times. But he was so enthralled with wanting to get her to the point where she'd let him punish her the way he wanted, that he forgot all reason as well. In his defense, he did start out saying that he behaved stupidly. But did you not want him to bring up the fact that she didn't safe-word in that situation? They needed to work that part out, so that they could trust each other to stop when either reached their limits. Should he have just ignored that part? They were trying to be honest and lay everything out in the open, so they could hopefully move on and have a future.
- What made this scene disturbing to me was that he was asking her to come back to him. He was admitting that he didn't want to punish her again. So why blame her?

220

It's not exactly the best strategy to win someone back. When you're sorry, you don't make excuses, and you most certainly don't blame someone else. You take responsibility. He didn't. He should have.

- Good points. Yeah at that point maybe it didn't matter. That could've been brought up later when they were back together, and he could ask her without being accusatory.
- Now I don't feel so loving toward Christian. I know he is flawed. I'll bet he didn't want to make her feel the way he did.
- I think he was trying to push her away, don't you?
- I don't know. I always thought it was so self-destructive the way he acted when he first saw her after the breakup. But I really don't think he consciously was trying to push her away. Maybe subconsciously because he still felt that he didn't deserve her.
- I agree with Christian, though he shouldn't have gotten ballistic about it. They had an agreement to use a safe-word; Ana just wanted to see how bad it could get. When it got too bad, instead of letting Christian know through the BDSM line of communication of using a safe-word, she jumped off the table. I do understand how Christian was confused (that look on his face in the movie says it all).
- Bottom line, he should have known better. He was the experienced one in most aspects. He allowed himself to get caught up in the moment. It was totally wrong for him to make that claim with her, especially the way he worded it. But then again, that is all he knows. They were both limited.
- Considering who he is, and the particular ways about him, I understand his statement. I can also see, from Ana's POV, how she felt hearing that from him. So, my question is, what did you think and feel when you read that?
- I don't remember how I felt the first time I read it because I've read it so many times. But, reading it again recently, I felt like he knew what made up a good relationship.

221

Having trust was important, even to him. I'm sure that was important in the BDSM relationships too. But, for him to let her know that if they were to move on, he would need to have her be honest about everything. To me, it meant that he was letting her know that he really wanted this relationship to work. He also was angry because, as he put it, "Maybe we could have avoided all this suffering."

Taking the Initiative

In *Freed*, Ana hesitates to take the initiative to kiss her new husband. How did you feel about this?

- I felt sad that Ana had to feel this way. To me, this reaffirms that they married too quickly. She didn't even feel comfortable walking in to kiss her husband goodbye? Very sad that she has to talk herself in to being a "normal" wife.
- I remember this happening, in *Freed* I think. How I felt about it was not that they got married too soon, but because they didn't show too much affection in public besides holding hands. Christian and Ana kept most of that stuff private. Then when they got engaged and married they had to be normal (especially Christian), and act like a normal married couple in the public eye. I think this scene Ana realized that it was okay to be affectionate with her husband outside of Escala.
- It was when they were still on their honeymoon, on the boat. It was just Ana and Christian in the study with Taylor just outside. Christian was on the phone with Andrea at the time. I feel sad for her that she felt like she had to have a reason to kiss.
- To me, it says she was still looking for his approval, which is sad to me.
- I always felt like that with my dad. When I called him or went by, I always felt like I had to have something to show or talk about. It's sad to feel like you have to get approval from someone all the time. So, I totally know how Ana felt here.

- Interesting comment. I guess I was that way with my mom. Though, ultimately, I realized that nothing I could do could make her not hate me.
- I guess, eventually I felt that way about my dad, or I figured it out. I don't remember him ever saying he was proud of me, though there were plenty of things to be proud of. I guess, all my life I wanted his approval. He was always negative. Such an unhappy man. I remember my mom saying that he wasn't happy if someone wasn't pissed off. God, I hope my kids don't think that way about me when they grow up. *Sigh*.
- I think that was her shyness, as well as her insecurity talking. She was still unsure how he would react if she were to show affection first.
- Don't you think that's sad?
- Extremely. Even after getting married, she still didn't feel comfortable around him.
- They will get there though.
- Do you guys remember when they came home from their honeymoon, Christian and Ana went to Christian's parents' house? Ana and Christian were teasing and then he says, "This feels so normal." Ana then says "After three weeks of being married?" It upset Christian. I think it was really hard for him to be normal. From what Ana could see, it made her insecure. It was sad for both of them because they didn't even know how to be normal with each other.
- They had a long way to go. And yet, even by this point, they had both also come so far (and yes - I can't resist adding the pun "and come so often!")
- That part made me sad for them both.
- It's hard to try to get his approval on how she should give him open and free affection. He's her husband, so why should she feel afraid to hug and kiss him whenever she wanted? He's so mercurial that she never knew how he would take her advances.
- Her ambivalence also surfaced when he came home due to Cocktailgate. He was angry, but in the aftermath of Hyde in the apartment. She wanted his comfort so she

crawled into his lap, because she was his wife. They did marry too soon, but I don't think more time would fix this issue. Premarital counselling might have helped.

- I think it's more that she was so used to Christian wanting to be in control and be the one to initiate any type of physical contact. She was still unsure about how he would respond.
- True - but don't you think that's sad?
- It really is. When they got married, they gave themselves to one another, and that means she should feel no fear in kissing or touching him.
- I think all marriages, in the beginning, go through the Honeymoon Stage where you're getting to know the other person. This can also go for couples when they first move in together.

"Please Don't Be Mad"

"Hi. It's me. Please don't be mad."

What are your thoughts about using that "please don't be mad" strategy? Do you think it works? Do you think it works for Ana with Christian?

- I think it works for Ana sometimes, and then it doesn't.
- Sometimes it does, but not always. On their honeymoon, Ana said it after she took her top off. Christian said it after giving her love bites. He turned the tables around on her.
- It depends on the situation. In Ana & Christian's case, it needed to be said because it gave him a moment to pause and think about what he was going to do next.
- I think it helps remind the person to calm down. Didn't she say "Please don't hate me?"
- It always helped Ana when it came to his mercurial moods. Seems that it always took him by surprise, and made him hold back a bit, but then his "revenge" got very intense.
- There's a 50/50 chance that it works. It depends on the situation! But I think it worked for Ana!

224

Withholding Affection

"'Don't hate me,' I whisper.
He grabs my hand. 'I don't hate you.'
'You haven't kissed me,' I whisper.

He eyes me suspiciously. 'I know,' he mutters."

What are your thoughts about Christian withholding affection? Is this an effective strategy for him? For you? When can it work - and when might it backfire?

- I think he is being a little immature here, but I think Flynn's words really resonate here. Remember, he said Christian is playing catch up. I think he should not do this, because, I'll bet he'd lose his sh*t if Ana did this to him.
- It can make you angry to see him sulking around whenever he is fighting with Ana. But there are reasons behind it, and we all know them. First, he was still learning about changing himself to not to overreact about everything. Second, he was afraid of hurting Ana. He was afraid that if he hurt her, she was going to leave him again. So, he thought it's better to sulk while he is angry, rather than do anything which he later regrets.
- I hate to say it, but he was really doing everything he could to rein in his temper. I think he was really, really scared that if he gave in to Ana, he really would hurt her. So, I think he did the right thing by pushing her away. But, he did end up punishing her later that day. I think it would've been a whole lot worse if he acted on his impulse in the shower, and even when she went off to work.
- Well, it can work in getting your point across. I do this too, but because I am an extremely affectionate person. It can backfire if you're not seeing the bigger picture. What if the other person's need for affection is more important than you making your point? That can cause more damage.
- I was hoping someone would say that.

225

- I don't know if it's more painful to withhold affection for security, or to let it flow, with the risk of being hurt. Withholding affection despite craving it - sometimes it hurts so much, it's almost a physical pain. For those of you who have the chance to have a lover, child or husband, don't neglect this part of your relationship. It's not a little nothing; it's huge and precious.
- I think it is effective. It got her attention, got her thinking, and helped her realize some things. She knows he's really mad if he is withholding affection.
- First he was sulking, then he was afraid to show his emotions. I think he was dying to touch her, as that was what he always craved, even when he feared for her safety.
- I agree with everyone's answers!
- He withheld affection because he was afraid he would hurt her. I think he did the right thing.
- I think he was at a loss as to what to do and say. One can sometimes get so mad that you can't even say a simple word such as "yes" or "no" because you're seething. It's a form of awareness of yourself and your partner. We do get confused, not just by the other person's deed, but by how we feel about what they had done for us to even get to that point. I do it all the time, and my challenge is "am I being open minded about this? Or am I just mad because it feels good to feel this way towards that person? Or, is it just me getting a rude awakening on the things I've been turning a blind eye to?

Walking On Eggshells

Scene from *Freed* after the hickey incident:
"He's not used to seeing me this mad. Can't he see what he's doing? Can't he see how ridiculous he is? I want to shout at him, but I refrain - I don't want to push him too far. Heaven knows what he'll do."

Why was she so apprehensive to really stand up to him? She'd already thrown a brush at him. Why was she worried that shouting at him would cause him to do something? Was she really that scared of what he would or could do? Do you think he knows how frightened she is of what he's capable of?

- I don't think Christian is aware. But over time, I think he learns. He probably had many therapy sessions with Flynn about this very issue.
- Christian probably suffers from "Borderline Personality Disorder." Here's the definition from Wikipedia, "Borderline personality disorder (BPD), also known as emotionally unstable personality disorder, is a long-term pattern of abnormal behavior characterized by unstable relationships with other people, unstable sense of self, and unstable emotions. There is often an extreme fear of abandonment, frequent dangerous behavior, a feeling of emptiness, and self-harm. Symptoms may be brought on by seemingly normal events." There's a book about it called "Walking on Eggshells."
- Thanks for sharing. My daughter was just diagnosed with it.
- Surely Flynn had thought about that disorder. It seems pretty in-line with Christian.
- People with Borderline Personality Disorder can really pull you in - and then push you out just as easily.
- Until that moment, he never saw that side of Ana. She was always the one who tamed him. Seeing her that mad confused him, and he didn't really understand what he did to make her that mad. And, yes, I agree that he really made me think that there was something more with him regarding his mental health.
- If you remember the day of the ball, Ana went to her room to look up Personality Disorder. When Christian came into the room, they had a wonderful Saturday afternoon in bed.
- Yes. multiple personalities, if I remember correctly.

Private Moments

"'Good. Do you need a private moment?' he asks sardonically.

"I snort. 'So coy, Mr. Grey. Yes, I need to pee.'
"He laughs. 'You expect me to leave?
"I giggle. 'You want to stay?'
"He cocks his head to one side, his expression amused.
"'You are one kinky son of a bitch. Out. I don't want you to watch me pee. That's a step too far.' I stand and wave him out of the bathroom."

What are your thoughts about this? For Ana and Christian? For yourself? What is "too far" for you? Do you think this changed for them over time?

- It does change over time for most people. It didn't bother me.
- No way that I would let someone watch me pee. It's just weird. Childhood was an exception - no way, as an adult. Even when I want to pee, I would hold it back because someone's watching. But I have to question why did Christian want to see Ana pee in front of him? Is that some kind of turn on? I watched so many men pee. Where I live, men are completely unashamed - they pee everywhere.
- I don't think he necessarily wanted to see her pee. However, when someone will pee around another person, you know they are very comfortable around them. I think Christian wanted to know that she was that comfortable. I can pee with a man or, or a woman in the bathroom. I don't care. I can only poop with my husband in there - nobody else. It's just too uncomfortable. I've made my husband leave when I wipe though. Lol.
- It doesn't bother me with my hubby and kids. But my mother-in- law, when I was dating my hubby, would do her business with the door open even while I was there, and she'd hold a whole conversation doing it. That was weird to me. I think, over time, that Ana wouldn't mind doing that front of Christian. I mean, he's been everywhere anyways.
- Eeep!
- That's weird to me too.

- See! I knew I wasn't weird thinking that was weird of her to keep the door open with guests around. Thanks y'all!
- It all comes down to personal preferences. My husband and I have been in the room for each other through it all. Lol.
- I can't imagine being with someone for 30 years and them not being in the bathroom at least once for peeing. We had to do that more years ago because we only had one bathroom when we were young. Now, not as much. We now have three bathrooms.
- I'd think after he sees you having a baby that shyness would go away. He has seen it all then. Lol.
- I think it's fascinating that when we're turned-on our filters for decency evaporate, but when we're "normal" we see things so differently!
- True!
- Maybe not for them, because they live in a huge place. In my one-bedroom apartment, my husband and I pretty much didn't have as much of an option.
- Hubby and I don't ever deliberately seek to walk in on the other while peeing. While we love intimacy, we both agree that watching the other is a step too far.
- My husband and I are in the bathroom with each other, but we don't watch each other. He might be shaving or in shower while I'm pottying.
- He was trying to see her reaction, maybe get another side of how much confidence she has, and how much she trusts him.
- I certainly can't imagine Christian doing this with anyone! Except maybe Lelliot when they were kids!
- I like my private moments.
- I do too, but I lost all of that when I became a mom.
- I don't think it had anything to do with trust.

Attention to Detail

On their trip to Aspen, Christian meticulously counts every drink Ana had had.

"Three glasses of white wine at dinner and two of champagne, after a strawberry daiquiri and two glasses of Frascati at lunchtime. Drink. Now, Ana."

As I read this, I imagined what it would feel like to be Christian. To feel obligated to be so attentive to every detail. It would seem so difficult to relax! Wdyt?

- I think it'd be hard to relax. He must have his bodyguards report everything to him. That would upset me.
- Christian is the kind of man I think every women wants. Love is not just about sex, it's also about noticing the little details about your partner. He knew Ana was carefree and does stupid stuff, so he had to be careful for her. He was always interested in everything related to Ana - even the little things. I want someone like that, someone who notices everything I do.
- I agree, which is why this series has been such a success and why we're all in love with the idea of Christian Grey.
- Christian likes to keep track of her alcohol consumption! He does know how she likes her tea!
- There are definitely many things I like about him too. I can't handle possessiveness though. I can handle some but not to Christian's extreme.
- I hear ya!
- Call me crazy, but I love his possessiveness. I think I fight when it's get to be too much, but I back off when I know he is right.
- Oh yeah, he definitely is very uptight. I notice he's usually most relaxed when it's only the two of them, and at home.
- I think paying attention to every detail was just his personality. That's why he was so successful in business. But it was difficult for him to relax. Again, I think that is his personality.
- It is him. He would be uncomfortable trying to ignore that stuff. He is a caretaker. Besides, I can see my

husband (if I drank, which I really don't) telling me..."Hey, maybe you've had enough?"

- Control freaks are also detail freaks! I doubt he'd ever get control of that. It's who he is.
- Sometimes it's too much. I would get crazy about his freaking control. Yet, we know it's always with good intentions.
- I think Christian is accustomed to being on high alert - it's his personality trait. He also cares deeply for Ana and is in protective mode because she truly doesn't know all that he knows. She is stubborn, and can behave in a child-like manner. Taking all of that into consideration, Christian is just taking care of Ana. It may be difficult, stressful and sometimes a pain, but I think he is used to being "on" a lot of the time.
- I think Mia might have mentioned the afternoon cocktails to Christian, as to what they did after shopping.
- It would drive me crazy. Completely nuts. It's one thing to have someone look over you and care for you, it's another for them to count every drink and every bite you eat. No. Not happening. Hard limit for me.

For Your Eyes Only

"Christian insisted I take Mia's trench coat to cover my behind."
How did you feel about this? After he told Ana she could wear the dress?

- He let her take it off eventually. I think he needed to get used to her wearing it and maybe also see how Elliot and Ethan reacted to her in it. I think if maybe the guys had said something inappropriate, he might have asked her to go change. But I agree that he was trying to not be so controlling.
- I really think after everything that happened with Jack, and then what happened in the Red Room, Christian wanted to show Ana he could be reasonable. Yes, he loved how she looked, but he also wanted to make sure

she was covered up. But I really think that he wanted to show her off and show everyone "she is mine."

- I think he only agreed to the dress because they've had "wardrobe" discussions before, that he lost (goes to picking your battles carefully). I think he really loved her in the dress, and was secretly wishing that they didn't have to go out, but rather he'd want to peel her out of it. The "covering up" with Mia's coat was a small compromise and goes back to the "for my eyes only" thing he keeps telling her.
- Well, really, she'd already bought it and he didn't want to spoil the fun. Especially, since things were a little tense right then. Yet, he was Christian. But, heck, why make her wear it outside, then not wear it in the club? I suppose Mia and Kate being there might have been a factor.
- Outside, it might've been cold but in the club it was very warm. Who would wear a trench coat in a club anyways?

I'm So Shy

"Why does he make me feel shy?"

Why DOES Christian make Ana feel shy?

- Because he is so unbelievably hot.
- Seeing how hot he looked, and how Ana's insecurities and lower self-esteem was why she felt shy.
- I think she's still shy about his wealth and their houses that they have!
- She's shy around him because, as nuts as she is about him, she's probably still wondering what the gorgeous Adonis sees in her, and the fact that the gorgeous Adonis wants her and only her.
- I think the sight of him and his sexy words and voice is enough to make her shy.
- I think since she went from a virgin to a *very* experienced woman so quickly, she's still adjusting to the thought - and shy and concerned that everyone could tell that about her!

- Good thought! And thinks, "I wonder what they think of me?"
- I think it was two things: 1. She was pregnant and didn't know it, so that was messing with her emotions. 2. She'd decided not to give Christian cause for concern, so she was on her best behavior. He still intimidated her and, by submitting to his will (even slightly), she felt shy because she wondered if she was being herself or if she was changing for him. And, she also wondered if she was pleasing him by trying to be good.

Carry Me Away

"'I don't want to hurt you. I got carried away.' He reaches down and kisses me. 'Lost in the moment." He kisses me again. 'Happens a lot with you.
"Oh? And for some bizarre reason the thought pleases me… I grin. Why does that make me happy?"

Why DOES it make her happy?

- Maybe because she realizes that she has a strong effect on Christian. It's not one-sided like she thought in *FSOG*.
- I think it makes her happy because it means she makes him lose his focus, his control. He is so into her that he loses all sense.
- He has that effect on all of us too! I'm sure I'd feel the same way around him!
- Good point!
- It makes her happy to know that she's able to make him so happy, considering that no one else has managed to do that for him until she came along.
- There's nothing more arousing and empowering than seeing a man so well put together with all his cards in place, loose it completely over you. Just saying.
- I would be happy and blown away at that moment when he said this, and knowing it is me - the only one who can make him lose his focus, even if I was scared before…

- It's a chink in his armor; an opening. It's like those quotes that say that it's our scars that let the light in. Loving someone's weaknesses and imperfections is true love.

Defiance

"'And yet you choose to defy me,' he murmurs baffled, his hand stilling in my hair.
I frown. Holy cow! Do I do that deliberately?'"

This passage suggests that Ana didn't consciously know she was defying him. Do you think that's true?

- I think there was times she knew that what she was going to do would piss Christian off, and she either did it anyway or didn't; but, there were a few times that she did things that he would overreact about. In those times, I don't think she deliberately did it to prove a point.
- At first, I think it was deliberate, but then it developed into habit. Habits usually become subconscious behaviors. But, she usually has a method to her madness; however, she loses control and takes it too far, or loses sight of Christian's side of reasoning.
- She did a lot of things impulsively, not really thinking through the consequences of her actions. Having said that, she could've been more forceful with Kate and insisted that they go back to Escala. Instead she opted to go out and knew on some level she was going to be punished.
- She did love defying him, and the consequences for it.

Girl Talk

"'I can't believe you spoke to my mother. Sh*t!' He lies down and puts his arm over his face again.
"'I didn't go into any specifics.'
"'I should hope not. Grace doesn't need all the gory details. Christ, Ana...'"

234

In *Freed*, Christian was surprised Ana had talked with Grace about Elena. Were you? How would you have felt if you were Christian?

- I was. I would feel violated.
- No, I wasn't surprised. They bonded over it. Ana needed someone to talk to about Elena. I'll bet that Grace brought it up, though. I probably would've felt violated if I was Christian, until she explained that she didn't reveal any details. Surely he wanted Ana and Grace to be friends.
- I wasn't surprised at all that Ana and Grace spoke about Elena. They have a common bond - they both hate Elena for what she did to Christian. Grace was also probably feeling an enormous amount of guilt and shame for not seeing what was going on under her nose. Ana and Grace were really each other's support system. Christian was feeling really uncomfortable that the two most important women in his life were judging him, and the decision he made to continue on with the sick relationship until he was 21 years old. Again, this is what HE was thinking, which wasn't the case at all.
- I wasn't surprised, but I wonder how Grace felt knowing Ana probably knew more than she did. I think Christian's reaction was appropriate.
- I hope that Grace felt happy that Christian had shared that part of his life with his soon-to-be wife. "No secrets in marriage" is the advice she gave him. We all want to think we know our kids well. But, once they have found a significant other, we realize that there are parts of their life they don't share with us. I'm sure she was sad and mad about the whole darn thing!
- Very true.
- I really don't think Grace would've wanted the gory details about what Elena did with Christian. Ana's too classy to give them to her, not wanting to hurt Christian further.
- Of course, they spoke about Elena! Ana had witnessed the whole thing. Grace might have wondered if Ana

knew, or if she was going to stop the wedding. Grace would've been worried about how Ana felt.

- I wasn't really surprised because they got along so well, and, in retrospect, Grace needed to find out, and maybe see Ana's reaction, even if she didn't tell her all the crap. But, I think, as a mother, she needed to see that Ana can deal with Christian's issues. Deep down, subconsciously, she knew that her son had stuff to hide. I think a mother always knows. So, it was reassuring for Ana as well that her fiancé's mother trusted her enough to confide in her. Entrusting her with her son's life because he'd changed ever since he'd met her. He was opening up.
- If I was Christian, I'd be royally pissed and freaked out!
- Well, he was, but when Ana reassured him that she withheld the details, he seemed to calm down. But only a story from his POV would confirm this.
- I had a history with my mother and sharing personal stuff with family members. Not this kind of thing, but they'd get me really pissed when I found out.
- Okay, Ana and Grace talked about it, and it was meant to be because Grace heard part of what was going between Christian, Elena and Ana the day of the engagement announcement and birthday party. I totally understand how ashamed and awful Christian felt, to know that his mother knows about his sex life. It's not very good feeling.
- Thankfully though, she didn't know everything, but if she did, screw her anti-gun stance, she'd go out and get a gun and wipe the bitch troll off the face of the earth.
- I wasn't surprised by Grace and Ana talking about Elena! I think Grace probably wanted to know how Ana felt about Elena!

Dom Jeans

Did anyone else think that Ana was in big trouble, and that this was going to be a punishment for her when Christian is standing in his Dom jeans and he says, "Good evening, Mrs. Grey. Good to have you home. I've been waiting for you."

236

- I'm willing to bet her heart rate spiked!
- I'm sure she had an "oh, crap" moment.
- I kind of had a feeling, when he said "I've been waiting for you." I was like "uh-oh! Ana is in big trouble." But I don't think it was more like punishment. It was fun, but kind of like he was out of control. It's like someone tickling you, and you are laughing, and begging them stop, but they are not stopping. I never thought Ana was going to end up crying, but even when being tickled too much, you start crying because it's out of control.
- Great analogy!
- Hahaha... Thanks.
- I agree!
- I imagined she was first taken aback by this sexy image, then went into panic mode.
- Her mind was going crazy thinking "what has she done to upset him?" That sexy teasing side of Mr. Grey was very unusual.

Questioning My Judgment

When Christian says, "You're making me question my judgement..." Judgment about what? Leaving her at home while he went on business? Not forcing the security team to make her go home (as if)? Not telling her the details of the increased risk to get safety? Leaving to come home early from New York? What are your thoughts?

- I think he thought he had it all under control, but adding Ana's decisions/judgment into the mix was like adding another chess piece to the board, which made him feel off-center. Speaking specifically, he was so sure that keeping her at home would ensure she was safe, and if she had stayed home, she might've been more vulnerable to Jack.
- So he was confused that the decision he made to keep her safe could have put her in harm's way. Do you think he trusted his security team more or less after this incident?

237

- Good question. I'm not sure what he felt. They did their job and kept Ana safe, but they also missed the gaps that allowed Jack to enter the apartment. What do you think?
- He didn't fire them, so if nothing else Taylor may have taken up for them. Maybe after things calmed down he realized that Ryan did the right thing. And, he also knew that the others really could not have "made" Ana go home. I mean, she might have left him if he had forced that.
- I think even if Ana was home, it would be really hard for Jack to kidnap Ana. Ryan already saw Jack on the CCTV cameras and let him in, and he sent Gail to the panic room. If Ana was home, he would've sent Ana with Gail into the panic room, or maybe never have let him in. Christian always made the right decisions for his company. This was way beyond what he could have thought could happen. This was the first time he made the wrong decision concerning his beloved wife. Maybe, it was this fact that made him angry, and is the reason he questions his judgement. Everything you said in your question is the reason.
- When things got out of control, Christian just got lost and confused, and questioned his judgment. This was so confusing for him, and now he's questioning if he could trust Ana, and be a bit less controlling with her about her safety or increased security. That didn't matter because crazy psycho Jack would've had time later to try to kidnap her. As I see it, Sawyer thought that letting him get in was a really good way to finally catch him, and once and for all, deal with him, and avoid major issues in the future.

Gun Control

"'Christian, there's no safety on that revolver. Don't you know anything about guns?'
"His eyes widen. 'Um ... no.'"

How do you think Christian felt in this moment? For once, Ana had more expertise than he did. Even though he had his opposition to guns, you would think, knowing Christian, he would at least educate himself.

- I guess he felt confident knowing that his security team knew enough about guns, but I think he should've had a bit more knowledge about firearms, just for information, even though he would never use one.
- For sure!
- I think Christian might've been surprised by the fact that Ana knew about guns!
- I think E.L. James was setting up the "guns vs. no-guns" debate. The UK looks at guns and gun ownership in America very differently than we do.
- Given his past, it didn't come as a big shock and surprise to me. It's not about whether Ana was more knowledgeable than Christian. It was his decision to stay away from those things. If he wanted, he could become more knowledgeable than Ana, but he made a decision and stuck to it.
- He probably felt Fifty Shades of Foolish because Ana had a point. He knew nothing about guns and really something awful (like the gun accidentally goes off!) could've happened. It shocks me that he never got rid of the gun, but it came in very handy when Mia was kidnapped. Christian should've taken Ana's advice and at least educate himself about guns, even though he's very anti-gun.
- He grew up with his parents talking anti-guns and he did say that his mom has taken care of too many gunshot victims, and that he is backing anti-gun laws.
- I would think that Taylor should have taken control of the gun after the Leila incident. It seemed odd to me that Christian hung on to it.
- This part was so confusing to me. With the way he felt about guns, you'd think he'd have had Taylor get rid of it, rather than keep it in the desk drawer in his study.

Flirting With Disaster?

"'I'm sure Miss Goody-Two-Shoes Prescott has told Christian I'm not at home. He'll be mad,' I mutter to Kate. And maybe he'll think of some delicious way to punish me... hopefully."

Ana had sure changed from the beginning of their relationship. Was she really thinking ahead and doing things on purpose that would make Christian angry? Or was that an afterthought? Her actions remind me how Leila would do things to get punishments from Christian too.

- It concerned me a bit. It's kind of like a kid that needs to act up to get attention. (I really think that was Leila's M.O.) But, I also think she was relaxing into the "give and take" of the relationship.
- I thought the same thing about Leila. She was always doing things to get his full attention.
- I think it was hard for Ana. She wanted her independence, but also liked Christian's controlling tendencies. But, his controlling tendencies also made her nuts as well. I think, in many ways through the Leila situation, they both were not telling each other everything, and it caused problems. COMMUNICATION!
- I agree; they were never on the same level. Sometimes, not even in the vicinity of one another. They were taking steps forward then back. They were all over the place a lot of the time. Communication is something they both needed to work on.
- I do think Ana started pushing Christian's buttons on purpose. She was comfortable in her new found confidence and sexuality and wanted to test him.
- Testing his limits like he tested hers. I guess that's kind of what we do in marriage.
- Interesting interpretation, I wonder.
- I think with Ana and Kate going out to the bar, they might've both been kidnapped by Jack!
- I mean, Kate knew it! Shameful of Christian!

240

- It does make you wonder what Christian would've done if that happened!
- She really really wanted to spend time with Kate. She missed her so much that she really didn't care what the consequence would be. She knew she'd be punished, and until that time, probably his punishments were very pleasurable (excepting the one where she left, of course). She didn't "disobey" Christian for the punishment. It was simply that she just wanted to spend time with her best friend, which according to Ana, had hardly spent any time with since they moved to Seattle.
- But they could've spent time at the apartment just the same.
- Kate loved the bar scene. She really wanted a girls' night out. I'm with Kate on this one. They desperately needed girl-time, and besides, Ana didn't have a true clue about the danger that Hyde was posing. That was a huge part of the fight she had with Christian the next day.

Role of Fun and Playfulness

"After a while, you just want to be with the one that makes you laugh."

This quote (from the TV show Sex & The City") explains one of the reasons Christian loved Ana – and why we loved FSOG. Hot sex is great, but it's the fun and playfulness that really brought – and kept – them together as a couple.

Playfulness

I really love Chapter 3 in *Darker* due to Christian's playfulness: acting his own age, genuinely smiling, joking, and bantering. Not to mention, the pissing contest, the trip to the grocery store with Ana, chopping vegetables, hot sex, and more hot sex with Ben & Jerry's, and the choice of "sex" or "breakfast." I always chuckle when I read the "Cook me some food, wench" bit. I find it totally out of character for Christian, yet so funny. Am I the only one?

- It's such a lovely and loving chapter. I'm with you. I personally don't need the thriller/drama aspect. I just love the love!
- I love it, too! He's so laid back, carefree, and fun. I know it made a huge impression on Ana. He really wants more!
- This is where Christian made the 180 turnaround, and I started liking him.
- Ana leaving Christian was pretty much like hitting his reset button. Once she took him back, it was like he decided to embrace that second chance with her, with everything he had. It meant trusting that they didn't need rules and/or punishments in place. In truth, he realized he had to relax, and could do that around Ana. The result was a playful, fun, and funny Christian.
- I loved his playfulness in this chapter too. It's where I finally realized he could be more.

I Scream, You Scream

"'Good. Where's the ice cream?'
"'In the oven.' I smile sweetly at him. He cocks his head to one side, sighs, and shakes his head at me. "'Sarcasm is the lowest form of wit, Miss Steele.' His eyes glitter."

Do you think he really felt that way about sarcasm? He followed with another sarcastic comment, and Ana shot his comment back at him. What do you think about sarcasm? Is his reference true in your opinion?

- I don't like sarcasm. I'm a very literal person, and sometimes I don't get when people are being sarcastic.
- For me, it depends on the spirit in which sarcasm is given. If it's intended to be playful, then it can be a lot of fun. But if it's snarky, or delivered with a superior attitude, then it bothers me.
- I think he wasn't used to anyone except family being sarcastic with him.
- I thought the repartee was cute and appropriate. I was raised to never, ever be sarcastic. When I wasn't around my parents, I'd let my sarcasm out, hell bent for leather. It is a part of my wit that is never hurtful or mean. Mostly, it's self-deprecating.
- I loved that part and laughed. He went with it and showed his playful side. I love sarcasm in a person. I love people with quick wit. It is fun to me. I grew up with it. Sarcasm online doesn't always work out so well because we can't hear tone of voice, see body language, or facial expressions.
- A little sarcasm might be okay. But basically, I hate it. One of my good friends has turned into a very sarcastic person in the last few months. As of now our friendship is hanging by a very thin thread.
- It depends on how a person uses it. Overusing can also be a bad thing.
- I like the sarcasm between both of them! It made me laugh when I read it!

The "Fifteen"

While Ana was an innocent virgin when they met, Christian was far from it. And his "past" often came back to, um, haunt him (so to speak). While we don't know a whole lot about his ex-submissives, we do know enough to speculate and discuss...

Mischievous and Lively

Christian said Leila was "mischievous and lively." This statement always stuck with me. It didn't seem to fit. Thoughts?

- It seemed odd to me too.
- Surely, he wouldn't have tolerated that behavior. Although it must have been a change for him, having a sub always behaving and at his beck and call. Maybe, he just enjoyed dishing out the punishments, so he tolerated it for a while to make it more pleasurable when he did punish her.
- I think she liked the punishments, and did things to rile him up and get his attention.
- She knew what type of sub he liked. (They all look like us.) Did he tell her, or did she find the picture stash too? He also let her put songs on the iPod. I just wonder about their relationship.
- I wonder about all that too. She was friends with Susannah, so they must have looked alike too. Maybe, she made the connection with just the two of them and Ana looking alike. I wonder how many were between Leila and Susannah. Christian and Leila emailed each other. That was weird to me.
- I think Master was sometimes kinder than he let on.
- Probably so. Do you feel that may make his relationship with Ana a little less unique than we want to believe?
- I think he wanted to love or felt a need to BE loved, before Ana. But, he felt unworthy and held back. He still had the desire to hurt "little brown haired girls" like his mother, but I think Ana's virginity is what clinched

it. He felt she was pure, and he couldn't grasp the concept that someone so innocent could care about him - Let alone love him. I still want to feel it was special because she went further than anyone else had.

- Sometimes, I think he could've had something with Leila, but being someone's first is irreplaceable. Christian and Ana shared a lot of firsts.
- You are right! I've started reading *Grey* again, and I think he was ready. Ana was the right one who came at exactly the right time, like it was meant to be. He fell so hard, so quickly, that it scared and mesmerized him.
- I think Leila was a consummate manipulator. She was lively and mischievous when it suited her (though we never saw it), and totally and completely submissive the rest of the time. She really knew how to push Christian's buttons because she knew him well. She knew him well as Ana did, and maybe better.
- Definitely differently!
- I think that description of Leila was E.L. James' way of letting us, the readers, know that Christian liked Leila. It was a glimpse at his other side.

Emotional Connection

"'I knew several women who like doing what I like to do. None of them appealed to me the way you do. I've never had an emotional connection with any of them. It's only ever been you, Ana.'
"'Because you never gave them a chance. You've spent too long locked up in your fortress, Christian.'"

Do you think this is true? If he'd given any of his subs a chance, or even other women he'd known, could it have worked? That people can work as couples, if they try? Or, do you believe there was only "one" for him, someone destined to help "break him free?" And that was Ana?

- I don't believe this is true. He didn't plan it with Ana. The chemistry was just there. If the chemistry had been there with one of the other subs, then he may have never met Ana, because she too could've changed him.

- I don't believe he felt anything until Ana, and that she was the one who turned his life upside down. So, yes, I do believe Ana is the one for him.

- He may have eventually felt an emotional connection with other subs like Leila, and that's why he broke it off. But, to have a connection from the start, I think that was only with Ana. She was "the one."

- If he had let his walls fall, it could've worked with another. I think he did have an emotional connection with Leila. I'm certain he had chemistry with her, but he just ignored some of it. I am convinced that one of the main reasons that Ana had an advantage was because she stimulated his interest without Elena's help. I don't think Christian would have let his interest in Leila, if there was any, get serious because of the way they began. Ana secured her fate by resisting the "sub idea."

- I think it was only Ana. He obviously cared for Leila, but he didn't have that spark and chemistry with her. The spark and chemistry is what made him want "more" with Ana. He kept giving more and trying harder. He felt a desperation to keep Ana. He didn't have that with Leila.

- Chemistry.

- No, I believe with him, it was a mindset. It took someone to come in and change that mindset.

- As most of you know, I believe in destiny, in the confluence of both fate and free will. I believe Ana was his destiny. He could've messed it up (and nearly did), but he knew down to his soul level that she'd be the one he'd love, who he'd known and loved before. Could he have loved others? Yes, but his destiny would've taken a different turn.

- No. They were a distraction. Thanks to Elena, it was all he knew. He was afraid of love.

- Ana is his soulmate. He just didn't get the memo until she left, then he won her back in *Darker*!

- We know next to nothing about most of his subs, so there's no way to really know if any of them would've worked out. The only one that I think MIGHT have had a chance with him was Leila. He didn't have one negative thing to say about her. He thought she was "exemplary" in the playroom, at the same time as being mischievous and full of life. Again, we have no way of knowing what would've happened if he hadn't been closed off to the idea of a relationship.

- Leila wanted more, and he said no to her. The chemistry wasn't there. He wasn't drawn to her like a moth to a flame. He was drawn to Ana. He couldn't stay away from her. There was a chemistry there for him.
- I think it was more than chemistry. I think it was "purpose." Don't you?
- Definitely both.

How Close is Close?

It seems like a lot of us have vastly different thoughts on Leila and her relationship with Christian. I tend to think that they were a lot closer than Christian let on. After all, he kept and displayed her paintings and still had her songs on his iPod. What do you think?

- I agree that there probably was a bit more to their relationship than Christian will admit. But, reading in *Grey* how she still had to kneel at his desk while he worked for who knows how long, makes me wonder how much more. I think he still kept to the rules with her. He may have been a bit lenient on some things like allowing her to use his iPod, but I think, for the most part, she stayed in her role as sub. Mostly. Unless she wanted to be punished.
- Yes, but it irritated me.
- If I try to put myself in Leila's position, I envision her spending hour upon hour, month after month alone or ignored in that apartment. She was there to just be at Christian's beck and call for sex and to cook for him and that's all. I'd go CRAZY if I had that much idle time! I'd probably stealthily explore the apartment. And if I

was, indeed, "crazy" like Leila, I could see myself plotting, in case he ended things.

- She was only there Friday through Sunday.
- Yes, but I'd still go crazy from boredom.
- She was ecstatic to be there. Wasn't he there with her all weekend, with the exception, that on occasion, on Fridays, he might have had an event to attend. I think she was given more liberties than she thought she would get, when Elena introduced her to Christian.
- I think she probably was content in the role of Dom/sub, and she also was as twisted as Christian wanted her to be. She could handle anything Christian dished out.
- I agree that it was more than a Dom/sub relationship, at least for a bit. She knew the apartment like the back of her hand (Christian's words). It seems to me she did more than subbing for him. She spent a lot of time in his apartment, and she knew a lot. She did as she pleased, like adding music to his iPod, exploring all around the apartment, and probably changing little things here and there. I think she did this very subtly; that way she wouldn't upset Christian.
- Very simply, even though he denies it, he had/has very strong feelings for Leila. He never had a bad thing to say about her ever, except when she pointed a gun at Ana.

Generous? Or Insensitive?

What was it about Christian paying for Leila's art classes? What does it say about him? About her? Did it make you angry?

- I think it shows he has compassion. Those expenses were pocket change for him.
- That isn't the point. I don't care about pocket change. What about the fact that he's still supporting his ex-submissive?
- I can understand, from Ana's point of view, how that would infuriate her. I just like the way that E.L. James put it in the book, so that we could know that he had compassion for Leila. He didn't have that dark heart that

248

he claimed to have. I do think it would matter, if money was a concern. Then, I would be livid.

- I guess we're all different. Because I don't care about Christian's money or compassion. When I'm in a relationship, I better not see anything that prompts me to think of his ex. Otherwise, I'll go crazy.
- Oh, I have my limits, like the bathing scene. But helping her out financially, especially helping her (a) get healthy and (b) in a career is kind of like a "consolation prize." "You don't get Christian, but here are your parting gifts!"
- I have a few parting gifts for her. Like sticking my boot up her *ss for assuming my man will take care of her just because he can "afford it." And someone might suggest that she didn't "expect" it. I am so irritated. Ugh! Haha.
- I wonder if she did expect it from him. How damn long would he have supported her, had he not married Ana?
- I thought he knew no compassion until he met Ana.
- I totally get what you are saying. And I don't think it's okay either. But, I think about how Ana forced him to admit that he cared about Leila later on in the book. How much more proof did it take to know he was paying for her art classes, insurance, and mental health facility? That's all the proof she needed, in my opinion.
- I think he should have cut the ties when the contract ended. But I think helping Leila tapped into that part of him that's also compassionate for helping poverty stricken countries. She had issues, and he took care of her because he could.
- I did not understand why he was paying for her education either. I do think he must have done some very twisted things to her, and felt guilty. Remember, she was really shocked by how he treated Ana. For example, she was shocked that Ana was allowed to sleep in his bed, or call him by his first name.
- Helping her get the psychiatric care she needed was the first priority for Christian. When she got better, maybe it was suggested that she look for an outlet to channel her "positive energy," hence the art school. Knowing

Christian, he felt obligated to take her treatment further, and pay for art school. Would I like it? Probably not, but Christian found a new emotion and embraced it: compassion.

- Even though he tried to deny it. You've made me see a different side of him with your comments.
- He just wants her to get better as quickly as possible. His soft heart was showing.
- Believe me, I totally get his reasoning, and the guilt behind it. But I feel it isn't his guilt to bear. However, no, this is not something I could be okay with.
- Up to a point, I agree, but I'm a bit more with Ana. At first, I would've been shocked and mad as hell to find out. But, after asking many questions I would find I'm comfortable with his answers. And, knowing my soft heart, I'd see his point.
- My heart is soft too, but a soft heart doesn't mean I'd let him hurt me or stress me out.
- And even then, not liking the whole idea, I'm not sure that I would've him cut her off right away. I'd give him a very short timeframe.
- We know so little of their relationship. But there's a huge part of me that tells me that he was so close to feeling the "L" word that once she left him, he felt guilty enough to still take care of her.

Show Me the Money

Billionaire. A single word that speaks volumes – and tells us a lot about the life of Christian Grey. Generous philanthropist or powerful megalomaniac, his money influenced us (the readers), as much as it affected his relationship with Ana.

Sudden Wealth

"As we follow Miss Kelly up the magnificent main stairs to the second floor, I can hardly contain my excitement. This house has everything I could ever wish for in a home."

Do you think Ana had secretly fantasized about wealth and/or being taken care of? Do you think she'd ever had any monetary insecurity when she was younger?

- I think we all have fantasies of living in the "ultimate" house. Ana's no different. For her though, her fantasy can easily become reality, and she hasn't quite wrapped her head around that quite yet.
- I think at some point we all probably think about our fantasy home.
- I think societal norms present fantasy worlds to us all, including what E.L. James presented through Ana's eyes. Ana undoubtedly had lived a life that was not extravagant. I'm not sure if she felt insecure. I don't recall any statements or questions in the trilogy that would speak to insecurity.
- Do you think Carla's bouncing around to multiple husbands might've had an effect?
- I don't feel very judgmental about Carla's multiple marriages. You have to have been in her shoes to know why things didn't work out. Her first husband died. Ray may be an exemplary father to Ana, but perhaps the marriage with Carla wasn't a good match. He may not have been "husband material." Something wasn't quite right in her third relationship, even with Ana, which was the point at which she moved away to live with Ray. All

seemed well with her fourth husband. We don't have a clue as to the financial effect multiple marriages had on either Carla or Ana. Ray did buy her a used VW bug at some point in her life. It wasn't an Audi, but it was transportation. So, I don't think that Carla's multiple husbands had a negative financial effect causing insecurity on Ana. Rich doesn't equate with security.

- Well, it does indicate that Carla wasn't very financially stable on her own. She certainly didn't seem to have a career. So, every time she left a husband she had to find another. I do think that Ray would've taken care of Ana, no matter what. That certainly would've helped Ana feel more secure, yet also wanting to be independent and have her own career.
- I guess she was just focused on getting a great job, being more independent, having a good future, and not struggling. But, yes, maybe she did dream at some point of having a bigger home for her future family. I think that idea got more stuck in her head, after she started living with Christian. She fantasized about it.

Prenuptial

One misconception about prenups is that they're for the wealthier person, but in reality they're usually in the best interest of the one without the money. What do you think? If you were wealthy, would you want one? If you were marrying someone wealthy, would you?

- Not sure I understand that prenups are for the benefit of the person with no wealth.
- Yes, they are. If you think about it, it makes sense. The poorer person needs to be protected. They couldn't hire the best lawyers.
- If I was wealthy and truly loved the person I'm with, and know for sure that they really feel the same about me, I wouldn't want them to sign a prenup.
- I always assumed prenups were to prevent the spouse with less money from leaving with half of the wealthier

spouse's money if they divorced. With that being said, I don't know if I would or wouldn't sign one.

- I think if the couple is truly in love, they don't need one.
- I'd sign one if it made my rich, future husband feel better. However, every month, I'd grab some money, and put it in a private bank account, just in case we broke up.
- I think people make a big deal of this. Christian was worth millions, so, of course she should have signed something. That doesn't mean that he thinks it won't work, it just protects him. I do love that he fought against it. That's romantic, but realistically it's smart to cover his assets. Same goes if the woman is wealthy.
- I'm with you. It might be romantic to assume you'll be together forever, but it's not practical. If the "equal distribution of income during the marriage" law was easy to uphold, it wouldn't be necessary. The problem is that rich people know how to hide income and assets to keep themselves protected.
- It's the fair thing, I think.
- He made how much money an hour? Even if she left, it wouldn't take long for him to build up lots of money quickly. And, she wouldn't get all of his money if she left. I guess I'd sign a prenup if he insisted, but I'd hire a lawyer using his money beforehand, to be certain it was fair. Surely, he'd agree to that if he loves me, and wants me protected too.

Playing Dress Up

"Yes. Famished. All the… er… activity has given me an appetite. But I'm not dressed for dinner. I'm sure my sweatpants and camisole would be frowned upon in the dining room."

I thought it was interesting how Ana was already conditioned to dressing up, even on their own boat, when she'd been a "jeans and t-shirt kind of girl." Do you think this kind of changing is normal? Or, do you think she adapted to his "lifestyle" a bit too quickly? What about you?

If you married a gazillionaire, would you start wearing a different wardrobe?

- When going out, my wardrobe would change. But, I think in my own home or on a boat (honeymoon), I'd wear the clothes that I am most comfortable in. I found that statement strange since they were on their honeymoon and not leaving the boat.
- I always like to dress up, even in my home. Then, I don't have to change when I go out. But, let's face it, I'm not Ana. I think Ana doesn't want to let Christian down in any way. She might have thought because of her wardrobe, he'd get embarrassed in front of his staff. Ana was always so unsure, and all of his wealth seemed unreal to her. She was afraid that if she did something stupid, Christian might divorce her. It could be her insecurity.
- She adopted the fancy clothes quickly, but I think it was to please Christian.
- I thought it was strange that she thought about changing when they were staying on the boat. I was glad that Christian told her she looked fine in her comfortable clothes. She was trying to adapt so quickly to this new lifestyle, and I think I'd adapt quickly too. I'd love to dress in the fanciest of clothing! I might even bathe in diamonds.
- In some homes sweatpants and a camisole (lingerie) are not proper attire for the dinner table. I don't think she's changing for Christian. It was her own upbringing.
- The more Ana integrated into Christian's life, the greater her need to dress the part. Kate was right about Ana's wardrobe for the interview, and on some level Ana knew that. She was also becoming a sexual being, transitioning from a girl to a woman, and her wardrobe reflected it.
- The bigger questions to ask are, was she just changing to please Christian? Was she losing herself in the process? A little bit is healthy; too much is, well, too much. The younger we are, the more vulnerable we are. Did she

"give in" to keep the peace? Did she ever feel uncomfortable in her new surroundings? We know she did, on more than one occasion. Yet, we also know she pushed back. Let's hope that continued.

- She was still the same Ana, even with all the fancy things.
- I think anytime someone changes themselves dramatically for a relationship, it's a red flag. I do think that, in some ways, Ana accommodated Christian too much, but in others she pushed back. The same goes for him; he changed and adapted for her.
- Christian fell in love with her when she wasn't "dressed up," so to speak.
- Yes, but he judged her a lot for that. Really put her down for her wardrobe.
- He did call her clothes cheap.
- I don't think he cared about what his subs wore outside of their time with him, only if he was seen out with them.
- We all judged her clothing at first, but he later admitted she looked hot in tight jeans and a T-shirt when he showed up at Clayton's.
- I don't think wardrobe is a huge issue, especially in private. In public though, Christian always wanted her to look her best. There's nothing wrong with that.
- I'm not crazy about how harshly he judged her wardrobe.
- We all judged her wardrobe. He didn't really judge though. He just thought she could be better dressed. Also, I don't think he ever told her how awful she looked when she fell into his office. He kept that opinion to himself. He did have huge issues with modesty, and that I take issue with. He'd have the personal shopper get her short dresses, yet when she'd wear them, he'd freak out. That I have a problem with.
- I have to disagree. He seriously judged her wardrobe. He judged the brands (Walmart, Old Navy), and the "shapeless shit" comment.
- But he didn't say those things to Ana. He did think in his thoughts that they looked cheap.

- True. I don't know about you, but when someone is judging me that harshly, I can feel it.
- At some point, I think I'd have to change the way I dressed. On this occasion, I don't feel it would matter that much given that they were on the boat. Also, it was evening, and she just had a nap. Maybe she thought it was best to ask, knowing how he always looks awesomely handsome and well-dressed, no matter where they were. I guess it was one of the changes she was getting used to without even noticing.

The Sex

Sex. Probably the most compelling three-letter word in the English language. It's as controversial as it is universal. It's the one thing we don't often talk about, yet it's one thing we all have in common. The *Fifty Shades of Grey* series gave us a peek into Ana and Christian's unique, complex, and absorbing world of pain and pleasure, both emotional and physical. And we can't stop talking about it.

Open Up

We've discussed how *FSOG* opened our minds, and gave us a little push to be more adventurous. There are many topics which still seem a little taboo. Like Christian being totally casual with kissing Ana, or performing oral sex right after he ejaculates. What surprised or shocked you the most?

- I think the most "radical" idea, to me at least, was the tampon scene. Not that there's anything wrong with it. Just more that it opened up dialogue about something that should be natural, but is considered "taboo."
- I can't think of anything that shocked me, except how explicit E.L. James was in the books.
- The Ginger Root! I still don't know what to think of that!
- We *have* to ask E.L. James where she got *that* idea!
- In *Grey*, he was thinking about how Leila loved the kinky fuckery, and how he used ginger root in her anus. That was shocking!
- Ginger root has a very nice aroma, but as a spice is a little hot. I wonder if it would feel hot and spicy, similar to warming lube?
-
- Sounds like it would be a VERY spicy feeling, if he'd use it to keep her from clenching her buttocks.
- Even if she tried to clench, she couldn't because of the root. But I'm talking about a secondary feeling down there. Would it burn a little?
- I didn't think about not being physically able to clench because of the root, but that makes sense. I'm thinking,

it would burn, but I'm not going to try it out anytime soon.

- I'd think it'd burn like hell, which I think is the point.
- It's so you cannot clench your cheeks when being spanked. It's a double-edged sword. You clench so it burns, but the smack is not as bad. Or you relax so it doesn't burn, but the smack hurts more. Sexual sadism at its best!
- It's not bad, if not left in too long.
- No wonder he thought Leila was an excellent submissive. She did everything he wanted. She loved the kinky fuckery, just like Ana. Ana was shocking, too. She had an inner freak.
- The only thing he did that surprised me is when he pulled out her tampon. Other than that, I already knew about the lifestyle, so not much of a shocker for me.
- Elena subbing for Christian while he was training to be a Dom was surprising.
- The tampon scene. It's so natural, but somehow I think all women are really private about it, and would react exactly like Ana. I completely missed the ginger root thing in *Grey*. How could I have missed that?
- I missed it, too! I was even convinced it wasn't in my copy, since I couldn't find it when I searched for it! I found it eventually. It's funny how it was so elusive.
- I have had my tampon pulled out, and it leaves you feeling like the person pulling the tampon out has an immense amount of command over you. I really liked it. It was a very vulnerable feeling.
- I loved the tampon scene because it meant that Christian was very accustomed to being intimate in that regard. It cut to the chase. I guess the ginger root kind of made me squirm a little. I've never experienced it, and don't want to. Imagining some of the stuff Elena and Christian did made me uneasy mostly because of his age. I think anytime there is a power dynamic, it is a moral issue and verboten.
- I was shocked and surprised that Christian admitted to Ana that Elena used the big rubber dildo on him, and that

he found it pleasurable. Also, at Ana's age and level of inexperience, that she was so willing to suck his fingers and "taste herself," and that she was so eager to perform oral sex on him. You *hit the hail on the nead* with the bit about him performing oral on her right after he ejaculated. I can almost guarantee Elena made him do that. And he figured it's no biggie now.

Shift Change

I felt uneasy when Christian wanted to have sex when he had just informed Ana that she was being stalked by his ex-sub. I'd want to discuss the situation, too. What was your reaction?

- Sex seems to be his way of escaping reality. Not that I'd complain!
- Haha. I'd just need a moment to transition my mood. Although, I am sure that he'd be of great help with that.
- He doesn't like facing problems. Having sex is his way of dealing with stress. I definitely wouldn't say "no," but, when the time is right, try discussing it again.
- Sex has always been Christian's coping mechanism. He hides behind his discomfort, and that's not healthy.
- I think having sex is his way of feeling close to her. In a way, he is able to open up to her and "release" his frustration. He thinks it works the same with Ana.
- It's a way of bonding.
- I'm not against it at all. After sex, he does open up. It's some sort of coping mechanism. It works for him, and it was another way of actually telling Ana that, even though he wouldn't admit it, was scared.
- After sex, Christian does talk to Ana; so, in a way, it works.

Shout! Shout! Let It All Out!

"'Yes, baby, let me hear you,' he murmurs against my overheated skin."

Do you think Ana was naturally vocal? Or, do you think this kind of encouragement helped bring that out? Have you ever held yourself back from being as vocal as you'd like? Does your volume indicate your degree of pleasure?

- I don't think Ana was vocal, hence the encouragement. I've had to bite my lip so frigging hard, it bled! Yes, volume rises as my orgasm intensifies. This has led to a couple of embarrassing times - in the summer, when the neighbors unexpectedly come home and your window is near their driveway, or when the landscapers show up. Thank God lawnmowers are noisy!
- I think she was vocal. Who can hide that kind of pleasure, especially when you are new to experiencing orgasms? I have to try to keep quiet because our kids' rooms are right next to ours. It's very difficult to keep quiet! Hubby has to keep shushing me. Sometimes, even the shushing can't quiet me down.
- She was quiet, but did have some breathy responses. Christian brought it out of her, a little bit. I assume she was always a bit sweet and hushed, but still vocal.
- I think Ana is naturally vocal. Her reaction to him brought that out. His encouragement only accentuated that.
- I think Christian just brought that out in her. She was a virgin. It was all new to her, so I think she just learned as she went. He helped her to be honest and comfortable with her body, so her being vocal was natural. Overall, I have a shy personality (until I get to know you), so I was always quiet. After reading *FSOG,* I am becoming more comfortable with myself and my body, and I am more vocal; way more than I was before. If you're comfortable with your spouse and what you are experiencing, then I think it's just a natural reaction. I don't like the screaming, yelling, and constant noise. Moans and natural sounds are hot!
- There's nothing worse than a fake orgasm scream!
- Being loud and obnoxious is a turn off for me. But, a natural moan or "Oh God," now that's a turn on!

- I think she was somewhat vocal, but Christian encouraged her not to hold back. Personally, I can be pretty vocal, as well. Less so now that my kids are a certain age, but I've developed tricks to muffle my sounds.
- What kind of tricks?
- Muffle the sounds in pillows, biting my lip, things like that.
- I don't think it was natural for Ana to be vocal, which is why he had to encourage her. I'm vocal, when I can be.
- I think Ana was a little vocal, but not loud on her own. He encouraged her to do it more and be louder. He was vocal, so that helped her to be, as well. I wasn't vocal before my last ex-fiancé and my husband. Nobody gave me orgasms like they did and do. They were always just little ones compared to what I get with these two men. With my ex and hubby, it is more like explosions. I can be too loud, sometimes. I definitely have to use a pillow when my daughter is home. I thought the same thing about the loudness, before my husband. Now, I can't help it. The orgasms are just really intense.
- Aren't you a lucky girl!
- I know exactly how you feel.
- Love it! Happy for you!
- Christian wasn't vocal. He was very quiet, until he was with Ana for a while. Then, he was vocal, calling her name.
- I thought he was vocal with her right away.
- I did too. Maybe not so many moans, but definitely a lot of orgasm alerts.
- I think Christian brought it out in Ana.
- I believe Ana was vocal from the first time. Of course, Christian talking like that would encourage her to be more so. Sometimes, being vocal does indicate the degree of pleasure.

Not So Fast!

Christian often told Ana when to "come," and when not to. In fact, he threatened her with punishment if she came too quickly. Have you ever tried to hold off or prevent an orgasm?

- It's called "edging"! I just started trying it. It's difficult, but most definitely can be done! Women are lucky, because we can have multiple orgasms! Men not so much, which is why I think they try to do this more than women!
- Never, because, as women we can climax many times before a man finishes. I know my husband tries to prolong it because he doesn't want it to end.
- I love it! Staying at a nine without coming. When you do, it's explosive.
- I totally understand wanting it to go on and on, but men are almost guaranteed a climax. We are not that fortunate, though we are fortunate that we can climax many times in one session, if we're lucky.
- What if we hold off too long, and he can't hold it anymore? We're screwed.
- It's quite hot to think a man would want to contain himself because he feels so good inside his partner.
- Yes, but they need to learn how, otherwise it's over too soon and the woman never gets there!
- True, but they can help using other body parts like fingers, tongue, or toys, even if it's not really the same. But still, it's better than doing it alone with no caress, kiss, or words.
- The problem is, once they ejaculate all that testosterone, they get weak and tired. So they really should believe in "Ladies First."
- Oh, really!? Completely out!?
- Often, yes. The strange thing is that we absorb the testosterone, making us stronger.

Sex Therapy

"I need to know we're okay. This is the only way I know how."

262

Christian, like most other men, need sex to feel intimacy. Yet most women need intimacy in order to want sex. Why do you think the genders are so different?

Maybe I should have been a man, because in order for me to feel loved, I need to have sex. My sex drive is really high, when I'm single. When I feel safe within a relationship, I want sex less, but I like snuggling more.

- I'm similar. If my husband and I go without sex for too long, I feel a disconnect. Once we have relations again, I feel reassured. When I say too long, it's not really long at all.
- It should be the other way around because that could hurt a relationship. My father-in-law always said, "Sex is only 10% of a relationship until you aren't getting any. Then it becomes 90%."
- That might explain why I'm not in a relationship.
- I asked my husband about this one. He said it's just a man thing. He said, women need a reason to get intimate. Men just need a place! It's not that men don't like intimacy; they just don't need the build-up. My husband loves to cuddle, and is definitely into intimacy. But, he also will stop whatever he's doing, if I flash him that signal that I'm up for doing anything. Christian only knew sex as his way to get his feelings across to Ana, in the beginning. He never had intimacy with anyone else. But as time went by, Ana showed him other ways to show his intimacy. This is what makes this story so special and beautiful! They grow and learn together.
- I think I should be a man too. If I don't get sex, I'm so moody and miserable, and feel unloved. Thankfully, my hubby understands my moods.
- This is me, too. If I go a few days without sex, you can tell. My husband will look at me and say, "I know what you need!" It seems the more sex I get, the more I want!
- I'm so glad it's not just me! I really understand what you mean. I always seem to want more!

- After my Grey-session started, my husband was so on board. The last almost four years have been unreal. But, I do feel that the more you do together - share and connect, the more you want it. Not just the sex, but the connection, too! We've been married for 25 years, this June!
- Keep it going, honey. I've been married for 54 years. Believe me, you miss it. Take care and stay healthy.
- My husband is the same as Christian. Let's have sex, then we can talk.
- Lately, I feel like I need sex to feel intimate with my husband. It's not the only way I feel close to him, but my drive is really high lately. I get really moody, and feel unloved, if I don't get sex on a regular basis.

Make-Up Sex

Did you notice that it seemed like Christian always got love-dovey and opened up more after they had a big fight? Why do you think that is? Does it happen with you? Share your stories!

- I think he was lovey-dovey out of remorse. He often felt guilty for letting his anger get the best of him. He opened up because I think he felt he owed Ana something in return for tolerating his craziness and extremism.
- I guess it has to do with him being more relaxed after sex.
- Making up after a fight is the best sex ever.
- He is so afraid of losing her, he opens up a little at a time. Not so with us.
- Oh, I'm very familiar with Christian's behavior. When hubby and I have fights, and we have doozies, I shut him out. Much like Ana did, when she was super-angry, after she told Christian she was pregnant, and he went and got drunk with Mrs. Robinson. When my hubby wants to make nice, he's quite the suck-up. He's so nice and sweet, and incredibly affectionate. He always says, "Time to make up. I wanna play." My hubby is a real

charmer, and knows that I have trouble resisting his charms. So, again, I can totally relate.

- Christian feels more vulnerable after sex.

It Takes Time

Virginity/Orgasm/Oral Sex all rolled into one in Ana's first time! Remember how shy she was about being a virgin? With her being a virgin, and not really even kissing many guys, do you think she would've been that comfortable with her nudity and with giving and receiving oral sex? She had no experience, and yet she had no hesitation! How was your first time? Was it like Ana's?

- My first time was horrible. My first orgasm was years later, and someone showed me how pleasurable it could be. I hated oral sex at first, and again years later that same man performed it on me, and I loved it. Is it just me and my bad early experiences? Or, maybe, was it that I grew up in a time when no one really discussed sex, and the pleasures to be found in it?
- For Ana, as first experiences go, it could've gone either way for her - horrid versus off the scale wow! It was a "wow" experience for her because she really, really wanted Christian. He also knew that this was her first time, so he was very careful with her, and made sure her first experience was everything she hoped it would be.
- No one discussed sex with me, ever. I was brought up by a relative. When I was married, I never had any problems. I love it and think it's great. Sometimes, it depends on your partner and their experiences, too. I agree with you, about Ana!
- They are, obviously, both natural talents when it comes to sex. Maybe it's not so realistic. Because of their chemistry, and because of Christian's experience with sex, I guess, it makes it somehow realistic. I didn't have my greatest experience until 15 years after my debut. I had the wrong partner. The more experience you have, you get to know yourself better, as a woman. Ana's one lucky girl to have experienced all this in her first 14 days.

I hope they will always be together because pity the poor guy who comes after Mr. Grey. That guy is doomed to fail. No one talked to me about this stuff. It comes with experience, knowledge, and being comfortable with the guy, and yourself.

- In my opinion, Ana's experience was totally fictional. After talking in this group, I do understand that orgasms happen in all sorts of ways. But, it was unlikely that she was that bold her first time. How could she be so "unashamed of her nakedness" so quickly? It wasn't until my 6th or 7th partner that I got naked for a man. I didn't have an orgasm for the longest time. I really doubt that she was that good at giving oral with no previous experience or training. But, I am glad the story was written this way.

- My ex-husband was my first, and we didn't have sex until six months or so before we were married. So, everything I did and learned was through his experience. Mostly, it was good. I had an orgasm the first time we had intercourse. I was a little shy about letting myself enjoy cunnilingus, but eventually let go. I always felt like I couldn't just relax. I felt pressured, and that took away the pleasure. I can be my own worst enemy. I still like giving head. Ana was a very lucky young woman. I always wondered if Kate discussed her own experiences with Ana, so that Ana had "an idea" of what to do. I got the impression she was a little embarrassed about her nakedness, or else, why would Christian mention that he wanted her to be unashamed of her nakedness?

- Ana had some serious body image issues, and I think Christian picked up on it right away. I loved how he really made Ana feel good about herself, and eventually she relaxed. Christian never stopped making her feel very good about herself.

- Trust me, it takes the right man. Christian knew a lot about women and how their bodies react. He had never been with a virgin either, so he was extra careful and made sure he did it right. I think he wanted to show her how good it could be from the beginning, because he wanted her so bad. She also wanted him more than she had ever wanted any man. It's not so crazy that things were perfect from the beginning. I wish I would've waited for my husband because, looking back now, I was wasting of my time, until I met him.

- I think Christian knew what to do and how to do it because of his training. I also think he made more of an effort with Ana. He wanted to please her.
- I love all of these thoughts! Personally, even though he was damned near perfect, I feel it should have portrayed her as a little shier.
- I agree, he knew how to please a woman, and that's what he did. I think she could've acted a little more shy, but she was past the point of no return because she wanted him pretty badly. My husband and I had an incredible sex life, right up until he died. We married at 18, so we did a lot of experimenting, but we found out what each other liked. We learned together. I have to admit that I never climaxed having my nipples being played with, but I climaxed every time. My husband made sure of it.
- As far as oral goes, I much prefer giving to receiving. There's something powerful about doing that. I love it!
- I'm the same way.
- My husband and I were each other's firsts. My husband was more knowledgeable about sex than I was, as far as how things worked, because of watching "movies." I knew about stuff, but not how do it right. I was so critical of myself back then. I've always been a fan of cunnilingus. It's one of the first things we did together. It took me a long time to enjoy giving oral to him though. I love doing it now, and I'm chalking that up to years of practice. Sex has always been wonderful between us, and it's gotten better and kinkier over the years. We were quite adventurous before we started having kids. No complaints when it comes to orgasms, I've always been able to have multiple orgasms during sex. I've been told that's rare. As for nudity, I was very self-conscious when I was younger, especially when it came to revealing myself to my husband for the first time. I was afraid he wouldn't be attracted to me because I'm curvy, but I'm not concerned with that anymore.

I Can't Resist

In *Freed*, Christian admits to having a fantasy of Ana resisting his sexual advances. How did you feel about this? Have you been with someone who wanted "resistance" or something more?

- It turns him on, plain and simple. She's always challenging otherwise. Why not bring her natural tendencies into the bedroom that offer him some pleasure? My husband also likes resistance sometimes. He likes me feisty and sassy. I think it gives them permission to be a little rough, and to implement some force as well.
- Maybe he wanted to see how far he could go with her? We know he enjoys resistance as a Dom, but Ana was new to all this. Could it be that he wanted her as a Dom and he be the sub? Crazy, I know; but he's mercurial. Why not try it with Ana?
- He did say she was "topping from the bottom." Maybe he secretly (or not so secretly) likes that.
- I think he was testing himself to see if he could get a bit rough with Ana, but not so rough that he'd hurt her. But mostly, he was really just playing with Ana. They both got off on it!
- I used to date a guy who confessed to having a rape fantasy. It freaked me out!
- Wow! That would definitely freak me out. There's nothing okay about rape. It's not fantasy not matter how you put it. It's still rape. Scary!
- I see it as **way** more than freaky. How could a rape induce someone's fantasies, to get turned on? Wow.
- At least he felt secure enough with you to tell you his fantasy. If it's a fantasy, it doesn't mean he'd do it in real life. Think about one of your fantasies. Would you really do them all if you could?
- I think there's a continuum. There are some things that might turn me on when I read about them, but would never try in a million years. Some that I might consider,

but might not share with someone I'm dating, and some that I'd share with a lover.

- Actually, yes I have resisted and it was fun, exciting, and different.
- I loved this scene in the book! They both got off on it. Resisting my hubby is one of my fantasies, too.
- When I first read this part, I thought Christian was weird for having this fantasy! But now that I've read this book more than once, he is not weird at all!
- I loved this scene. What is wrong with a rape fantasy? It's fiction, just like any other fantasy. I don't have problems with any kinds of fantasies. Why should I judge someone for something that turns them on while we are having sex?
- It's not rape as long as both consent. I think "rape" is the wrong word to use.
- Just because it's a fantasy doesn't mean they would do that in real life, out of the relationship with you.

I've Lost Count

Since *FSOG* is from Ana's point of view, we know each of her orgasms. And of course, Christian's "attentiveness" makes him know, too. Do you think most men "know" and keep count? Do you think Christian kept count with his other subs? Or do you think he cared that much? Do you think he could tell if one of his subs faked an orgasm? What might he do if he found out?

- I think most men really don't count unless you're having a lot! Christian might've kept count at times, but probably not all the time, unless that just came naturally for him. With Christian I really think you don't need to fake it. If one of his subs did, I think he'd want to know why, or figure out what went wrong, and try to fix it.
- Elena trained him well, and to be tuned in to all sensations and physiological responses. He had experienced years of intense sexual activity. In the books, he can feel Ana's body change when she's about to orgasm, and he can feel her vagina clench down on

269

him. I think he'd know if the subs were faking, and I think he'd punish them.

- I don't think he cared enough to keep track until Ana.
- I can definitely see Christian withholding orgasms from his subs, as a form of manipulation. As I'm sure Elena did to him.
- Wasn't his number one punishment that if you disobeyed him that he wouldn't let you come? I think he only counted Ana's because he was the only one that ever gave them to her, and it was all new to both of them. I also think that with the subs, he'd punish them if they faked it.
- I think for all intents and purposes, he probably didn't care if the subs had an orgasm or not. I think it was important and special with Ana was because she was an innocent virgin. When he told her he "fucked hard," and he was simply "rectifying the situation," it still mattered to him that she experienced the sensations to the fullest that go into "making love."
- I think he counted Ana's because he was responsible for them. As for other subs, I think he would've only counted orgasms if he was giving multiples in a session. I think, if he knew a sub well enough he could tell, but the first couple of times, probably not.
- In answer to your first question, I don't think most men know if you have had an orgasm, unless they have been schooled in this stuff. Most guys are oblivious.
- My man seems to know, because I'm pretty obvious. I think Christian probably didn't count when he was with the subs. I think was all tied up with the fact that Ana was a virgin.
- I don't think he'd count the orgasms with his submissives because they were already sexually active and trained in the art of BDSM. They were like staff to him, but I think Doms take pride in controlling a sub's body, and giving orgasms is powerful, just as denying them is. He said that when the sub is gagged, the only indication of what is happening is by watching their body's response very carefully, so I doubt a sub could

fake an orgasm. Since Doms know how to get you nearly there, and then stop as punishment, I should think they are very good at it. He counted Ana's because he had her first orgasm, and they mattered to him because she mattered to him. In his point of view, he thanked God every time he got her to reach orgasm. Her pleasure meant more to him than his own. My partner knows when I've orgasmed. We've been together for 24 years, he knows my body very well. But most men, in the beginning of a relationship can be easily fooled by faking it, and a lot of young men only worry about their own orgasm!

- Sad. but SO true about men who are only concerned with their own "O!"

Butt Really?

Christian was serious about prepping Ana for anal sex. Why would anyone want to have anal sex? What's your experience with anal sex and butt plugs?

- I have no idea, but I guess would feel shy and shocked about it, like Ana was.
- If used correctly, butt plugs don't hurt.
- It HURT LIKE HELL, but once it settled, in it was interesting.
- They don't hurt, if lubricated properly.
- I haven't had the experience, but it's interesting to think about. In the story it sounds so pleasurable; I guess preparation makes the difference.
- I haven't had the pleasure yet.
- I've done this once, and used a lubricant called Anal Ease, which numbs the area.
- I've never had anal sex, and used to think, "No way," but now? Let's just say, I'm more "open" to it! Anal licking? NO! Yuck!
- I'm up for it more than my hubby, and that makes it difficult sometimes. But I'm not opposed to trying this. I did have a life before I got married many moons ago.

- I don't mind the licking part, giving or receiving. It can be very erotic! I feel fresher, though, if we do it in the shower or bath.
- I've never tried it, and never will. That area has only one task to do, and that's what I'm letting mine do. Nothing is going to be put up my ass!
- Taboo or not, I enjoy anal sex. But no licking! I've never done it, never will. Maybe a bit of a finger, but no more than that, and not my finger! Yuck!
- Outie, not innie!
- I like it, and it's very enjoyable with the right man.
- I've done it many times. There are times when it will hurt, and times it's so pleasurable. I guess it depends on how intense your mood is. I've never done the licking, and don't think I ever will.
- The orgasm is way different and very intense. It is great! Sometimes it's good and doesn't hurt much. Other times, it hurts too much and we stop. It does typically hurt a little going in, but after a certain point it stops hurting and feels good. I won't do any licking there. The thought makes me want to vomit. My husband doesn't seem to mind if I'm fresh out of the shower. It feels good when he does it.
- I'm an anal virgin. I used to think, "No way!" but once again *FSOG* changed my way of thinking. Now I'm more like, "Maybe, with the right person."
- I've had anal sex, but not with a very thoughtful partner. It wasn't very satisfying for me. He chose to do it because he didn't believe in having vaginal intercourse when I was having my period!
- Boo on him!
- I know. I was too naive or dumb to have a say-so in the matter.
- Been there, done that. I leave it for very special occasions when I owe my husband something, or when I'm in trouble. I really don't enjoy it at all.
- I use it as a bargaining tool.
- Me, too, and it actually works. Even if we don't deliver in full.

- I always deliver or try my damnedest. If I don't, it doesn't work anymore.
- Wow, thanks so much for all this information. I've had anal sex only a few times. I've enjoyed some, and some not so much. It just depends.
- My ex put his little finger up there, and I hated it. I'm a huge baby about pain. I did like when he touched me there by kind of poking at it. That felt really good.
- Thanks for the information. I was one of those that said ABSOLUTELY NEVER to anal sex. Well, never say never. After *FSOG, t*hings changed, and two years ago we tried it, and it was quite enjoyable. It's not a constant thing we do, but sometimes it just seems to be the right moment. My advice is, if you try it, and don't like it, try it at least one more time. Also make sure you trust your partner, and you take it slow and prepare that area. You have control of this situation. Don't knock it until you try it.
- I found drinking helps to relax me. The more relaxed, the less it hurts.
- My best friend says the same thing.
- Anal sex really intrigues me. I hope to find someone who would like to try it.

Now That We're Married...

As we read in *Freed*, we're experiencing their lovemaking as a married couple. Does that make it sexier for you? Or, was it sexier at the beginning?

- It's not as descriptive as it was in the other two books. I was disappointed that it seemed like the scenes were cut off more in *Freed*. The sex is still hot. Just not as much of it being described in the third book.
- As crazy as it sounds, I was a little bit okay with that because their sex scenes didn't feel repetitive. I think sex as a married couple was very sexy because of how much Christian liked that Ana was officially his forever. I feel like sex when your dating is hot and wonderful because it's new and spontaneous. When you get

married, there's another layer of wonderful because that person is *yours*.

- That absolutely makes sense! I just wanted different types of sex scenes between them. Things they hadn't done together yet; and, we did get some of those.
- Yes! I'm down with that!
- They were both sexy for different reasons.
- It's all sexy to me!
- I'm loving them as a married couple. To me it's a more intimate peek into their lives.
- I love the sex they have as a married couple. In particular, I loved the rumble sex they had in Aspen! That was totally hot!

The Sleeping Together

Ana was the first woman that Christian "slept with." He wrapped himself around her like a vine. She kept his nightmares away. What are your thoughts about these words? Would they mean anything to Christian?

- I think, for the first time in his life, she made him feel cherished and safe. Although, I don't think he recognized those feelings because he's always in control and has never had to rely on others for anything. I think he learned the importance of all the components of a relationship, including all the little things, besides just sex.
- Sometimes sleeping with someone, really sleeping, can be really difficult! And, the inability to sleep can seriously impact a relationship/marriage!
- Christian never did allow himself that comfort with anyone else. However, with Ana there was that connection, something special they both had in their own little world. The effect she had on him was life-altering, and she gave him so many firsts. I need my companion to sleep well. I feel protected. It can be a task to fall asleep if he's not there.
- From the start, when he brought her to the Heathman, and slept with her, he knew something had changed from

that time on. Surely, the Heathman had somewhere else he could've slept, if he had stuck to his guns and enforced his "rule" about not sleeping with anyone. Also, he "couldn't seem to stay away from her," he desperately needed her. He wanted to be wrapped in her warmth - something he didn't get, even from his family, no matter how loving they were.

- There was no touching. It's funny how he'd cocoon himself around Ana, but didn't let her touch him at that time.
- It's so sweet, yet sad, knowing she really wants to comfort him.
- I believe that his heart trusted Ana right from the beginning. It just took his head a while to catch up because it was still so ingrained with his "rules." Those rules had been put in place in order for him to survive his past ordeals, and to get to where he was today.
- "Paging Dr. Flynn!"
- Yes, that was amazing! Which is why I think it was his heart trusting Ana. He couldn't control his head while he was asleep.
- At the same time, she kept wanting it to be a romance novel in her sleep. "Like Icarus flying too close to the sun."

Pregnancy and Children

Most "happily ever after" stories end with "and baby makes three." Yet in typical Ana and Christian style, there are a few bumps (if not blips) on the road to "forever."

Oops!

In *Darker*, after Ana and Christian got back together, he asked her if she was still taking her pill. She hadn't. Would you have stopped, if you were in Ana's position?

- I would've stopped. When a relationship is over, it's over. Why continue on the pill?
- Totally! And, if we're on a pill topic, I've always disliked Christian's pushing Ana to take the pill and how he'd arrange it all. Yes, he might've not liked condoms, but it was Ana's body after all.
- He's such an ass! Sometimes I can't understand why I fell for him. What does that say about me? Hmmm.
- I don't know that she intentionally stopped. I think she was so emotionally torn apart that she honestly forgot.
- That's what I think too.
- I would've stopped; I have stopped in the past. It just makes sense with a breakup.
- I would have stopped.
- I don't think she stopped purposely. I think it just didn't occur to her to remember. And if you recall, her alarm was set on the phone she left with him.
- I think the only reason she stopped taking the pill was because she was so heartbroken that she couldn't function at all. Taking a birth control pill was the absolute last thing on her mind at that time. I would've been the exact same way.
- Actually, Ana's stopping the pill frustrated me. I think Dr. Greene would've explained how the pill works and how she needed to take them every day. She had made love with Christian the night before they broke up. She should have known better than to stop the pill until the

end of the pack. I know Ana was inexperienced, but she was also smart. Which is why this frustrated me.

- Okay, yes; they had sex the night before, but come on, she was so extremely heartbroken, felt lost, her world was falling apart and thinking that they were never going to be together again because she wasn't going to be able to fulfill his need. How could I blame her for not taking the pill, or even think of it?
- I also would've stopped taking it. I think Ana was in a state of shock, and taking the pill was the last thing on her mind.
- It would've been irresponsible to stop for sure, but completely normal for an inexperienced 21-year-old going through a traumatic experience and not wanting a daily reminder.
- My Choice
- When Ana finds out she's pregnant, she tells Christian, "I do choose this defenseless baby over you. That's what any loving parent does. That's what your mother should have done for you." Do you think it was right for Ana to give him an ultimatum like this? When is it okay to give an ultimatum, and when can it backfire?
- While I understand where she was coming from, this scene really bothered me. I think it's really dangerous for her to threaten to leave him again. And, I also think it's dangerous for her to place the unborn child's welfare over Christian's.
- I think in this instance she was right. Christian was acting like a child.
- I think ultimatums are good if you are prepared to do what you're saying. If not, it can definitely backfire. I do think Ana was prepared to raise Teddy on her own. She is very strong in this moment, and Christian is being a total *sshole.
- I understand why she did it, but I think it was a mistake; even borderline cruel, given Christian's insecurity with abandonment.
- I think she was coming from a place of fear; she did not want to have a baby yet.

- They were both scared. She was lashing out from anger. They were so new to all this relationship stuff. She didn't really know what she wanted, but she was also afraid he'd leave her over the baby. They were both insecure at this point.
- I don't know if it was right for her to do this, but she didn't really know what to do. After he ran to Elena, she was confused and worried, and wanted him to choose her and the baby over Elena.
- I've learned that, especially with kids, (and Christian was acting as one), if you give an ultimatum you better be prepared to follow through with it, or you lose all credibility and control.
- As long as you are confident to act on the ultimatum.
- Do you think she would have? Should have?
- I think she would have. Reluctantly. If even to prove to Christian that it's what his mother should have done. He would've respected her for doing so. In the end, I think she was acting on impulse and needed to give him time to acclimate to having a child. That apartment was big enough for them both to live there while they worked things out.
- Isn't it a bit ironic that she might've done that to show him "what his mother should have done" but by doing it, she was doing exactly what his mother had done – abandon him?
- Oh, you gave me chills with that thought! Good God, that's deep.
- Full circle.
- To me, it was a slap in the face. A wake-up call for him.
- I feel it was to make him realize that it was not about only him anymore; that there was a real baby to think about now and to stop acting childish.
- As far as her abandoning him, I can see your point; but on the other hand it could also fall on him. He'd be the one abandoning his child.
- I wonder if she'd had the opportunity to show him the ultrasound, if that would've halted his anger and fear.

- I don't think, at this point, Christian thought of it as his child. To him it was an inconvenience and a betrayal (Ana not keeping up with her shots). He hadn't seen the "blip." He had no connection (yet) to it becoming a person.
- He thought of it as a "thing that will mess their lives," not as a real person.
- This whole part makes my blood boil to the point that I have to say that Ana was 1000% correct in making this ultimatum! He was being a total horse's arse, and she had so much to deal with! (especially with Ray in the hospital). The last thing she needed was Christian's stupid temper, and his ridiculous accusations. She was totally justified in making the ultimatum, and it would only backfire if Christian would say, "Fine, go ahead and raise the kid on your own."
- She was 100% right. He didn't want the baby. She felt unloved and alone, after how he acted. They were married. Give an ultimatum only if you mean to go through with it, and she did.
- I completely agree with Ana, giving Christian the ultimatum. I think Ana knew Christian was upset and she hoped that he just needed time to cool down, and then talk to her. However, after reading the text from Elena, she had every right to be pissed. I was so happy she stood her ground. I'm sure if Ana had gone to see Jose, Christian would've been just as (if not even more) pissed.
- Given the way he reacted, I would've had the same comeback. Both of them could've handled the whole situation better in a lot of ways.
- Good for you Ana. Christian needed to grow up.
- Ana has the right to be mad at Christian! I would be too, if it happened to me!
- I don't like that Ana threatened to leave him. That was a bit mean. But I like that she said she'd choose the child over him, and that she said she was sorry his mother didn't do that for him. I think pointing out that it's what any loving parent would do was the wake-up call he

needed. To remember what it was like being neglected by a parent, not just for him to deal with the hurt, so that he can be the type of father I'm sure Ana knows he can be. The type of parent that Blip deserves.

- Most mothers would (and should) put their child's welfare above everyone else. If he was unable to accept this child, then she should leave him. Thankfully, he finally came around.

- Ana isn't saying that Christian isn't important. She doesn't want to make the choice. But, if she had to, any parent, especially a mother, would and should choose the child born or unborn. I mean, tell me Grace wouldn't have chosen her kids over her husband. Also, we all say Carla should have chosen Ana over her husbands, but the minute Ana does, it's wrong. The only reason many would feel it's wrong is because he's Christian Grey. Who would want to leave him, right? If he couldn't accept a new life coming into theirs, and he was angry about it all the time, why should she stay? It's not good to live in an environment like that. Yes, Christian has been through a lot, and the last thing he needs is someone leaving him, especially the love of his life. But, he's not the only person that matters. The world doesn't revolve around him. You say it's dangerous for him, but imagine that child growing up feeling unwanted by Christian because he didn't care for him or love him. Then, imagine Ana and Christian arguing all the time because of it. It would be hell for them and the child. Thankfully it didn't turn out like this, and he did eventually come around. Ana and little Blip deserve someone who would accept them both, and until he did accept the situation, Christian wasn't that guy. As I said, thankfully, he did come around because he made a great dad even though he thought he wouldn't.

- I still think threatening to leave a spouse over an unborn child is a dangerous thing to do. I believe that the couple's relationship should be a priority and that threatening to leave, especially someone as insecure as Christian, is cruel. She could've made her point in a more mature and considerate way, and her being angry at his behavior is no excuse to lower herself to his level. It worked because it's fiction.

- I still disagree. She had to shock him into thinking differently. Who knows if it would've really worked? The thing that finally brought him around was her kidnapping by Jack. What might've happened to their relationship if that had never occurred? Would he have still come around to accepting the child? I think he would have, if for no other reason than he couldn't live without Ana. But, if he never did come around, then she should have left his *ss in a heartbeat. Neither she nor the child deserve to live with a man who resents, and does not accept his own child. But, because it is fiction, there was a happy ending. Unfortunately, in real life things don't always end so happily.
- Every book and article I've ever read, and all the advice I've ever gotten, says to never *ever* use threatening to leave as a manipulation tool.
- Normally, I would agree with you. Threatening to leave is certainly not something to be done lightly. But there are certain circumstances where I believe it is warranted. If the spouse is abusive, or cheating on you, or addicted to something and refusing to get help, and certainly not accepting your child is another one. But I sure don't think it should be done just because you're pissed at your spouse, and are trying to manipulate them into doing something they don't want to do. And, if you ever do make that threat, you should be fully prepared to actually do it.
- I think Ana was very serious here. If he was unable to accept the child, I do think she would've left him. It was not an idle threat from her. I think Christian knew that, too.
- I don't think she was trying to manipulate him. I think she was serious. If he didn't come around, she would've left him to raise their child alone.
- Just because she chose the baby, it doesn't mean Ana doesn't think her relationship with Christian isn't a priority. I think, if we thought only about keeping our spouses as a priority, none of us would be here. I'm kind

of like Christian, where I went through a lot, very similar to him. Although it would be hard on me if I acted like Christian, I'd eventually understand why my spouse would say what Ana did.

- I have a personal situation similar to this. My sister was dating a guy and she got pregnant. He and his family wanted her to abort the baby. I told her that if she decided to not keep the baby she should have it and I'd adopt it before she killed it. Needless to say, the guy wasn't around the baby's first year and half of their lives. They have since married and are raising their daughter together, as a family. It took some time for him to come around, but they're now a happy family. My niece is my little unicorn. She put color and light in our world. Obviously, he and his family were *ssholes, until he finally came around. To kill a defenseless baby who didn't ask to come into this world is even more cruel than breaking someone's heart. So to me, for Ana to put the baby before Christian was absolutely the right thing to do.

- This part does show the level of immaturity that both Christian and Ana have. They got married quickly and are both still young. Yes, Christian is older, but men don't mature as quickly as women, so to me they're both on the same level with immaturity. Like most couples, they have to learn to talk to each other instead of running away.

- I've been a mother to children that aren't mine, in addition to my own. I have a wonderful husband and love him very much, but if he was a jerk like that, I'd leave him in a flat second. I came into the relationship with two children that weren't mine, my ex-fiancé's daughter, and my niece. My husband embraced them and helped me raise them. My children always have come first, and he fell in love with me for that. I definitely know my biological children would be first. Children are always first to me.

- Ana had every right to choose the baby, and put it first. That's why God created women to have babies. They are much stronger, loving, protective, and can be fierce when it comes to their young. It doesn't take away any love from the father. It's a different love for the child. She explained it very well to him, even while being furious. She loved him to the moon and back, and always will.

- I think Ana should've given Christian more time to adjust, before threatening him. He had to feel like he had some choice in the matter, that it wasn't just forced on him.
- I think she was just pissed, and needed to scare him a little.
- But I think scaring someone, especially someone like Christian, especially with his history, is kind of cruel. It would make him even more insecure.
- She was feeling insecure too. But she needed to be strong for herself, and the baby.
- It's a tricky situation. I can relate to that. I'm total crap at relationships.
- I think Ana is channeling her mama-bear instinct; being protective to her unborn child. On top of feeling frustrated about knowing that Christian met Mrs. Robinson that night, and seeing the message from her, I think I'd react the same.
- I just can't ever imagine being with a man who would react that way. I could never put a man like that first. My baby would always be first.
- That is Ana! Speaking her mind, and now defending her little Blip. Christian had that coming. I know he was shocked, but she couldn't have said it any better. Good for you, Ana.

Avoidance Tactic

Christian decides to come home late the evening after he found out about Blip.
Why did Christian change his mind about coming home that evening?

- I don't know, but it was really stupid and childish of him! I want to know where Flynn was this whole time!

- It pissed me off. Guys do that bullsh*t. They screw up, and then go run and hide, which only makes it worse by staying away, and not facing their mistakes.
- Damn it to hell. He says one thing, then goes into his office to avoid seeing her. Now, he's the one who's upset and tries to make Ana pay for it? He should've been there earlier and talked with Ana, and told her that he was with her and the baby. That it was scary, but together they will learn.
- I think they both acted immature and childish, every time they had a fight. Ana loved to provoke him and he acted like a typical man, and avoided the situation. I got pissed at both of them, while reading the book.
- Me too.
- That's so right; both need to be spanked, sometimes.
- But, of course, he should have told her that he'd be there for her A LOT sooner.
- He was out of control, and he didn't want to see Ana until he felt he was prepared to address things accordingly. It wasn't right, and it pissed me off too, but I believe that was the reasoning behind the behavior.
- Do you think that's an excuse?
- Oh no, not at all, but I'm explaining why I think he did it. Just because I understand it, that doesn't mean I condone it.
- I don't think he can be excused, whatever his reasoning. If the tables were turned, how would he have acted if she did the same thing to him? If she left him the same way? I really felt sorry for Ana – her husband dismissing her like that. How vulnerable and alone and betrayed she felt.
- My husband never did this to me when I told him I was pregnant, but the behavior throughout the book resonated with me on so many levels. Have I ever mentioned that Christian reminds me a lot of my husband? It is both a good and a bad thing. Very similar personalities. I have stories.
-

- I think Christian is holding back, and waiting definitely fits his personality. If he had suddenly become all gooey and sweet, and tender, and attentive, and accepting of her, it just wouldn't fit who Christian Grey is. It would have been way too fast a transformation.
- That's what I was thinking.
- I think that's why I love this series so much; because I'm very much like Ana and my husband is very much like Christian. Though, I wish we had Christian's bank account sometimes.
- I was about to write the same thing. I'd take a few hours' worth of his pay.
- A few hours of his pay would be good!
- I believe he didn't come home because he didn't want an evening of more drama. He knew that Ana was super-pissed at him, and he knew that they weren't ready to talk, to heal the rift between them. I was really touched that even in this f*cked up scenario, he felt the need to let Ana know that he hasn't abandoned her, and that he watched over her while she slept.
- That was very sweet.
- I think he didn't come home because he was too embarrassed about acting like a child, and he didn't know how to make it up to her.
- He was probably also afraid of himself. Afraid of his reaction and that he could push her away further.

Family Matters

"Okay … I steel myself to ask the million-dollar question. 'Do you want to put in a playroom?'
"…'Let's leave our options open for the moment. After all, this will be a family home.'"

Why do you think that Christian thought they couldn't have a playroom in a "family home?"

- He was worried that the kids might see it, and ask questions.

- I think that the kids would be curious enough to ask "why is that the only room that is locked all the time?"
- Maybe they could have one of those hidden doors that rich people in movies have? So the kids wouldn't even know it was there?
- Wow! I love that idea. Since Ana loves to read, it could be part of the library.
- Great idea! Let's call Gia and get it done!
- Gia put in the playroom? I think not. It would have to be someone much more discreet than Gia. Maybe, the door entrance but NOT the playroom.
- I like the idea of a secret passage from their walk-in closet. They would be in their bedroom and have easy access. Kids are asleep, they would never know. But, they would have to give Gia an explanation. Maybe, tell her it's a safe room like the one Christian had at the penthouse.
- I think he was leaving that life behind. He could do those things just about anywhere with Ana. He didn't have to hide. He didn't need a special room. (Plus they weren't selling the apartment at Escala.)
- Would you want your kids to wonder why mommy and daddy can go to the playroom, but they can't?
- Did you see my "hidden room" idea above?
- Escala would always be there. But, then the children would also want to go there, at some point. It would be rather unnatural for them to not go. And then there would be the question as to why that room is the only one locked! I don't know if there is a right answer.
- Did you see my ideas above for a hidden room? The rich people in movies have them all the time! I can definitely see Christian and Ana building one!
- I did, but I guess I'd wonder whether children might not eventually discover it. Sexual activities are such very personal behaviorisms, and I don't believe they can easily be shared with children, such that they aren't understood.
- Christian had a hard time blending his old way of life with the new. Maybe, he thought it would tarnish this

286

new image he had of the life he was moving forward with.

- Kids are super curious, especially when it comes to closed doors. The last thing he'd want is for either Teddy or Phoebe to find the keys and open the door. It could be quite traumatizing; not to mention, how do you explain a room like that to a child? So, it's best the playroom stay at Escala.
- I would find it really sad that the parents couldn't have a (secret hidden) playroom in the bigger house.
- I'm all for a secret place. Sounds good.
- They should have a secret room!
- Knowing Christian, he'd have the latest in security - eye scanners, fingerprints, the works, to make sure the kiddies don't have a chance!
- Not worth it. He'd probably do it, but that would only make his kids even more determined to figure out a way to get in there, and see what Mom and Dad are hiding. Do not underestimate the craftiness of kids!
- They will get through EVERY wall, door, partition, the more curious they will be. If Mom and Dad are willing to go to these extremes, it must be something so wild, and freaky that we gotta be patient, and peel those onion layers. It's gotta be something mind-blowing!
- We can write the TV show episode right now! Soo funny!

And The Baby...?

"'And the baby?' The words are anguished, breathless. "'The baby's fine, Mr. Grey.'
"'Oh, thank God.' The words are a litany... a prayer. 'Oh, thank God.'

Do you think Christian was more worried about losing the baby - or worried that Ana would be upset if she lost the baby (Blip)?"

- He was genuinely concerned for the baby.

- A bit of both, I think. He was probably scared that if Ana lost the baby, she'd leave him.
- I think both. Once it set in that Ana and the baby were in danger, he realized how much he actually cared about the baby. He also worried about Ana's feelings, if the baby didn't survive.
- Both. But, I think he changed his focus a lot when Ana was hurt. His focus shifted from how he felt to caring for both her and the baby.
- I think even though he had a horrid reaction to the news that he was going to be a dad, he loves Ana and would never want anything tragic to happen to Ana or his child. Seeing Ana out cold snapped him out of his anger, and made him realize how much he really wanted her and their child. Also, Grace was amazing with him too!

When Change Occurs

At what point did Christian's feelings change about the baby?

- I think it might've been at that very moment when Ana's life was at risk after the kidnapping.
- I think it was after Elena made a pass at him.
- When Elena made a pass at him and he realized how he'd feel if his child was put in the same situation he was in when Elena first took advantage of him.
- Why then did it take him so long to talk to Ana about that realization?
- Because it's Christian, and he's never forthcoming with his emotions.
- Stubborn.
- I think his feelings changed when Elena crossed this line, but things really changed once he saw Ana unconscious on the pavement and thought he lost everything. From that moment on, his protective mode kicked in huge, and his feelings for his child intensified.

Pink or Blue

"'You know,' I mutter between mouthfuls, 'Blip might be a girl.'
"Christian runs his hand through his hair. 'Two women, eh?' Alarm flashes across his face, and his dark look vanishes.
"Oh crap. 'Do you have a preference?'
"'Preference?'
"'Boy or girl.'"

Christian gives the "politically correct" answer - but do you think he was relieved his first child was a boy? If so, why?

* The whole man thing, and what they want to do to your little girl when they grow up. It's hard for a man to see his little girl as a grown woman. Men often think back to how they acted, the thoughts they had about women, and what they did to women. Can you imagine his thoughts? Plus, he feels he'd have to protect a female more. Look at his experience. Ana and Mia were both very stubborn and uncooperative, when it came to security.
* I can't explain why, but I have to come out and say how annoyed I was that she called it a blip this whole time.
* Yeah, he did give Ana the politically correct answer, but I think he really wanted Blip to be a boy. I think he considers girls fragile and delicate, and in constant need of protecting. It would probably put his mind at ease if he didn't have to worry about boys, and their intentions towards any daughter of his. All I can say is "poor Phoebe!"
* I LOVE Phoebe! A lot of you know why.
* I think Phoebe is going to be stubborn and strong like Ana! He's not going to have to worry about her very much. (But I know he will.)
* Yes, I think he was relieved they had a boy first.
* A boy who will likely grow up to be just like Daddy in so many ways - controlling, smart, and very likely, sexy as f*ck!
* You know it.

Impact of Fatherhood

In the *Freed* epilogue, Ana marvels at Christian's patience and capacity for play.
Why do you think Christian is more patient with Teddy than he is with Ana? Would that bother you if you were Ana?

- I think a parent should, to the best of their ability, be patient with kids. I'm more patient with my husband than I am with our kids, but I'm with them 24/7. I'm working on being more patient with them. If I were Ana, I'd be happy that he turned out to be a great father.
- I think Christian wanted only the best childhood for Teddy, and didn't want him tainted with his awful memories, so decided that he'd create beautiful and loving memories for his son. I think that in the beginning, Christian wasn't very patient with Ana and for the same reasons, decided to also create beautiful memories with her as well. Ana loved Christian unconditionally and did everything she could to understand his issues. I think, more than anything, Ana was relieved and grateful that Christian was the amazing father she knew he could be.
- It shouldn't bother her, not only should one always have more patience with children, but he wants to fulfill the role of being a father, in every way, for all the obvious reasons.

Fast-Forward

Fast forward 12 years or so and Teddy and Phoebe are starting to have friends and starting to "socialize" a bit. Do you think Ana and Christian will host hangouts at their place, or will they prefer to have the kids go "out?" Christian is in fact more of the private type right now. But will that change? Will he be really trusting of his kids? Or over-protective?

- Both trusting and over-protective. I think he'll have hang-outs at his house since the kids have their own security teams. They can't have them going to sleepovers without them.

- Wouldn't the kids want to get out on their own at some point? I'd think it would feel claustrophobic to stay at home the whole time – or to have to bring their security team.
- I'm sure they will want to hang out, but I think Christian and Ana raised them to understand why they have their own security teams.
- Right, just like celebrities, it's probably part of their normal life. Something they have to deal with. They'll probably also be surrounded by people in an equal social class.
- Christian will want to host everything, in order to keep control, and keep everyone in line.
- Ana will host, but I think Christian will sit in the background, carefully observing and complaining to Ana, "Did you see this, did you hear that?" Ana will have to tell him he's being a megalomaniac, and that they're just kids.
- I love this! I'm imagining now.
- I can see Christian leering menacingly at any boy who gives Phoebe a second glance.
- They would hang out there. He's going to be very protective, more so with Phoebe. Also, having the kids, I think by then he's not so private. Can you imagine the parties and hangouts there? Fun times. And the friends would probably want the parties there. Who wouldn't?
- Christian is totally going to be one of "those dads."
- All of Phoebe's friends will have mad crushes on Christian! Even the mothers! Here's a scenario. Kid: "Phoebe's having a get together today…" The mom is already in the car before her daughter finished the question! Mom's applying lipstick, and honking the horn. Dad shrugs, looks at the daughter. You must be going over to Phoebe's. "Bye, daddy."
- I think he'll still be over-protective. Only a select few will be allowed to visit. I suspect most socializing will be done away from the home for the kids.
- Ana would let them go out, Christian not so much.

- When he brings them to Aspen they can be a lot freer because it's so safe there. When they go skiing, they will have their own private ski instructor. And their friends would all ski together.
- He will host so he knows the kids are safe. I think he will be over-protective.
- Protective, at their house, and under security
- I also think one of the reasons he wanted to them to stay at home, and bring their friends there is because this is something he missed out on himself, as a kid or teenager.
- I think Christian would have the hangout at their place. I also think that even though it might be a bit embarrassing for the kids to have the team there, they would probably get used to it. And I'm sure Christian has had all their friends or their parents background-checked, unless they are children of the team members.
- Becoming a parent changes everything. You have to let them have their own friends, and also become part of their friends' parents' lives. Christian changed so much, and I think 12 years is a long time. By then, not only Ana but also Phoebe will have him wrapped around her finger, and be Daddy's little princess. He can be protective, and be private, and also trust his children. I can imagine Phoebe giving pretty pouts to daddy Christian, and his heart melting. The same goes with Teddy.
- I definitely think Christian will be over-protective, especially with Phoebe. But I think Ana will ground him, and they will have some functions at their house. The Greys were ones to socialize, so I think Christian will allow it. Plus, this way, he can keep an eye on the kids and their friends.
- Yes, he might trust them, just like he trusts Ana, but he will never get over the need to protect them.

Dangerous?

Ana debated when to tell Christian about "Blip." She considered telling him while they were having sex but then thought, "that might be dangerous for both of us." What do you think she meant by "dangerous for both of us?"

- I honestly think she was scared to tell him because she did not know how badly he was going to react. At times, he can be a little bit of a "negative nelly."
- Can you imagine telling him news like this with him on top of you?
- She was afraid he'd lose it. Maybe physically. She was still concerned about how far he'd go. Even though she didn't think he'd hurt her physically (or maybe hoped), she felt she still needed to be careful about how and when she told him things that would upset him. I think she also felt some responsibility to help him keep his precious temper in check. Remember, in Aspen, how upset she was that blonde giant made him lose his cool?
- Christian has a history of reacting badly to unexpected news, and he takes it out on Ana in the RROP (Cocktailgate is a prime example of this). She was scared that the same thing would happen, and that he'd punish her with a whip or belt; physically hurting her and emotionally hurting him.
- He'd take her in the red room of pain and torture her somehow.
- She was afraid that maybe he'd really hurt her physically, and then he'd get more emotionally damaged for hurting her.
- Surely, she didn't mean her and the baby!

Power and Control

Many relationships go through a tug-of-war of power at one time or another. BDSM takes this dynamic to a whole new level. Who really has the control in a D/s relationship? And who had more power – Ana or Christian? These questions are explored in this chapter.

I'm Soooo Bored

When Christian said to Ana he was used to getting his own way, she responded, "That must get really boring." Why do you think Ana said this? Do you think she really thought it (or he) was boring? Would you agree?

- Thinking about it, I have to agree with her. To get your own way all the time, where's the challenge? It doesn't even sound like fun - more of a power play move, I think. Anyone else see this?
- I think what she means is that it must be very boring for him to have women agreeing with him all the time. That's why he actually loved her smart mouth from the beginning. Finally, a woman who speaks up to him!
- She said it because if you only experience what you like and know, you miss out on a lot of what this world has to show you.
- I love how she just calls it, straight. I think, he was rather taken by that. Likewise, I don't think she thought he was boring at all. I think that she knew getting your own way all the time is predictable. If she didn't know consciously, certainly her subconscious was being drawn to him, to bring about the change/growth they both needed.
- That's very interesting! We should delve more into Ana's "selves" for another post. Regarding this one, it's almost like being around him brings out a side of her that might've been suppressed. What do you think?
- I think it surprised even herself! It's like that moment that you realize you strongly feel the way you do, and you don't ever remember "when" you started to believe

it so strongly. It happens, sometimes, because of those we choose to invite into our lives, and how they impact on our views, challenge them, even if subconsciously. He brought that out in her, much to both their surprise! She was already so affected by his presence/spirit/closeness, it was so much fun to read her 'inner goddess' thoughts throughout the story.

- I love that, too! The Inner Goddess.
- I love a challenge.
- Variety is engaging. Routine is predictable. Yet, in his case, it involved another person, and that changes it every time.
- I'm thinking about it, and I love the fact that Ana wasn't impressed by his wealth, even from the start. She was smitten with him when she fell in the office, yet, she had no problem telling him how she truly felt. She was a force to be reckoned with, right out of the gate!
- I think when everything goes your way, it could be very boring because everything is so predictable. Also, I think she said it because she was trying to be snarky with him.
- He liked her because Ana is smart, and knows not to be bossed around. She called him out. I loved it.
- As Christian himself said, Ana really doesn't have a submissive bone in her body. And I think he loved that about her.
- He was at a place in his life where he was bored with the subs and the life. He hadn't had a sub in several months, when Ana literally fell into his life. It happened at the most perfect time in his life. She was everything he never knew he always wanted.
- I think you hit the "hail on the nead." If she showed up a couple of years earlier, he probably wouldn't have been ready for her.
- I agree about perfect timing for him. Though, with their undeniable invisible draw to each other, I think he would've stopped his lifestyle to pursue her any way he could. They were destined to be together.

- Yes - and she wouldn't have been ready, either! She was only 21 when they met, right? I wonder what Ana was like at 18 or 19. I wonder how Ana and Kate met. Anybody have a clue? Has there been any good fanfiction about that?
- Didn't they meet when they started college?
- I'm pretty sure they met during freshman year, in college.
- Do we know how they met? Any back stories?
- I think they met when Ana stumbled at the local coffee shop, and spilled her Twinings English Breakfast tea all over Kate. Kate took it in stride, and felt an instant connection to this clumsy geeky English Literature major. After Ana apologized all over herself, they began talking and soon realized they were both looking for a place to stay. They decided to move in together, and the rest is history!

Why Did Christian Use the Belt?

Do you think Christian used the belt to show "who's in charge?"

- And my boot, and knee to his genitalia, would make him think again.
- I don't think so.
- Maybe beforehand. He said he liked to make his subs' fair skin pink up, but in Ana's case, with the cuff marks, definitely not. He felt really bad for leaving visible marks on her perfect skin.
- I don't think he was thinking, too much. He reacted out of anger.
- Not a control thing. It's more of a release thing for him.
- I actually think it was a control thing for him - not only to punish her/put her into her place - but also to seize control of himself, too. To prove to himself (as well as to her) that he was in control.
- He felt his heart getting soft, and he wanted to harden it back up a bit. Sometimes it's hard to let people in, not knowing whether or not they're going to stay. It's a

296

struggle. Sometimes it's easier to push them away, or shut them out.

- No, I don't think he was thinking that. I think he just wanted to fulfill Ana's request. I think he was thinking something else. His look was one of a very angry man.
- What was prompting the anger? (To me it was because he felt like he was losing control.)
- I've read where some readers thought that his mind was on Leila, and the amount of danger he was putting Ana in, and he was trying to push her away. I can see that but that was not my first impression. I think he was pissed because she was infiltrating the little, quiet, non-chaotic, comfortable predictable world he had created.
- It became a power of wills that should never have happened. Ana wanting so desperately to be what he wanted, and having to know the "worst." Christian struggling, as he tries to settle his Dom side, yet really wanting to feel the release of belting her. They were both wrong - Christian, as a Dom, should have never let it get to that point. Ana as a "sub" should have safe-worded, yet didn't. It was like she argued with him to do it, didn't safe-word, then got pissed because he didn't stop. I believe she really thought he wasn't going to do it, that he loved her enough not to belt her. But you can't put a Dom in that position.
- I think she thought he'd "finish" belting her, and that he'd make the connection automatically, and not want to hurt her.
- Personally, I couldn't cross the line that would lead to what this is saying (I've been slapped in the face, once, for my insolence). But, I think I understand another one of the "why's" for Christian wanting to give Ana "a good hiding," as he claimed.
- They certainly do. Hehe.
- He definitely should have been more clear with Ana from the start. I would NEVER touch my subs until we had talked and signed contracts. But, that's because he had an instant attraction to Ana. Any good Dom would never have taken the belt to her in anger, and he didn't

even warm her up with the softer spanks. It was done wrong, but then, it's a love story, with a little kink.

- He screwed up.
- He's not into leaving marks. That does nothing for him, it's inflicting the pain that gets him off.
- No, the they weren't about control. The welts were more about evidence of inflicting pain.
- He thought, right from the first time he met her, how a few welts from a crop would help her. He liked his hand print on her ass, as he was spanking her. He didn't mind marks that would go away overnight. Nothing permanent. He had to have control.
- I think he mentioned marks from the cane. But, you make a very good point. He definitely liked leaving redness.
- I believe he liked pink.

Rules

So, I'm reading through *Freed,* and a thought occurs to me. Christian breaks his own rule when he marks Ana's body with hickeys, in order to prevent her from showing excess skin during the remainder of their honeymoon (wasn't leaving marks on a sub's skin a no go?). So the thought occurred to me, what other, not so, obvious rules did Christian break in his relationship with Ana?

- Falling in love.
- Remember, in *Freed* she is no longer his sub. She is his wife and he sees her as his property.
- They married so fast, I think he wanted to keep her. After they were married, I think he was still learning, and falling deeper in love.
- He couldn't help but fall in love with her.
- That's why he feels so guilty.
- And that's a problem, in, and, of itself. He had to learn that Ana was his wife, not his property. That was the essence of their argument over her wanting to keep her maiden name at the office. Remember, when he came to see her to deal with his "errant wife/asset", she kept

yelling in her head "I AM NOT AN ASSET!'"? She's no one's property. Christian had yet to learn that.

- He does learn it though. I think he actually changes and compromises a lot more than she does.
- I'm not so sure about that. He wouldn't leave her office until she agreed to change her name to Grey. Then, there's his possessive jealousy issues. Ana, on the other hand, needed to grow up too. Going out with Kate against his wishes, with crazy Jack out there, really did put her at risk, and she didn't realize it.
- I think she did know. I don't think she is as innocent in her mind as we believe. Controversial, I know, but don't all women like to push boundaries, even if just in our heads? Men are more physical, and react as such.
- If we go back even further...in *Darker*, Christian insisted that Ana use her Blackberry for personal texts, as opposed to her work computer (he kept telling her that emails were being monitored), Ana was pushing boundaries at that time, but didn't realize the ramifications, until it's too late. For both of them, I believe their actions were somewhat childish, and both needed to explore what "growing up" meant.
- There was, of course, a rule that nobody slept in his bed, which he rather willing broke, when he realized he actually loved sleeping next to Ana. She'd kept his nightmares away.
- The double standard of eye-rolling, too.
- Speaking of the Blackberry...whenever he'd tell her to USE HER BLACKBERRY, that drove me crazy. If he wanted her to use the flippin' thing, why was he e-mailing her on her work e-mail? All he had to do was e-mail her on her Blackberry, and she'd have to respond using it, too. So, he's as much at fault for her not using it, as she is, in fact he's more at fault.
- That's why I said they both needed to explore what growing up was about. I agree, Christian was as guilty as Ana for doing that. But, I think, at that time, the "control freak" was surfacing.

- They certainly knew nothing about relationships. They dove in head first, and being their first relationship, they had loads to learn. I totally agree about them being rather childish, at times. In Ana's case, how careless she was about her own safety, to the point of behaving like a kid? But, it's good they were learning together.
- He broke all of his rules from the get-go!
- So, the question is: Who spanks him when *he* breaks the rules?
- He broke all his rules. He had so many firsts with her.
- Yes, he did break all his rules with Ana. He chased her, and he never chased a girl before Ana. That was #1, many more followed, after that. All the firsts they had together, were all rule breakers.

The Little Woman

Christian says Ana doesn't need to work for a living. He obviously sees nothing wrong with supporting her, but isn't that yet another subconscious attempt at "forever?" His working and bringing home the bacon, and her at home waiting for him? Quite a little family unit on his terms. Hmmm.

- That was most definitely his wanting, so much, to take care of her. For her part, she was feeling more like a "kept" woman rather than his girlfriend. At this point, the marriage proposal was probably brewing in his head, but wasn't even on Ana's radar.
- I think he did want the fairytale, possibly more so than Ana. But, I also think that he wanted her all to himself. He hated other men ogling her.
- Totally, that too! He was a bit of a caveman.
- If he makes her stay at home, he won't have to worry about her, about any problems with Leila, with other men, with Jack, etc.
- Except her unhappiness.
- I was glad when she thought, "He's mad and I don't give a sh*t!"

- Christian had an awful lot to learn. His mother worked. Like a lot of men, they tend to not realize that both men and women have life goals of enjoying work; finding something that makes you feel good about your contribution to the world. What I didn't enjoy reading was how they fought over that issue. Ana was rather ready to explode about Christian's already explosive nature. It will take them a while to learn how to discuss inflammatory issues in a reasonable way.
- Another example of "Christian The King of Contradictions." Pissed me off. One minute he wants her to run the company, and the next he wants her to stay home. How about this, Christian? Let HER decide!

Making Waves

Was Ana going too far by going out on the jet ski without telling Christian? Or, was he being too over-protective?

- I think it is another situation with his controlling tendencies. She loves it, but also hates it. I am glad that she did it without telling him, but when she falls, I, kind of, saw Christian's point of view.
- He was over-protective and afraid that Ana might hurt herself.
- I think Christian knows Ana better than she cares to admit. He knows her risk-taking tendencies, and seems to almost be able to predict problems that she doesn't seem to see. I'm not sure it has to do with control issues rather than experience and knowledge issues. I think Christian would've been willing to teach Ana so that she'd be more aware. She reminds me of a recalcitrant teenager!
- Don't you think the harder he held on, the more she struggled to get free? That one behavior prompted the other?
- I think Ana was much less a risk-taker than a typical 21-year-old. Most college students have gone to clubs, gotten drunk, slept with more than one partner, and some have tried drugs. Ana was more of a quiet introvert.

- Most? I don't think you can say most. That was never my scene. And, I think that's part of the problem with people today. They think most people are doing these things, so I guess I'll do it too. Ana was not a risk taker. But she did not consider her safety, like she should have.
- I'll give my answer. Statistically, a majority of girls lose their virginity before 21, especially these days. Not sure about the partying part, but I'm sure most have also had a drink or two. That being said, "average" differs for each person.
- The way I see it, if you, as a parent, think it's normal to do those things by 21, then that's what you pass on to your children. Of course, we all make our own choices. But, in my opinion, if one is permissive or accepting of things as normal, that's what our children will see as normal, and okay to do. If you tell them from early on that these things are not normal, it gives them a different mindset that hopefully will stay with them as they become teens.
- As a Christian who went to a Christian school, I rebelled everything I had been taught. I tried everything, and took a lot of risks. I saw a lot more people like Kate and Elliot, than virgins, like Ana.
- I think there are a lot more "loners" than people realize. Because they're loners. They don't stand out. But they're there. And that's okay! It's great to be whoever you are!
- I'm not a parent, so take this however you want, but I think it's best if they're there for their kids to help them with whatever choices they make. We all make mistakes, and many of us make them when we're young. We just need to learn from them.
- That's true. My sister made choices that scared me. She and I are totally different with regards to the risks we took as teens. I couldn't imagine doing some of the things she did. And, I wasn't perfect. I did do a few of the things you mentioned. I'm not judging the choices others have made. We all think differently and what's okay for me may not be okay for you. I'm definitely not going to be one of those parents who disowns my child for a choice they make. But, I will let them know what I

think right and wrong are. My ideas of those just may be different from other's.

- The dynamic worked for them. The push-and-pull allowed them to test the boundaries and find a place in the middle (eventually).
- Ana tried to teach him to compromise. She was trying to see how far he'd go.
- I think the timing was off because he was already upset about what just happened at GEH. She didn't need to add to that worry.
- Maybe he was worried that she was still independent, and didn't need him all of the time?
- Good point. Makes me think.
- I think she is a little rebellious. I think she probably got worse as she grew more confident, and more secure.
- He probably had the security issues going on at home, and was worried even more about her safety.
- I think Ana was trying to flirt with Christian. Maybe she was hoping he'd get on the jet ski with her!

Hit the Reset Button

In this excerpt from *Freed* Ana says, "He closes his eyes and shakes his head as if it's a great effort of will. When he opens them again, his eyes are bright with his resolve." Do you think he learned this technique to hold off his emotions from Flynn? What do you think was Christian's "inner dialogue" during this moment?

- Sadly, I think he learned it from Elena. She taught him so much about control on so many levels. Again... sadly.
- Perhaps in this moment he was trying to de-program Elena's thoughts from his head.
- He did this in other instances, if I remember correctly. He had to reset his brain so that he was not being selfish, and thought about Ana's needs instead of his own. I think he wanted to be intimate with Ana as much as she wanted it, but he had to rethink that so that he thought of her

needs of rest and recuperation being more important at this point.

- "Reset his brain." I like that.

Openness, Deception and Privacy

As a relationship evolves, we reveal more and more of ourselves. The more we trust, the more we share. The more comfortable we feel around someone, the more they learn about us. As we followed the evolution of Ana and Christian's relationship, we saw how they stumbled and grew along the way.

Fear of...?

When Christian said, "I keep a lot of sh*t to myself, because in reality, nobody gives a f*ck," do you think Christian was reluctant to be open because he really thought this about people?

- I think he really didn't care what other people thought, for the most part. Only for the people close to him, of which there were very few.
- In his case, people did give a f*ck. That was his problem...he hated anyone sticking their nose in his business...that's why he was so careful about everything and did background checks on anyone who crossed his path.
- He kept many things to himself especially his particular pursuits. But the statement is right. Nobody gives a sh*t about one's problems.
- I keep everything to myself because I don't trust people. I've been stabbed in back so many times; I never open up. I think he feels the same. People only want him for either his looks or his money. Ana wants him for who he is inside, which is why he opens up to her.
- Truer words were never spoken.
- He kept a lot to himself because he didn't trust a lot of people. But isn't that true of most of us?
- Yes, sadly.

Big Lies Little Lies

"Is this one of those times when you want me to lie to protect your delicate emotions?"

Let's talk lies. Big lies, little lies. What are some things Ana and Christian might've lied to each other about? How do you feel about lying?

- I absolutely abhor being lied to. It ruins trust. Don't do it if you don't want it done to you.
- Lying is unacceptable. I know when he lied to her about where the Tess books came from it was a little lie, but it never sat well with me. I wonder if he ever confessed to that lie.
- You should always fess up. That's what I call a white lie. It doesn't really hurt anyone. It's a lie of omission. But I see what you mean. Sometimes you think if someone will lie about one thing, they'll lie about another. He probably eventually told her when they were lying in bed, after one of their romps, I'd imagine. It seems like a good time to come clean about it.
- Yes, he did seem very talkative after sex.
- Hehe!
- Exactly. In *Grey*, after that lie, I kept expecting to see him lie about more things. Bigger things. I guess one thing would be not telling her about Leila. Like you said, a lie of omission. And, we see what problems that lie caused.
- Yes those are the kind of lies that can be hurtful and detrimental to a relationship.
- Lies are a deal-breaker for me.
- Me, too. I can deal with any truth. Just don't lie to me.
- Don't want to be with a liar at all. Been there, done that, and I'm not able to always tell, and I get snookered every time. No more. I didn't even like that Christian evaded telling Ana about Leila. That would've saved a whole lot of grief.

- Ana lied about going out with Jose for drinks that Friday night. Remember, Kate busted her at the dinner with the Greys.
- I don't think she did it to be deceitful. She just wanted to hang out with a friend and clear her mind. Another lie of omission.
- But she knew how Christian would react.
- I only remember Christian's lies, and that always creates problems. Lies, like not telling her about Leila; not telling her everything about his birth mom; and, how he got her the books. Some of them might be small lies. But the truth puts him in a different light, compared to how he'd be seen with his lies. So, telling lies is a no-go for me. I've been in a relationship with little white lies all the time. It breaks you in the end, when you can't trust your loved one.
- Lying through omission is a form of manipulation, to avoid facing something (or telling the truth.)
- I think that's why he lied to her in the beginning. He didn't know if he could trust her. Not yet. He didn't think he was loveable, and I think his lies kept her at arm's reach. He did this with everyone. He was a manipulator, and I'm sure he used lies as part of that. I don't like that part of him, but I think that after he let himself love, and be loved, especially after Ana was hurt by Jack, and was in the coma, he realized how important being honest was in a relationship.
- A lie is a lie! Christian's lies of omission, about being with Elena and Leila. Ana would've been spared a lot of misery if he told her right from the start. And, she may have been safer. He wanted her out of danger. Hmm. By the way, I hate liars. I would rather be alone, than be with a liar.

Tell Me No Secrets

Where do you think Christian got the idea that if he told Ana his secrets that she'd run? Is that just something he made up in his head, or do you think there's a back story we don't know about where he actually opened up, not necessarily that he loved that person but felt comfortable enough to say, and got that reaction? Then, he was so surprised when Ana didn't run.

- I think he and Flynn talked about it - a lot. And, frankly, he SHOULD have been worried to share something like that.
- I get that, and I agree, but maybe it's just me, but those aren't reasons for me to run. And, if he's opening up, it's because he has the notion that the person is ready for that information. I could never turn my back on him had he confessed that to me. I'd feel hurt for him to have to go through such emotions and thoughts. Like Ana, I'd want understanding. Did Flynn encourage to keep it to himself?
- I think Flynn probably suggested that not everyone could handle that kind of news - and I think he'd be right.
- Even the first time I read his confession, I didn't find it as appalling as everyone else seemed to. It seemed to be a natural reason for his actions. It didn't bother me as much as it seemed to bother others. He was opening up to her, and that was a wonderful thing. I don't think he told anyone else, except Flynn. I wondered if he told Elena, and she told him not to tell anyone else because they would judge and hate him. I can't recall if he told Ana, and had never told anyone else what he shared with her. If the listener wanted to truly understand and love him, I don't think they could turn their back on him. He's human like everyone else.
- I think the reason we weren't as appalled is that E.L. James set it up perfectly. When someone sets us up to think it's "the worst thing ever" and our minds go crazy, we're relieved that it's not as bad as we imagined. But if he'd said something to her right away, we would've been shocked.
- To me, it wasn't that big of a deal. Who cares about his background, or why he's doing it? The bigger deal was his sadism, and how he withheld any emotional connection from the women he was f*cking in the

RROP. He also enslaved them, forcing them kneel at his feet, to not move until he returned after God-knows-how-long. Making them stay in his apartment the entire weekend, being at his beck and call.

- It was consensual; they wanted him to control them. It was a game. A play. Even if it was an act, they both believed, at the time, that it was real.
- That's why I think the distinction of "why" is important. If it was just a game, then it's one thing. But if the underlying reason is to act out his anger and punish his mother, then it's no longer a game.
- I just wanted to write the same - you read my mind. For the submissive, it was a kind of role play, but for him, well, he had his reasons.
- Elena probably knew the reason and used it to control him. She probably made him afraid to reveal the reason to anyone. Plus, she wanted to be the only who knew the truth.
- I agree that Elena probably encouraged this reaction in him, but honestly, he felt like he was basically admitting that he was sexually attracted to his mother, or at least to women who looked like his mother. That, alone, is enough to cause him to wonder if any woman could handle the news.
- Interesting point. Oedipus. Hamlet, too.
- What I think is interesting is how Grace also had the same physical appearance (dark hair, etc.). What is *that* saying?
- Grace looked like Ana? I don't recall that.
- I don't think that was an accident on E.L. James's part. I think she intended for the "Madonna/whore" comparison between the two mothers.
- Perhaps, but he didn't exactly have a say in who adopted him.
- I'm not saying that. I'm talking about how it influenced Christian's perception of the kind of women he chose. On one hand, they looked like his birth mother, so he treated them that way, on the other, they looked like Grace.

- I still don't see the connection. I don't think every brunette looked like his mother. They had to be small of build, with long straight hair. And young. I really do not think Christian looked at Grace and thought of his birth mother.
- Grace had long, dark hair. In the books, Ana's hair was wayward, and not straight at all.
- I really think he viewed Grace as his savior, almost with reverence, and not sexually, in any way, whatsoever.
- As I said - Madonna/Whore. He wanted a woman like Grace - but he also wanted his mother's love.
- I'm not sure how horrible it is to be attracted to someone who looks like your mother, or your father. Isn't there an old saying about a woman marrying a man who reminds them of their father, or something like that? I think the terrible part is that he felt like he needed to punish them, almost as surrogates for the mother who did him wrong.
- I didn't say it was horrible. I just said it explains Christian's choice of women. And that E.L. James made them similar in appearance to make that point.
- It was the connection between the two the messed with his head. It blurred lines for him. But truly I don't believe it was quite that connection. I thought maybe also deep down inside he wanted to be loved and accepted by his mother, which is why he was attracted to the pale skinned brunettes.
- Well there's something in it. He wanted his submissives to look like his mother; to punish them. And he was also jealous of his natural mother, seeing her with the pimp and other men. I doubt she was hiding her liaisons. And I'm sure their apartment was small.
- I think, in Christian's mind, he had trepidation about his BDSM life and therefore thought others would too.
- Christian never thinks positively about *any* situation. You really get that loud and clear in *Grey*! He's so full of self-doubt that it truly is heart-breaking. He may have, in the past, confided in previous subs and they went screaming for the hills. Also, Ana is so naive and

innocent, that he had convinced himself that there was no way she was ever going to take this information about himself and ever be okay with it. It also goes back to him feeling that he doesn't deserve to be loved. He really didn't understand how much Ana loved him unconditionally. Truly sad.

- Ana reacted the way she did because she saw how broken he was. The other submissives didn't see that, only his money.
- Let's not forget, Ana left - and it devastated him. And she left because of how he hit her with the belt. The news about WHY he wanted to hit her with the belt was much worse (in my opinion). He had every right to be afraid. (I also think he was afraid that he'd still desire to hit her - and that would be the double-whammy for her to leave and never take him back).
- Yeah, I think it was in his head. He always had negative thoughts about himself. He thought of himself as a monster, and thought that if Ana knew, she'd leave.
- If you're talking about when he finally tells Ana: "I like to whip brown hair girls because they remind me of the crack whore," yes; I think this comment would make some people freak out. If I was Ana, it would shock me but I don't think I'd stop loving him. I do agree that Elena used it as a way to keep him close to her, which is pretty messed up. I do think he did probably open up to someone to a degree, and they let him down.
- I think if he'd told her in the first book, it would've been very different from the second one.
- I think she would've flipped out and never come back. It's a big moment for both of them.

Stalking?

Let's talk stalking!
Do you think Christian was stalking Ana when:
- he had the background check done?
- he visited her at Clayton's?
- he did a "run-by?"

Have you done any of these things - or something similar? Google search, perhaps? Drive-by?

- Technically, each of those are signs of a (potential) stalker. But that doesn't mean it's uncommon. Many of us (I'm sure) have tried to choreograph another meeting, either stopping by their favorite hangout or where they work. The difference with *FSOG* was Christian's access to more information than the average person.
- I think with a man in the same position as Christian Grey, any woman he had become interested in would totally be checked out, for obvious reasons. However, if the question is, did he go beyond the norm? I'd have to say yes, and no. Yes, because these were emotions that were so foreign to him, it was like waves crashing in on him. No, because regular "normal" people just don't behave that way.
- Yes, in my opinion he was stalking Ana. I wonder if he did this to his previous subs. But, I think he was more than seriously interested in her. Maybe didn't even realize this himself; he wanted to know everything about her.
Ana also found that he was stalking.
- No, it's the way he works. He's a public figure, and rich. He has to protect himself.
- No, I don't think so. He was really interested in her, and wanted to see her again. He probably does a lot of background checks. He couldn't stay away from her, and had to see her, so went to her work, just to do so. He's very controlling, but that is just his way. I wouldn't really say he was stalking her. At times, it might appear that he was, but that was just his way. I don't think he means to be stalking, though to some, it may seem that way.
- Myself, I confess to doing an online search about someone I'm interested in. I look on FB and Linkedin, for sure. Stalking, or research? I do usually confess to it, when I meet them. I have also been known to do a D-B (drive-by). It's fun!

- Christian was new to feelings. He had no real sphere of reference to know what was normal behavior, and what wasn't. A man in his position, first of all, has to be careful. On the flip side though, a "normal" guy who hasn't been emotionally damaged will go up to a girl, chat her up, ask her out. Christian really didn't seem to realize that's the normal thing to do. He's so ingrained in his behavior, he probably didn't realize that showing up where she works, running by her apartment, etc., wasn't necessarily the right thing to do. In his own way, he was just showing he cared.

- Background check, no - it's normal to Google search people, and he does need to protect himself. The running is a bit stalkerish, but sometimes I drive by my sister's house, which is just a block or two out of the way, to make sure all is well. And, there is no intent like you need for criminal stalking. Clayton's crosses the line a bit, as much as I love it. Obviously, out of his way to go there, by a couple hours, and he didn't need anything. In real life, I might be a bit freaked out. But, it's part of the fun of the story.

- For the Clayton's scene, did anyone else notice that he was just standing there between the aisles? Like, he knew she'd be passing by there, or something? My 12-year-old noticed that, and thought it was creepy.

- I agree that the way he stood there was creepy. But not so much that he was there. I remember when I was in high school, I worked at a store in the mall, and had boys stop by to see me. Not creepy in the least! I loved it. Okay, maybe not the time two came at once.

- As odd as it may seem, I thought the way he just *had* to see her again (going to Clayton's), was endearing. He couldn't get her out of his head, or from under his skin. I kind of thought that he was 'stuck in his shoes' and not able to approach her, just hoping she'd walk by. So boyishly charming, in a deviated kind of way, what with the cable ties, masking tape and rope.

- While I don't think the run-by, or background check, or even showing up at Claytons was all that unusually stalker-ish, I DO think that tracking her phone, and showing up at the bar WAS creepy! Useful and helpful, but creepy!

- That was so bossy of him! When he called her after she hung up and said, "Stay there I'm coming to get you," in a creepy in a way. But also hot!
- As he said, "I'm used to getting my own way," and he "likes to control all things."
- Sorry, but to me, he wasn't stalking her. There was just something about her that called to him, and like I've already mentioned, he is seriously rich, so he has to take precautions like background checks, and even more with his lifestyle. But, he knew that there was something special about Ana. He wasn't stalking, he just couldn't keep away from her.
- He was mesmerized and drawn to her. It wasn't stalking.
- I mean, let's admit it, we are not going to call the police any time soon if Christian was stalking us. I mean, just look at him. With my luck, I'd have to stalk him, and he'd call the police, and off to jail, in the wrong person's handcuffs, and not a red room in sight. Happens to me all the time. I know all the officers by their first name, and I have my own cell, but they still refuse to paint it red, and leave me the handcuffs. I've even asked to be tazered for a kick start, but they just laughed all the way down the corridor, bastards.
- My ex-husband came to my work once, when I was out at lunch, and he waited for me to get back. I almost got fired for it. However, I think that because Christian purchased something, it was cool. Even though he really came to see Ana. I don't think he was stalking her. At least not until he knew where she was, when she was drunk. I think that was stalking.
- I think Christian has stalker tendencies. He wants what he wants when he wants it. Just my impression...and yes, I've been stalked, but didn't know it until after-the-fact. It was an ex-boyfriend who was keeping tabs on my comings and goings with the person I currently was dating. It didn't freak me out. I ended up marrying the stalker, and was with him for 25 years. Ended.

- Uh, yeah. In the movie, it's endearing. In real life, not so much. Where I work, they'd have to get past security, and I'd be appalled if that were to happen. I keep my professional and personal lives separate, and each one is sacred.
- I'd love for him to come where I work. I wouldn't mind measuring him for a tux. I'd spend extra time to measure every inch of his body.
- I think it's different if someone works in a private office, or a public place. After that, it depends on the relationship and what they do there. In this case, they both had an interest in each other, and he bought stuff. He created an opportunity, instead of the "following her around" type stalking. But, that also assumes you're in the same area. So, definitely a but fuzzy on this, if it was real life.
- No I have not. I don't think Christian purposely meant to be stalking, though he can be that way. He needed an excuse to see her again.
- He desperately wanted to see her again. It made me laugh, because as he said himself he normally did not visit those places. I don't think it was necessarily stalking, since he really saw Ana (and didn't just watch from afar).
- This sort of happened to me...before I met hubby. I was fairly new in town (months!), and was starting to make friends. One of the girls I became friendly with, was dating a guy from my home town (I didn't know him!), and he was also new in town. He was a nice guy, and we were chatting. Several days later, I was working in the local department store, and he shows up, and we were making very small talk (really!). Several days after that, I saw the girl he was dating, and naively told her that her boyfriend was at the store and we chatted. Very quickly, I became public enemy number one because she thought I was trying to steal her boyfriend away from her. I mean, he was nice, but really not my type at all.

So You're a Sadist?

In the book Christian lies to Anastasia about his true self when she asks him if he's a sadist and he replies, 'I'm a Dominant." Okay, it was a lie by omission and we know he wanted her more than anything. He didn't want to risk losing her when he nearly had her. But, was it acceptable? Would you lie for your own gain?

- Everyone does at some point. That's been my experience anyway.
- I don't think it was acceptable to lie. In Christian's case though, he was so scared that if he told the truth, Ana would run for the hills, and he really wanted her...bad. So, he told her what he thought she wanted to hear and what would make her stay. Of course, we all know that only he thought of himself as a sadist, which Flynn pointed out to him many times, that he wasn't. I'm not sure if I wouldn't have lied about something like that if losing something/someone was at stake. Interesting dilemma.
- I abhor lying. Though in his case, timing is everything and it wasn't the right time to tell her.
- I do give him props for coming clean with her right before the proposal though.
- I don't think he was lying for gain, though it was lying, nevertheless. He wanted her so badly, he didn't want to risk losing her at that point.
- Isn't the terminology "Dominant" a more progressive way of expressing the person, as opposed to a "Sadist?" I think of the latter as being a tad judgmental and outdated. But, I don't know for sure. My frame of reference comes from the Marquis de Sade. I think he should have acknowledged that some call the person a sadist, but that he prefers to use Dominant. And, before she freaked out, he should have talked a little about it. But, at that point in getting to know Ana, he wasn't a great communicator.

- Actually, I think there is a big distinction between being a Dominant and a sadist. Certainly, not all Dominants aren't sadists. What does everyone else think?
- You're right, for the both of them "language" was a barrier. He was used to his subs knowing or "appreciating" what he was about, while Ana was trying to understand. Sex, in itself, was all new to her...and to be taken into a room with all these strange contraptions, he had to have noticed the "shock and awe" in Ana that made her ask that question.
- Didn't Flynn use the terminology sexual sadist, setting it aside as different than a sadist?
- He didn't lie, per se. He was a Dom; that was the truth. He was a sexual sadist, which is different.
- I don't fault him for lying. He just said what he thought he needed to, at the time, not wanting to scare her off. Dominant was bad enough, I guess. After all, she saw all of his "play things" as she walked through the room. She didn't leave, as he said she could, if it was all too much for her.

Not Keeping Your Word

Let's talk "Cocktailgate" – when Ana went out with Kate instead of staying at home while Christian was out of town. Christian was furious, telling Ana, "Because you went back on your word, and you defied me, putting yourself at unnecessary risk." She couldn't believe he said she "went back on her word" and, instead, thought he was overreacting. Do you think Christian was overreacting? How would you have felt, if you were him? How do you feel about Ana "changing her mind" without telling him?

- This whole situation could've been handled so differently. They both had so much to learn about each other, and I think that's the crux of the problem. Ana knew she'd piss Christian off by going out, but she didn't seem to care, knowing that he'd punish her...yet, she went ahead and ignored his instruction. Having said that, Kate has her share of blame in this, too. She shouldn't have pushed and cajoled Ana into going out, but she did, and that had so much to do with Ana changing her mind. As for Christian, he should've had Prescott give her phone to Ana so he could talk to her. The fact that he didn't, really bugged me. It was like he was setting Ana up for punishment...not cool. Again, they both needed to grow up!

- I also think Ana was a bit too easily manipulated by others. She was learning to stand up to Christian, but still had challenges with asserting herself with Kate.

- With all that he worried about, as a public figure, in general, he also worried about her. Add in some lunatic making trouble, and the fact that he never lets her know the real truth about all the dangers around her - if he did, she would've understood why she needed to be careful and act accordingly. And, how about the fact that she is, what, 22-23? So, how much does he expect her to read his mind? He keeps expecting her to act like she's like 35.

- I also think that if he'd given her a bit more information regarding what was going on, it would've helped her make the right decision, and at least to be more careful and alert.

- Sadly, Christian incorrectly believed that he was protecting Ana, by keeping things from her. He learned VERY quickly that the silent approach only causes more problems. It comes down to learning how to communicate. That was something they had trouble with from the very beginning. One would hope that as time goes on, they worked on that big time, not just for their sakes, but for the sake of their two young children!

- He should start trusting and share more with his wife. Poor girl, always being in the dark about so much.

- Ana should've known better. If she was in a normal relationship with a normal man, maybe it would've been okay. But Christian isn't normal. He's over-protective and controlling, and fifty shades of f*cked-up. Besides, she *promised*. She made a commitment. As soon as Kate came around she "changed her mind." Not cool.

- I also think that making a promise to someone and not doing everything you can to keep it is very close to a lie.
- Absolutely. She didn't even try to keep her commitment; so yes, she basically lied.
- You are so right. What the hell? A drink in a bar vs your own house? They could be more intimate and discuss all kinds of things at home. Plus, like you all said, she made a promise. To me, that is telling a lie.
- Yes, and no, to Christian overreacting! The "yes" part is that Ana changed her mind to staying at home. Kate talked *her* into going out! The fact that Kate did that saved both of them from being kidnapped by Jack, when he showed up at Christian's apartment! The "no" part: I think Christian should've realized that when he found out that Jack was at their apartment, and Ana and Kate weren't there, in harm's way, and Jack doing something bad to them! Okay, since they weren't at the apartment, he should've been a little relieved that Jack didn't get a chance to do anything to them!
- Yes, she needed a reminder about who she was dealing with (control freak Christian). Yet, in a way, Kate saved Ana, which was a relief. I'm confused what to think now. I still think Christian should have shared more information.

It's Off to Work I Go

When Ana and Christian got back from their honeymoon, Christian tried to keep her from going back to work. Ana argued, "How can you expect me to run the business if I'm never there?" Then Christian stopped and changed the subject mid-discussion. Why do you think he changed the subject, and didn't elaborate on what he was thinking or feeling in this moment? I think if he would've expressed himself, it could've been another tiny moment of bonding and understanding for them.

- Christian was still trying to get used to being with an intelligent woman who challenged him. He probably

319

stopped because he realized she was right, which shocked him.

- The way Ana explained it, there must have been something that made him not want to comment!
- I love when arguments are "broken" in this way - with something kind of sweet and disarming.
- True. It takes someone with a lot of inner strength to gracefully bow out of a situation when you're wrong.
- This was a matter of picking your battles carefully. Christian knew how much Ana loved her work. The selfish part of him wanted her with him, but he also knew that it wasn't a battle he was going to win. I also think that there was a part of him that was proud to have a woman who wanted to succeed, and he didn't want to stand in her way.

In Your Pocket

After Ana told Christian about Blip and he ran off, she got tempted and read the emails and texts on his Blackberry. When is it "okay" to read your mate's text messages and/or emails? Have you done it? Were you glad? Or, did you regret it? How about the other way around? Have you had anyone read yours? What was your reaction?

- I wouldn't be in a relationship where I couldn't read his texts, and I'd fully allow him to read mine. Transparency is the key to trust. Without it, the relationship won't last.
- I read my hubby's texts about two years ago. I'm glad I did. It changed things for us, and made me realize that I needed to be a better wife. It wasn't anything serious, but serious enough for me to take action. We've had many heart to hearts since then, and I'm glad I checked his phone that day. And, I'd do it again. I don't care if he checks my phone. If there is something on our phones that we'd be embarrassed about, it shouldn't have ever been sent.
- I think it's important to be completely open in a relationship.

- I've read them - both my husband's, and my son's. With my husband, it was a complicated situation, but I don't regret it. With my son, it's a learning process for him to understand the responsibility of having a phone, so I do it to teach him about his etiquette, and how things can affect him.
- I think it's a two-sided issue. If one partner doesn't want the other to read their emails or texts, then there's an issue. But I also think if a partner wants to read their partner's emails and texts, it's also an issue. There has to be trust.
- Trust is only created by full disclosure, openness and transparency, and only built over time. Re-building trust takes even longer, and sometimes it's broken beyond repair. If one partner isn't willing to open up and share everything, they shouldn't be in a relationship.
- Neither should read the other's phone. The only exception would be if one person couldn't take care of themselves.
- I can say that although I would never ever cheat, I would also never ever want to be with someone who wanted to spy on me that way. I like my privacy - probably why I'm single. I'm also transparent - but want to choose what and when I tell someone something.

- I once accidentally read hubby's messages, and he was super-pissed. After that, I never did it again. I'm not sure if he extends the same courtesy to me. I've "almost" caught him eyeing my phone. Of course, he denies it.
- I've read my husband's after I had a disagreement with his parents. Of course, they said all the things I thought they would say about me (because I put my foot down about something I felt was wrong.) But, other than that time, I've never checked his phone.
- I think there should be some boundaries. If there is a trust issue to the point that you have to check on a partner's phone, then something may not be right. I don't like it if my boyfriend reads my group texts with my girls

because there are private issues they talk about, and I wouldn't want anyone else to see.

Tell Me No Secrets

Ana says she wants to know everything - everything - related to what's going on with the security and investigations. But do you really think she does? Would you?

- She should. I would. You can't be prepared, if you're not informed.
- Christian talks about keeping her in a cage. The only way she can be free is if he shares everything with her. Everything. And yes, I would want to know it all, good or bad.
- I believe she does. I would also. He can't just give her the luxurious parts of his life. These things that are happening are, unfortunately, also part of his world. He made her a part of his world, so it's necessary for him to provide her with the proper information, especially if it's something that could be detrimental to her. If she knows what's going on, then she can be proactive about it.
- I think it's a case of "be careful what you ask for." She might want to know more - but not everything.
- For example?
- It's like the "making sausage" analogy. Example: Does she want to know Hyde's experience with weapons? His every move? His knowledge of bomb-making? I think it could become very overwhelming.
- The more she knows, the less likely it will be that she underestimates him.
- It's not necessarily that she wants to know all the details, in that sense. It's that she wants him to be forthcoming with information that pertains to her and his well-being. As the conversation is happening, she could say "I don't care for that information. Tell me the important things." I think it's necessary to know exactly how dangerous Hyde is, and the extent of his background knowledge. It may seem like it, but Ana doesn't intimidate easily - she just requires some time to process.

- Yes. And yes. How can she know how, or when to protect herself, if she's constantly in the dark?
- I think, yes. He should give her a bit more information about things regarding her safety; that way, she'd be more alert, and a bit less careless, and accept that the security team had to be with her for a good reason.
- Yes - I really believe that she does want to know. It would help her set boundaries for herself and help her act appropriately. Without them, she does things like going out with Kate, when she doesn't have all the information, then Christian comes home and tortures the hell out of her.
- Yes, if I'm in danger, I should know what it is, so that I can take precautions of my own, with my own brain. She would've been even safer if Christian would've told her, from the start, about Leila, and what they found in Jack's van.
- I think Ana just didn't want to be left in the dark about things going on. I'm also like that.
- To be informed is knowledge. Maybe things would have played out differently if Christian was honest and upfront with his information. He said he didn't tell her to protect her. How is that protecting her? Kate knew more than Ana did, and she's married to the Stalking, Megalomaniac CEO, Control Freak.

Spill It!

More examples of Christian not being fully open with Ana with regards to his people interviewing Hyde's assistants and the note Hyde left in the van. How frustrating for her! Would you have handled that situation differently than she did? Do you think she was right to wait for Christian to open up, instead of badgering him about it?

- I think it can be difficult to know when to push - and know when you're nagging.
- I'm the kind of person who asks when something seems off or wrong. If you don't give me that feeling, I probably won't ask. If I do, just like "hear anything new

on..." If someone tells me, "No," I drop it. Tell me yes, and that's a whole different story, I'll go on and on with it.

- Since this had so much to do with Ana, Christian should've been much, much more open with her, and told her everything. Hiding information only comes back to bite him in his gorgeous ass!
- You can only badger a man so much before he tells you to F--- off.
- The main thing for Ana to remember is - if she doesn't say anything, she needs to be careful not to "hold it in" and resent him. That can lead to becoming passive-aggressive, which is a lot more damaging than speaking up.
- I've been like that in the past.
- I guess she was trying to make him trust her more and be patient, but he's so stubborn when it comes to sharing with her. It really pisses me off that she's always in the dark regarding what's happening around them.

Christian's Mothers

By all accounts, Christian two "mothers" portrayed two extremes of parenting. Ella, the crack-addicted prostitute who neglected (if not abused) her son, and Grace, the epitome of the qualities her name suggests: elegance, beauty, kindness and generosity.

Suicide or Overdose?

In the chapter where Christian tells Ana that his mother killed herself, I first thought it was an overdose. But as I read it again, it sounds like deliberate suicide. What are your thoughts about that?

- That part always confuses me, but I think she killed herself and that's why he couldn't bring himself to forgive her. She didn't protect him when he was getting hit. And, she also killed herself and left him alone!
- Exactly. If it was deliberate, she has no excuse for not finding him another home. (Not that she had any excuse to keep him in the first place).
- You're totally right!
- Maybe it's all speculation; perhaps they don't really know?
- I would think she killed herself because somehow she knew that she couldn't give Christian a better life. And, he was angry that she took the easy way out.
- That fits what I think, too.
- Were there passages in the book that led you to believe it was suicide?
- When Christian said she "killed herself."
- I don't think she did commit suicide as we traditionally think. I had a college roommate who still smokes cigarettes, and I often remark that she is trying to kill herself. I look at Christian's comment the same way. Call me a tree-hugging softie. I don't have personal experience with addiction, but have counseled in the arena of sexuality education. Often, drugs and alcohol are part of the problem when it comes to unintended

pregnancies. Addiction is a very, very difficult situation. Drugs are often laced with other foreign elements and it's not as easy to dose the same amount that one has been told is safe. Not sure if I'm being clear. I have a lot of compassion for situations, and people in this situation. I'd say it was an overdose.

- I don't think she committed suicide. I think she was so addicted to crack that she simply OD'd. I think when Christian said that "she killed herself," it was more about her losing control to the point of where she died by letting the drugs control her.
- She overdosed to free herself from the pain and guilt of her miserable life. She knew "Maggot" would be better off without her.
- I always felt that he'd always feel she killed herself because he hated her so much for not protecting him.
- I always thought it was an accidental overdose.
- I think it was accidental, but suicide wouldn't surprise me because she was going through a lot. Mostly her fault, but still going through a lot.
- It must have been accidental as I cannot imagine any mother, no matter her condition, leaving a 4-year old child an orphan.
- I can't imagine anything she did in regard to Christian.
- I think she was so stoned most of the time, that she didn't realize what she was going through. Just pop another pill, instead of dealing with her problems. Accidental all the way.
- I think it was an accident. Sometimes she couldn't feed Christian. She couldn't take care of him, so who knows?
- I always thought she was murdered by her pimp.
- No, He came in and found her. He called her a f*cked up bitch. He kicked Christian, made one call, then left. He called the police because they came soon after. So sad!!
- I completely think it was an accident. But it was sure to happen eventually!

- I always assumed it was accidental because not all of Christian's memories of her were awful; just most of them.
- Well if it was suicide, it ended up being the best thing for Christian. She wasn't equipped to raise him and should have realized it a lot sooner.
- I classify it like they do some murders, as "reckless disregard for human life." She didn't care if she lived or died.
- I believe she was so drug addicted that she took too much of something. I think she got to a point in her life that she really didn't care about anything more than getting her next fix. She had no regard for Christian and his needs. She was completely fixated on her addiction, and paid no attention to what, or how much she was taking.
- She loved him. I don't think she'd have done it on purpose.
- She may have loved him, but I'll never forgive her for calling little Christian "Maggot."

Is Suicide Selfish?

Christian's mother also committed suicide when he was 4 years old scarring him for life. I don't want to upset you with this post. I never really considered it, but I heard it so many times, people saying suicide is a selfish action. I would love to hear your thoughts about this. Again, I apologize that this is not a lighthearted post.

- Like Christian, it's my family that prevents me from suicide, because they don't deserve to suffer. Yet, sometimes, when you suffer too much, it seems to be the answer to your problems.
- Your comment strikes right into my heart. I feel exactly the same. I knew some people for which it was the only escape. They suffered greatly, and even the family was relieved that the person was out of his misery. But, I agree having a family can be a huge reason for not going through with it.

- When I was young I came close to committing suicide many times. The one thing that also stopped me is the love from the people around me. Unfortunately, many people fail to see that love.
- Its not selfish, I know, I don't want to go into details, but I just KNOW. It takes a lot to break a person completely to cause them to no longer want to live. It can be drugs, family problems, or life in general. It isn't always the person's 'fault' that they feel this way. It can creep up on you without you knowing, and that's when no one else sees it, unless they are really looking. It's not a selfish act. In some cases, it's not even a cry for help its…an escape from the pain.
- To tell the truth, about three years ago, I was considering it because of this terrible ongoing noise in my head 24/7 – a condition called Tinnitus. I panicked and thought, *How am I ever going to deal with this*? I somehow got used to it.
- Maybe you don't actually want to die, but just rest and escape from the pain. When I am in pain, I like to sleep a lot just to forget.
- I will say one thing about my experience of this, sometimes a total stranger walking a dog in the early hours of the morning is suddenly the light that guides you back.
- I was close to suicide one or two times in my life... And I often commit scarification in the past...
- The same thing happens with drug addiction. It's proven that the lack of love causes the person to dive more deeply into the addiction. Love helps in the rehabilitation process. Normally, people who commit suicide are not selfish simply because they're doing it for their own benefit. It's more because there is no one that would care. In their state of mind, by doing it, they shouldn't be hurting anybody. When you don't commit suicide, or stop yourself from doing it, that's because you see the support and love around you.
- I do believe that Christian's mum was too far gone with the drugs. It's very hard to think straight with that. Did

she love Christian? She probably did, but she didn't feel worth it. She didn't love herself. She didn't know what giving love or receiving love was. I do believe it was an overdose that caused her to die, and if she committed suicide, if was just a sense of giving up. But I don't think she did kill herself, as the only thing that keep her alive was that child. But the fact that she felt impotent to protect him also gave her a lot of pain, she felt trapped in a hole.

- Having a child (or someone to love) can eventually prevent you from doing it. I knew someone who was manic-depressive, and it was his only escape, after trying all sorts of treatments and medications. His wife understood and was relieved for him too.

- But it's also very sad that support and love do not always help.

- Yes, Ella did overdose. Though, I don't think it was revealed whether it was accidental or intentional.

- I think when many people get to the point of committing suicide they don't really think of others. Not because they don't care; they're just not able to. They could possibly be so mentally far-gone, that they can't think logically.

- Yes; I think when you are that far-gone, there's just nothing on your mind anymore.

- I've tried it in the past. I didn't actually want to die, I just needed help to survive my days with pain and suffering.

- If a person is just considering it, they may be able to think logically.

- Very true. It usually gets to a point where all they can think of is the pain or sadness. Nothing, and no one else matters, just the relief from the pain. I think Christian's mum had enough of the way she was living, and she knew he'd be looked after better if she were gone. So, in her case, doing it was not selfish at all.

- That's just it; you don't want to die, but you don't want to feel any pain and suffering anymore.

- You are normally not in the right state of mind, when you make such a decision. The driver can be depression, and this leads to alcohol and drug addiction, and all this leads to destruction. Nobody just makes a decision, saying "hey, I will end my life." It's always how a situation develops.
- When times were hard, I tried tranquillizers. They took away the rough edges, but I didn't feel emotions anymore. No joy, no sadness, just one dull emotionless feeling.
- When you are depressed, you are less likely to be able to solve problems. That's why, when in pain or depressed, people simply give up, and if they don't have support around to remind them that they are loved, or that there is a light at the end of the tunnel, this is when people make such an end. That's why it's very important to make our loved ones know how much we love them. This loving and caring can be the difference in many people's decisions.
- There are always triggers, and if you have ever felt this way, and have stopped yourself, you KNOW what the triggers are, and are, hopefully, able to recognize them again. I do. I read now, to escape.
- You are truly blessed when you have such people surrounding you. I feel so sorry for the ones who don't have them.
- That's why, when people fall into drug addiction and parents decide to ignore them, it gets worse because of the lack of love and support. I just saw a documentary about this. Many kids, these days, are exposed to drugs and many parents turn their backs when they find it hard. Those kids are less likely to make a comeback. They stay in that hole, and in many cases, end up suiciding. Not giving up is the key. No giving up for the person that is thinking of taking their life, but also for the people around them, not giving up on them.
- The people around them need support, too. It's very hard to deal with.

- Yes, of course it is hard, but in many cases people give up. They think that the people committing suicide or, en-route to it, are being selfish, but they don't realize that they just need more attention and love.
- So true. Nowadays, I see so many kids having to figure it out on their own, with their parents working, etc.
- So many teens these days kill themselves because they feel depressed and bullied. It all comes to lack of love. 80% of those cases show that the parents admit they had no clue their kids were suffering. Why? Because the parents were too busy. Oh, they're teenagers; that will pass, etc. Then, it's too late when they realize what's going on. I've seen a lot of people also overcome depression, and it's thanks to the support of the loved ones.
- I cherish the days when I came home from school, and my mum was always there with a cup of tea and listening ears.
- I do believe Christian hated his mum because he felt that she didn't love him and didn't protect him. Even if she didn't mean to kill herself, for her to leave him behind like that...He can't forgive her, but she was also a victim of the circumstances. When he was born, she was probably already in that hole, not able to think straight and able to get out. Drugs can lead to a lot of destruction, and that lack of love at such an age; all the things that he endured thanks to the life his mum provided, I don't blame him for how troubled and angry he was.
- I don't blame him. How can anyone be "normal" when they have to go through this?
- Reading the last chapter of *Grey* put me in a bad, dark place. I didn't enjoy the end; it made me feel really depressed.
- I believe E.L. James wanted us to believe that Emma died of an overdose, which is indirectly a way of committing suicide, not overtly, but maybe covertly.
- Yes, dying slowly...letting go...
- I've had those very thoughts about my son. He'd be better off without me. After my 17-year-old daughter

committed suicide, I went downhill with depression. Every day is a battle for me to live. I have five tumors on my organs, but no way to get medical help because I can't work, due to PTSD. I've been raped, molested, physically and mentally abused. I found out recently that my husband has been having an affair. Some days I really don't want to go on. I don't have real friends or a family that cares anymore. I think they finally gave up on me too.

- Don't ever feel you are alone by talking about it. It helps to put things into perspective. I felt the same as you, that no one would miss me. But one kind word from a total stranger turned it around for me.

- Someone very close to me did. I don't think she was thinking about being selfish. She was so troubled and out of control. I don't know if she meant to, but I think she did. I believe she just couldn't take it anymore. So, now I don't have her. I rarely speak of this, if ever. You don't know what that person is thinking.

- From the outside, these people appear perfectly normal. Many are very good at hiding their troubles behind a smile - I know I am. I understand how you feel, but some people get to a point, as I said, where nothing else matters, just getting rid of the pain, no matter how many friends or family you have as a support. Sometimes, unfortunately, that isn't enough. I'm so sorry for your loss.

- I agree that an overdose is a form of suicide, intentional or not. As far as "selfishness" is concerned, I think some people who commit suicide might be doing it so that they're no longer a burden on other people, making it not selfish at all. I love the new semicolon tattoo trend. Such a powerful message to take a breather and reconsider what's next.

- "A semicolon is used when an author could've chosen to end their sentence, but chose not to. The author is you and the sentence is your life."

- Yes, I love that. I posted an article a few weeks ago, and even told my husband I'd like to get one! I don't have tattoos, but that's one I'd like.

- Me also. I'd get one in a skin color (like Jennifer Lawrence).
- So many insights and heartbreaking tragic comments on the topic!

Space Invaders

If this was your adopted child, would you do as Grace did and allow him his space? Or, would you think well, he is this way because of a horrible past, and it's now my job to help change things? Would you step away and let a 4-year-old do everything for himself? Or, step in and assure him that he was safe with her, that things were different now?

- I think that because of Christian's history, Grace parented from a distance. She wasn't trying to change Christian, but respected his space, even at a young age.
- Grace was an exceptional mother. She respected Christian's space and understood his limits. She didn't force him to speak; she didn't push his boundaries of touch. Should she have? Would it have been better if she had pushed harder? I don't know.
- It was almost like she left him to suffer in his past, alone instead of forcing him out of it. There are ways to ease into it.
- I, unfortunately, see kids like every day at my school. It breaks my heart hearing that a four-year-old, a baby still, fixed a bowl of cereal for dinner and sat down to watch television – by themselves! Grace was a good mother, but I do think she should have been a bit more involved in getting Christian to talk and slowly showing him loving touches. I realize he was scared, and who wouldn't be, but I just think other things could've been done. Just my opinion.
- I'm sure Grace hired the best child psychologists available and followed their guidance.
- I'm sure. And I do hope that they sought out other opinions from other therapists. She probably didn't rely on just one.

- Given that she was a pediatrician, I suspect she had both knowledge and experience of her own, too.
- I know that there are all these studies and methods that are developed to help, but I feel like it's so broad and that sometimes a mother has to do what fits the child best even if it isn't written in some guidelines. I have found that especially applies to educating.
- I think she should've been more physical with him. Slowly. He needed that motherly touch. All kids do. He needed to know that not everyone was there to hurt him. Poor kid.
- I would most definitely step up and show this ever so sweet and loving child that he was safe with me, and that nothing, and no one in the world would hurt him the way Ella, and the pimp did.
- I think she did right. I'm sure she let him know that she cared for him. You have to give them space, and they will eventually come to you. You parent, you love, you protect all from a distance. Push too hard, and they will run, or hide deeper within their own mind.
- Well, eventually, as we know, he came around. I actually like that Grace accepted his limitations and loved him anyway. That's unconditional love. I truly believe she did her best.
- He did somewhat. He started talking, and he slowly began to trust she wasn't going to hurt him. It took Ana to completely change him, when he finally let her hug him.
- I'd give him his space but he'd definitely know that I am his mother blood or not and I will be there and protect him. He'd know the unconditional love that is around him. I know it is hard to deal with adopted children that has a dark past. My aunt raised three girls and it was and still can be a difficult journey. Grace was exactly what he needed. It just took time and Ana for Christian to realize that.
- I think Grace was a good mom. It hurt her to not be able to touch him. I think that it had a lasting effect on both of them.

334

- She was so happy when he finally let her hold him.
- I can't imagine not being able to hold and comfort your child. It must be heartbreaking.
- I can answer this way. I'm not a mom, but I've worked with young children since I was ten. I think what Grace did was appropriate, but I think I would've done more things for him. I would've talked through what I was going to do. For instance, "Christian, I am going to wash your hair now. I want you to know that you are safe with me and that I love you." So, I'd give him space but gradually help him with things.
- I'm not a mother, either, and as I said, I think Grace did her best. I can imagine how many times she tried all of those techniques and had him go screaming and pitching a fit and running away from her, and how devastating that must have been to her. Remember, Christian has will of iron, and if he wasn't going to do something he wouldn't do it.
- I'm thinking that they already tried everything to help him. And hired the best professionals. But he didn't open up, so I guess they just took the best of him and showered him with love. By the way, I am a mother. I think mothers will always do everything in their power to help their children. Besides, we don't have many facts about his childhood.
- I'd give him some space, but I'd do any and everything to let him know he is safe and loved. I think Grace and Carrick did well with him. Things got a little better when Mia came along and he started speaking. Mia was someone who protected him from his past life.
- I think that a lot of people don't respond to formality. Eventually, people learn that if they act or react a certain way, they can draw certain reactions from people. They manipulate the situation to stay comfortable, so to speak. I think that Ana approached Christian the way Grace should have approached him. Ana had a great push and pull method, five steps forward two steps back, but always making progress. That's how I would've done it as his mother. I respect Grace's way and I don't think she furthered his damage, but she didn't push him to work on

it. I think she wanted so much to be accepted by him and for him not to lose trust in her, and in pushing him, there would have been short instances where Christian would've probably expressed negativity towards her, I don't think Grace could've handled that.

Shift in Perspective

In *Freed*, when Christian and Grace are talking, he says to his mother, "But seeing her finally put it all in perspective for me. You know...with the child. For the first time I felt... What we did... it was wrong." Grace corrects him and says, "What she did, darling..."

Do you think that Grace had forgiven Christian for his deception, at this point?

- I'm not sure she ever blamed Christian for what happened - just for keeping it from her. But, in the big picture - would many 15-year-olds tell their parents? Especially in a situation like Christian's - where he was enjoying it?
- No, but I'm sure he felt that she blamed him. He always thought the worst about himself. I'm sure she felt that she needed to remind him that it wasn't his fault. After all, do we blame kids who are molested? No. And, in my mind, he was molested by Elena. If he was enjoying the situation, I don't think he would've told anyone. But if he had felt at any time that it was wrong, I'd hope he'd speak up. I think he was a bit scared of Elena too. Scared of losing her, and of her punishing him, if he told. I wonder what she threatened him with, if he told. Or, did she even need that threat to keep him in line?
- I'm sure she "dominated" him in a number of ways, including both emotional and physical abuse.
- I think Grace is one of those mothers who is seriously pissed in the moment, but she truly, truly loves all of her children no matter what. She also knew that Elena had such undue influence over Christian that she really

couldn't totally fault him for what happened. Again, unconditional love is a very powerful thing!

Role Models

Ana talks about how Grace and Carrick are exemplary parents. Do you think they were? What about their not knowing that something was up with Christian for all those years when he was with Elena? Are there any other mistakes you think they made with regards to raising Christian?

- I do think they were exemplary. I don't blame them for not knowing what was happening. But, then again, I'm not a parent.
- I do believe they were exemplary parents. They adopted a little boy who was so damaged, in so many ways. They were patient with him, and let him come out of himself, as much as he could, without any pressure. He seemed to be doing okay, but then puberty hit and his hormones kicked in and screwed him up all over again. He was so messed up that he didn't feel he could relate to his family on any level. They had no way of really knowing how to deal with his pain...but really, what parent does?
- I don't think they were "exemplary parents." If they were, Christian wouldn't have had so many childhood issues as a grown man. They should have been more prepared to handle a difficult child, or they should never have adopted him. They may have loved him, but they made a lot of mistakes.
- I suspect that Grace and Carrick were within a hair of sending him off to military school; he was that out of control. Then Elena happened and things shifted dramatically, it's a shame they didn't scratch their heads and wonder what the change was all about. I do think they should've talked to him more and made themselves more available to him, rather than focus on their high powered careers. It might've prevented so much crap from happening when he was an adult.

Are You My Mother?

"It's from a kid's book. Christ. The Colliers had it. It was called...*Are You My Mother?* Sh*t." His eyes widen. "I loved that book."

Do you think it was appropriate for that particular book to be read to a child who just lost his mother? Do you think Ana and/or Christian will read that book to their children?

- I don't think it was appropriate. That is like pouring salt in the wound. I doubt they will read it to their kids. That would bring back bad memories for Christian.
- I don't know that it was inappropriate. Christian really seemed to love that book, maybe because someone was actually taking time to sit and read it to him. I think that meant a lot to him, much more than the content of the story. I think before Hyde perverted the story and used "Baby Bird" to taunt Christian, he might've read it to his kids, but not now and not ever.
- I think was an insensitive choice for an orphaned or adopted child. I can't see him reading that to his kids.
- It's interesting you see him as an orphan; and, I suppose in a very real way he was. Even if his biological father is alive, unless he can find out who he was, it's pretty much the same thing.
- I wouldn't agree on that specific book. It was very poor judgment. She did it with good intentions, and I don't think she ever thought of how bad it was for Christian. She just wanted to read to him.

No Means No

Ana and Christian argued about naming their daughter after his mother Ella, (the woman he called the "crack whore.") Whose side do you understand more in this discussion?

- I'm on Ana's side, here.

- I'm on Christian's side. He doesn't want to be reminded of that time in his life, even though he accepts it, and now sees it as an adult instead of a scared and abused child.
- Christian. I feel like I was tarnishing my child. Why honor somebody he thought neglected him and allowed him to be abused.? Why not honor the mother who loved him and raised him?
- Christian's side. Ana shouldn't have pushed the issue.
- Christian. Why would he name an innocent child after the woman who didn't protect him, and allowed her pimp to physically abuse him? If they were to name their daughter after her, Christian would have a daily reminder of his horrific childhood. I totally take his side on this.

Motherly Love

Ana repeatedly tries to get Christian to admit his love for his birth mother. Do you think a child is obligated to love his or her parent?

- I think a child would naturally feel love towards his/her parents, and the parents would feel love towards their kids. Unless, under some bizarre circumstances, they would feel otherwise.
- So, there are cases where a child won't be able to love his or her parent?
- Abuse cases, maybe.
- Do you think Ana was right to push him to admit these feelings? Or should she have accepted how he felt?
- That is what Flynn has been trying with Christian. But, Ana's the one that'd be able to break through to him.
- I think it is part of his therapy to learn that! Unconditional love is supposed to happen, but I can say, it's always not the case! For him, his character, I think it was important! Each case is different!
- I believe we are all designed to love and be loved in return. We learn to fear. A part of me will always love my parents. Even after all they've done to me. Though, I won't have anything to do with my dad, and my mum is on thin ice. I can only spend so much time around her.

- I know they say children are born to love, but as you get older and that love isn't reciprocated or your needs aren't met, you don't feel obligated to return it. That rejection can carry you through to your adult years.
- I have an adopted brother and another brother. I would, and did take care of my little brother. I don't think I could've cared any differently about him or my other brother! I loved them both!
- Obligated, no. But I think it's natural for a child to love their parents. A child. Now, as an adult, we can choose not to love our parents. As we all know, not all parents deserve our love.
- I think Christian was extremely conflicted about his feelings for his birth mother. As a little boy, he really did love her and then when she died, he felt abandoned and that feeling turned into anger as he got older. He started to feel that she let him down by not protecting him from her pimp and letting that animal lose on him. Ana was the first person who was really able to finally get him to have an honest conversation about his feelings about his mother, and that made him so uncomfortable.
- I think it was cruel - yes cruel - of Ana to try to force Christian to admit feelings he had when he was a toddler desperate for any kind of love or affection. He had no other outlet, no other source for "love" - even though it was from the worst excuse for a mother you can get. It bothers me when people post messages that say something like "all mothers love their kids" or some such crap. They don't. I'm sorry, but abandoning or abusing someone isn't love in any way, shape or form. Even if there was five minutes of "love" - the abuse overrides any of that possible emotion.
- This what I hate about Mother's Day. I love my mother, but all the Mother's Day cards go on about 'thanks for always being there for me in the hard times' or 'world's best mother'. I wouldn't necessarily have called it cruel of Ana to get Christian to admit he loved his mother. But my own mother (though she isn't a Crack whore) has a bit in common with Ella. Maybe my own view is a little out of order.

340

- I hear ya. And don't you think it's cruel when people try to force you to say that your mother was closer to the "ideal" when she wasn't? It's like they don't believe you. Christian had every reason to hate his mother - and Ana's forcing him to say differently is like she's dismissing all the horrific things that crack whore did to him (or allowed to be done to him). So freaking what if she let him brush her hair? He's supposed to overlook the other crap? No. In fact, that's the beginning of the cycle of abuse - to "forgive" the abuser by overlooking the abuse. That being said, there is a form of forgiveness that says, "It is what it is. Maybe she did her best; maybe she didn't. It's over, and I've moved on and wish her (soul) well."

- I wonder if Ana, trying to get Christian to admit to, at some point, loving his mother was her trying to help him make peace with it. The "it is what it is." To help him make peace with his past, so he can move on from it.

- Maybe, but I don't think forcing him to admit he loved her is the way to do that. And THANK GOD she didn't win by naming the child after her! I honestly think that some people don't get it - they don't see that some parents can be terrible parents, so they try to put it into a box they understand. Carla might not have put Ana as much of a priority as she could have, but she did love her daughter (just not as #1 in her life). But that is a far cry from what Ella did. As many of you have heard, my mother hated me. HATED. And it really pisses me off when people try to pretend otherwise. It's like they don't believe me, even when I give example after example.

- I hate when people seem to try to justify my mother's reaction to what her husband did to me. I've spent nearly 18 years being a parent to my own mother while she gets to act like a teenager.

- I also changed my name after I found out who my mother let my dad name me after.

- I think it was also dangerous of Ana. Christian was very fragile with this part of his life. Me, I had a wonderful childhood and grown-up relationship with my parents. I miss them both. When my father passed (almost 12 years, this month), I hated Father's Day, going to the store seeing the cards and knowing I couldn't buy one. Now my mom is gone (4 years), and I go through the same. I don't like Mother's Day. Of course, my daughters do.

- I loved my mum until the day she died. Yet, she didn't protect me from the abuse I went through from a cousin from the age of eight, onwards. I always have that in the back of my mind, and I hate her for it, even though I know it's not her fault.
- I think children always love their mom. He didn't ever know any other moms, so he thought that's what moms were like. It was too soon for her to force him to talk about that. She should have given him more time and patience.
- No, I don't think you're obligated at all. Situations are different for everyone. Some good and some bad. Maybe Christian would opened up more when and if he was ready. Ana just wanted to know so much about him and his childhood.

Breaking Point

I've thought about Christian's mother, Ella, all day. What made her life so bad that she had to turn to prostitution and then commit suicide? Leaving her little 4-year-old child behind and alone. She's only mentioned in the books four times and we don't know her name until the very end of *Freed*. Can we discuss this? What comes to mind for you?

- I'll just say here that addiction is a very scary thing.
- That's a tough one. For Ella, maybe her thinking of OD'ing, probably to end her misery, but I see it as being selfish act...for leaving her child alone in a world. Once the act is done, who really suffered? Christian did.
- I'm not sure. It could also be her boyfriend fooling her into trying it out, and by being tired of her life, she decides to end it, leaving a sad and hungry child all alone. Reading this part in the book was really sad.

- Who's to say what led her into that life...when or where she had Christian through it all... that was never divulged. Christian most likely a "trick baby." Sad, nevertheless.
- That's why I didn't mention how she got into that, because it was never said.

Christian's Family

When Ana first meets Christian (for the interview) she asks him about his family. He says, "I have a family. I have a brother and a sister and two loving parents." As the story unfolds, we learn more about his relationship with his family.

My Papa Was a ...?

We've talked a lot about Ella's behavior toward Christian, but we haven't discussed who his birth father (sperm donor) was - and his transgressions. Do you think his birth father knew he had a child? If not, why didn't Ella tell him? She could've gotten the financial support she so desperately needed. Do you think we'll ever know who his birth father was?

- She, herself, might not even know who the father is.
- Sadly, I agree.
- She might not have known who the father was. She did sleep around so knowing for sure might not have been possible. Even if she did know, and if she told him, knowing the kind of guys she slept with, they probably wouldn't have helped.
- Yeah, but they would have to - by law - if she could get a paternity test.
- Well, yeah, that's true, but she was a drug addicted prostitute, so I don't really think that she, or anyone else she hung around with were ones to follow the law.
- I don't think she knew.
- I've been thinking about this. What if his birth father is some businessman who happened to hire the use of a prostitute (Ella)? So, he never knew she was pregnant. Fast forward four years. As we know, Ella died, leaving Christian to be adopted by the Greys. What if, at some point, something happened to him, or Grace, and one of them needed a donor for some reason. But, because he, like his siblings, was adopted it's not likely there's a match. But then it turns out that not only is he a match,

but that Grace is blood related to him. I'm thinking maybe his aunt (his father's sister) or something. That would also give Ana a reason to say to Christian that he may have thought it's in his DNA to be a bad parent. But here's the proof it's in his DNA to be a good parent.

- Wow, that's actually a pretty good theory.
- She might've known, and thought he was a loser, or a threat, and that she and/or Christian were better off without him.
- Remember she was a serious addict, and probably wasn't able to distinguish reality very well. Even if she knew better, she wasn't able to *act* better.
- For a while, I've been convinced that Christian's birth dad is also Hyde's birth dad. There's so many similarities between Hyde and Christian...frankly, too many to ignore. The hair color (copper is not a stretch to red), the facial expressions. Also, when Christian says to Ana "we're cut from the same cloth", that sent a huge chill down my back. Both also had no father. I think we'll only ever find out the truth if there's another story that goes beyond *Freed*...if there's a scenario where a DNA test figures into the storyline...Jack could claim to be Christian's brother, not realizing that it's true, and when the results come back, they're shockingly a DNA match!
- I was thinking when Christian would've been conceived, in the 80s, there was no texting or social media. It may have been impossible for Ella to contact Christian's father, even if she did have an idea who he was. It was probably some client she met in a hotel, and never got his number, maybe not even a last name. It could've been someone just passing through Detroit.
- I think she didn't know; she was too far-gone into drugs. I think Christian was a crack baby. I'd love to read Ella's story.
- In my mind, I've already filled in her story. Ella was a beautiful young woman who fell in love with a man. She gave her virginity to him, and got pregnant, but he wanted nothing to do with kids, and left her. She never saw him again. She would've gotten an abortion, but she was just so devastated, and all she could think about was

the helpless child within her. She carried him to term, but after giving birth, she found that she could hardly look at him without thinking of the scumbag that left her. She tried her best to raise him, but it all finally got to be too much for her. She spiraled into a deep depression, and the only thing that seemed to help was numbing herself with drugs. It was all downhill from there. She started selling herself to get money for drugs, and food for little Christian, but eventually the drugs became more important to her than anything else. She continued to resent Christian and blamed him, and his absent father, for everything wrong in her life. She moved in with her pimp, and the rest is history. A very tragic story that is, unfortunately, far too common in this world.

- I envisioned her as being abused by her stepfather, running away from home and having to sell herself to stay alive. That led to drugs and her getting pregnant.

- I'm sure she was very attractive, in a hard, abused sort of way. It's interesting to consider what other traits Christian might've inherited from his birth parents, physically and mentally. Were either of them exceptionally intelligent? Was one of them also a control freak? Inclined to feel guilty? Self-deprecating? So many questions!

- I have no use for Ella, as she so completely neglected her son in the worst possible ways.

- I know she was a victim, too, but there's no excuse to allow that to happen to your child. If you can't handle being a mother, either don't have a kid or give it to someone worthy.

- I'm not defending her. She was a terrible mother, no doubt about that. I'm just curious about how she got to that place. People are not born terrible. Something had to happen to make her that way.

My Parents Love Me

"I have a family. I have a brother, a sister, and two loving parents. I'm not interested in extending my family beyond that."

346

Why do you think Christian emphasized "loving parents?"

- I'm sure he meant that they, in fact, were loving parents to him because he hadn't known love previously. And, maybe self-consciously he means "loving parents" to be the love his mom and dad have between themselves?
- Because Ana pointed out he was adopted, and I think he thought she was showing pity towards him (because his birth parents weren't around.) He probably knew the assumptions that went through people's heads when they learned that fact about him.
- Because, after being adopted and he felt like he wasn't really part of a family, and he missed his birth parents.
- He didn't know his birth father right?
- I think he referred to his adoptive parents as loving to maybe convince himself of that very fact...remember, he doesn't believe he's deserving of love...from anyone...even them.
- True.
- I thought it was interesting that he said that to Ana. On some level, he wanted to tell her he was "lovable."
- Yes!
- Nice!
- Because, I think on some level he does not feel worthy of his parents. I think when you are a child of abuse, your sense of worth is not that strong.
- Probably very true.
- This would be the "pat" answer to a question he was asked by a lot of interviewers. Also, his PR people might've told him to say it.
- Because his birth mom didn't seem to be as loving as she should have been!

Healing Powers

"'Mee a,' I whisper. 'Mee a.'"
"'Yes. Yes. Darling boy, Mia. Her name is Mia.'

"When Mia cries, Elliot ignores her. I hug her and I hold her and she stops. She falls asleep in my arms. 'Mii...a' I whisper."

What did you think about Mia's effect on Christian?

- This was one of the scenes where I actually choked up. All the sad flashbacks were heartbreaking, but this scene was hopeful, positive and such a milestone for that 6-year-old boy. Baby Mia, not being a threat, broke his barriers, so effortlessly.
- I love that part! It is so sad... But he feels the baby needs him and he's there for her... I guess that's why Christian and Mia are so close. It's a nice part.
- It is. Says so much.
- This part had me bawling. It shows that he is more than capable of love and protecting those he cares about most. I think it was always part of his "makeup." He just never realized it. He has it in him to protect those who can't protect themselves. He tried to protect his birth mother but was really too young to do it. So, he's making up for that by being a protector to Mia and Ana too. Such a sensitive soul...gotta love him.
- And it explains how Mia can touch him without reservation. Effortlessly.
- Beautiful insight into a troubled soul. It shows love and hope is there. Someone younger that he can care for that can bring out those feelings.
- These pictures, and this section of Grey is so heartwarming. Christian knew how to love, even as a small child.

Party Crasher

"As I glance anxiously around at the assembled crowd, I catch sight of Elena. Her mouth is open. She's stunned—horrified even, and I can't help a small but intense feeling of satisfaction to see her dumbstruck. What the hell is she doing here, anyway?"

What WAS Elena doing there? This was the only friend of the Greys there, right? Wasn't Grace even surprised that Christian and Elena were such good friends?

- I felt like this was probably the first time Elena was so aggressive towards Christian in front of the Greys. That's why Grace frowned when she saw the three of them talking together. Christian had been ignoring Elena's calls and messages, and she felt like she was losing her control over him. I'm sure she insisted on being at the party. Maybe even contacting Grace to ask about him, and inviting herself to the party.
- I think they just thought the two were good friends, and Mia invited her.
- I always wondered about that, too.
- From a writer's POV, it set the stage for an awesome conflict!
- I agree that they were good friends, and Mia invited her.
- Grace was totally clueless about the "friendship." I think that Elena was Grace's best friend. Probably because of the nature of her relationship with Christian, she was with Grace a lot, so she thought nothing of it. Sometimes, I think Grace was a total dolt about things, especially about her children and how to deal with them. What angered me the most was how disrespectful Elena was towards Grace when speaking with Christian. She seemed to have a rather spiteful tone when referring to Grace as "Mama Grey." I also resented that Christian didn't call her on it.
- I don't think Grace was totally clueless about the friendship. How could she be? Elena loaned him money to start his business and they were in business together. He worked for her at her house. That is how things got started. I think she knew they were good friends. I think she may have been clueless about the sexual part of their relationship.
- She was a family friend, and I bet she called Grace because of Charlie Tango the day before, and wrangled an invitation.

- Oooh! Good thought! Probably also asked if Grace was doing anything for Christian's birthday. She put Grace on the spot!
- I think Elena was always searching for information about Christian, and she called Grace. Then, she got invited to the party.

Ana's Family

While we learn considerably more about Christian's family than we do Ana's, we do get some hints into her background, including her mother's being an "incurable romantic" who married four times. In this chapter, we follow these clues to come up with some theories…

Dads and Step-Dads

"'Not really,' I scoff. 'By the time I was interested in learning, my mom was living with Husband Number Three in Mansfield, Texas. And Ray, well, he would've lived on toast and takeout if it wasn't for me.'"
"Christian gazes down at me. 'You didn't stay in Texas with your mom?'
"'No. Steve, her husband and I, we didn't get along. And I missed Ray. Her marriage to Steve didn't last long. She came to her senses, I think. She never talks about him,' I add quietly. I think that's a dark part of her life, which we've never discussed.'"

We don't know much about Steve. Let's make a few guesses about him and why and/or how they didn't get along. What do you think?

- I was curious about why she didn't get along with him. She also said her mom doesn't talk about him much because that was a dark time in her life. That's concerning.
- I don't know why, but I get a feeling Steve was abusive to Ana – or her mother. Maybe that's why she said her mother "finally came to her senses."
- I also thought he did something to Ana, or her mom.
- I think he was controlling in some aspects. Ana got out as soon as she could. With Ana gone, her mom saw what he was truly like, and left him not long after Ana left. Did they ever say how long after that that she married Bob?

351

- Do you think he was emotionally abusive? Physically abusive? If emotionally, how could that have influenced Ana and her future relationship with Christian? If physically, how might that have made things different for them?
- I think he was physically, emotionally, and verbally abusive. I always thought Steve made advances toward Ana, and that made her uncomfortable enough to want to leave.
- I wondered about that too.
- Maybe, her mom got her out of there before something bad happened so she wouldn't see it?
- I wish I could say I think so, but I don't see Carla as being that protective. She seems to have a pattern of choosing her man over her daughter.
- Very true. I'm leaning towards Ray getting her out in time. Carla always needed a man. She married Steve quickly after her divorce.
- I'm going to say emotionally and verbally, because I don't want to imagine the other for her and her mom. I think if it were physical, Ana may not have left because she wanted to protect her mom. I think it has to do with her low self-esteem. He was probably like my brother-in-law. He bought my niece a car, but told her she could only drive it to school. He checked the odometer every day when she got back home. He talked down to her about everything. She left as soon as she could. And, he didn't have kids. He was just a controlling ass, and still is. Probably like Steve. He was my sister's second husband.
- I think he made a pass or passes at Ana that were inappropriate.
- I think he was abusive to both of them.
- He was probably verbally and psychologically abusive towards both Ana and Carla. Ana had the sense to get out and live with Ray before Steve's behavior could escalate.

Tug of Love

Do you think Ana's reaction to the accident would've been the same if it had been her mother vs. Ray?

- I think so. She was a caregiver. She loved both of her parents immensely.
- She would've been even more upset, if it happened to Carla.
- I think so. Even though she and her mother weren't close, she wouldn't want anything bad to happen to her. She cares.
- Yes, maybe a bit more freaked out with Ray vs. Carla.
- I actually think she would've been more upset about Ray than Carla. Carla had so quickly blown her off about graduation. Plus - Carla had Bob, but Ray was alone. (I think it's one reason Ana stayed with Ray)
- She is closer to Ray personality wise. I think that's why they got along so well. She loves her mother, just not as much as she loves Ray.
- Yeah. And she gravitates more to people who need her vs. those who don't (as much), which explains it, too.
- I think she would've been more upset about Ray.
- Yes, because deep down, Ana loved her mother, and understood her, because they were both hopeless romantics.
- Ana had different feelings for Ray than she did for Carla. She took care of Ray, yet he was also her hero. Her rock. Her mother was the opposite: flighty and not dependable. Her mother dismissed her; Ray stood by her. Yet, Ana probably felt a similar bond and obligation to both of them.

Visitation

Did you find it odd or sweet that Carla wanted to go see Ray while he was still in the coma? Would Ray appreciate that visit, or would he feel embarrassed when he finds out?

- I think it's sweet, even if she only did it because she cared about Ana. I'd worry if Ray was still harboring feelings (positive or negative) for Carla. I suspect he's a man who isn't comfortable being fussed-over.
- Carla knows how Ana feels about Ray being a dad to her. Maybe she stills cares about him too!
- I really wonder about their relationship. I'm guessing that Ray got tired of Carla's flightiness and all her crafty ideas to make money. Otherwise, I really think they make better friends than lovers.
- I don't think Ray was exciting enough for Carla.
- I have a family member who's also a really good friend of mine (I met her before I met my husband - we were dating brothers!), who gave up a boring guy for another who she thought was more interesting/fun. It turns out he wasn't. Oddly, though, she won't leave him (and, their kids are all grown-up now).
- I'm not sure Carla knew what was best for her - though I do hope she and Bob are very happy!
- I think it was mainly because of Ana, and seeing how bad her daughter was in distress. Maybe she thought that by giving her a bit more support at times like this, especially given how little time she spends with Ana.
- I don't think it was odd at all because, deep down, she still had feelings for Ray, and how he took care of Ana while she lived with him.

Growing Up Too Early

"Kids! Hmm … and there it is again—a not-so-veiled reference to the fact that she had me so early."

It seems like Carla had lamented having Ana so young. How would you feel if your mom said that to you?

- Her mother was immature, all of Ana's life. She was somewhat self-centered, and she'd unload on a young Ana as if she were a best friend.
- I've actually witnessed conversations like this in my own family, and frankly, they are cringe-worthy. I feel awful

for the person in my family that was informed that they were an "accident." This relative found this out years ago, and is still understandably hurt. I totally get how Ana feels about all of this.

- My ex-mother-in-law had a difficult birth with her last son. She never let time go by without making her son feel responsible for the pain and suffering she endured during delivery. And he didn't have a clue. He just absorbed it all. I always felt so horrible for him.
- I think it's not fair of her to express that openly. I would never do that, as a mother. My mother-in-law often points out how my husband, who is the baby of the family wasn't planned, or wanted at first. It hurts his feelings even though their relationship is beyond repair.
- That is awful! I would be hurt if my mom said that. Although she isn't saying she wished she didn't have her, but she had her too early. I guess that isn't as bad.
- I would feel terrible. Reminded me of my ex-mother-in-law complaining in front of her last born how difficult her labor was with him. Poor guy ended up feeling responsible and guilty for the hard labor. I wanted to bop her on the head!
- It would make me feel uneasy, if she said it in a negative way.
- My mum said that sort of thing a number of times, when my half brother and sister were kids. She would say how she sometimes wishes she stopped with me, so she and my stepfather could holiday (vacation) whenever they wanted. She said it right in front of them, as well. I felt so bad for them. I don't know why she'd say that anyway. She clearly got the perfect daughter out of my sister. I love my sister, but mum does favor her and my younger brother.

Bringing Up Baby

Let's talk about Carla. Ana grew up with Ray, so he was more present in her life than her mum, why? Do you think Ana will follow her steps in the upbringing her children?

- I've seen women who jump from relationship to relationship. It's not so much about Ana, as her own selfish need. It's horrible that a mother can put herself first, ahead of her child, but it happens all the time
- We don't know how long Carla was with Ray, but I guessed Ana was in junior high or middle school. So she had 10-15 years with Ray. He loved Ana, but he might not have made Carla happy. We don't know. To me, her real offense was when she married Steve, and left Ana behind with Ray (though in the big picture, it was best for Ana). Good or bad, I think Carla was one of those women who couldn't stand not to be "attached" and had difficulty being independent. Ana actually took that as a sign, and went the opposite way. She became independent and self-sufficient. The interesting thing is that by marrying Christian so young, she was at risk for doing the same thing. Which, as we know, is why she fought so hard to keep her career.
- I couldn't stand that Carla didn't come for the graduation, because her husband twisted an ankle, and that's it? She couldn't leave him? Come on - Ana was disappointed, I felt it.
- Carla should've been there for Ana!
- Ana will be nothing like Carla! Christian will make sure of that! Carla is flighty, whereas, Ana is devoted and focused on her career. She's also devoted to her control freak who doesn't require the fawning over like Bob seems to need. Ana will be much more like Ray.
- I agree with you; she'll be quite opposite to her mum.
- When I was a child, my mum would go on holiday; she used to leave me with my granny first, and then my brother. I'm the contrary - I can't even leave my son alone for one day.
- I don't really get the story with Carla. How could she marry Steve and move so far away from her daughter? And, how could she cancel coming to the graduation because Bob broke his foot? Come on. Is Bob 6 years old? I'd be more pissed at her, if I were Ana. I don't

think she'll be anything like that, because she lived with Ray for so many years.

- It sure pissed me off! (Her blowing off graduation). I think Ana just took it as "par for the course." She knew her mother, and although she probably always hoped Carla would change, Ana probably just got to the point of lowering her expectations. (Or... am I talking about my own relationship with my mother? Hmmm...)
- I agree, you just get used to it, so you don't get hurt over and over again, and accept the reality, instead of being in denial.
- I am with you about the graduation. There is nothing on this planet that would make me miss my child's graduation.
- Especially an only child.
- I think Carla is too dependent on a man and seems to put them first, instead of Ana. I'd like to know what her third marriage was like that caused Ana to live with Ray. I always wondered if there was some type of abuse involved.
- It sure makes you wonder, doesn't it?
- I wonder if Steve made advances on Ana, but Carla denied the situation. I hope E.L. James will reveal what happened.
- Wouldn't it be awesome if she could tell us *Deeper* members?
- I hope so too. That was pretty awesome that she was looking for your group.
- OUR group!
- Yes, it would be awesome if she tells us!
- Here's the excerpt in Darker:

"Did you your mother teach you?" (to cook)
"Not really," I scoff. "By the time I was interested in learning, my mom was living with Husband Number Three in Mansfield, Texas. And Ray, well, he would've lived on toast and takeout if it wasn't for me."
Christian gazes down at me. "You didn't stay in Texas with your mom?"

"No. Steve, her husband and I, we didn't get along. And I missed Ray. Her marriage to Steve didn't last long. She came to her senses, I think. She never talks about him," I add quietly. I think that's a dark part of her life, which we've never discussed.

- Steve probably resented Ana being around, since she was not his child. He doesn't sound like a nice man, and wondered why they got married.

- I think Ana will be a way better mom to her children than Carla was. From what I read, and come up with, is that Carla resents Ana in some way. I believe that because she was so young when she had Ana, and since she is a hopeless romantic. Not all men want women with children. It is sad, but so true that most, not all, but most women, would rather have a sex life and a man with them than their kids. I also believe that Ray loved Ana so much, and she loved him that she'd rather be with Ray than her mom.

- I'd hope not! Carla was all about herself, and whatever man she had in her life to even bother with Ana. Ana should remember how Carla did things and do the exact opposite.

- Nope!

- I think, once Ana and Christian are married, and have kids she will see them as an extension of the man she loves so deeply. There's nothing that will stop her from being a fabulous mother to their children. Carla didn't have that - a man she was so in love with helping her raise their children. So, on to the next one and so on, with her. Ana is much more like Ray!

- This question makes me wonder...Ana's being a "romantic" with her English Lit major - yet going for the "darker" romances, and how her history with the "incurable romantic" mother shifted her perspective.

- Evolving?

- I think so. The sense I get from Ana is that she is going to be very active in her children's upbringing. I thought it was interesting that Ana told Gail that she wanted to cook her him on the weekends.

- What another poster said, made me think that Carla and Christian's mom were similar, in that they put their needs first, over their children's needs. Both, crappy moms. I'm sure that Christian and Ana will do the exact opposite for their kids.
- I like to think they'll have balance. Spending enough time on their own relationship, too. If a couple focuses too much on the kids, the relationship can suffer, and then it ends up damaging the kids anyway.
- I totally agree! We lost each other, after we had kids because we were so focused on getting through the day. Once we made our relationship a priority again, everyone is happier!

The Impact of Divorce

In what ways do you think that Ana, being a child of divorce, impacted the way she loves? Why do you think Carla divorced Ray? On a personal note, I think it can be worse to have parents who stay together, but shouldn't have. What do you think?

- I am very opinionated on this, but I believe it is a true statement that some are cautious, and enter into a relationship, and love differently. As for Carla, she tried to find what she lost in the one she truly loved first (Ana's father).
- I can't imagine why she left Ray. He seemed to be a great guy, he took good care of Ana. You could be right about Carla, looking for the love she felt for the first guy. I think if you can't get along with each other, break up! Don't involve the kids in your horror story.
- I don't think Ray was expressive and romantic. He was a rather taciturn guy. Carla was looking for romance.
- I was thinking that, too. Ray wasn't exciting enough for Carla, who craved drama and romance.
- Ray was too straight and narrow. Poor guy.
- With Ray, I'm betting he was romantic at the beginning. But, then, life keeps going on, and he was in real life. Carla was probably looking for the great romance to

continue (the hearts and flowers stuff) and didn't want to live in the "life happens" stuff. As a child of divorce, and living in the house in the last two years of my parents' marriage, I emphatically say, "Don't stay married for the kids." Stay married only because you believe in the marriage, and are willing to work on it. If you're staying for the kids, you're teaching them to not look for happiness for themselves. They'll learn to be afraid of moving on when the marriage is bad and getting worse, and the partner isn't willing to get help and/or admit then help is needed. I am living this now, and trying to work on it daily.

- My parents stayed together but never should have. I know it's the reason I never married. I didn't want to feel trapped/dependent. And now, in hindsight, I am glad I didn't marry the three that asked. That being said, if I met "the one" at the right time, I do think I'd be willing to give up my precious freedom and be willing to work at the relationship. He'd just have to be my champion, my friend, my lover. Otherwise, it wouldn't be worth it.

- My parent's where married for 47 years until my father passed. They had crazy times, but mostly good times. My husband and I are coming up on 26 years. Mostly good.

- Some of you know what I am going through. I'm trying to rectify what I just wrote in my own life. It is definitely easier said than done to leave, when you know that it isn't good anymore, and you and your child could be better off without the marriage but...

- Fortunately, I have no first-hand experience in the subject. But, I can say there's a lot of suffering on the part of children.

- I divorced my children's father eight years ago. When the children were 3 and 5 years of age. It was the best decision I ever made, because six years ago I met the man of my dreams. I didn't even know what real love was until I met him. I think children growing up with divorced parents may be more careful with love. But I also think they're stronger. I have a friend who she said she wished her parents divorced a lot sooner than they did. They divorced when she was grown up. She says she regrets growing up in a home where mum and dad never touched, or kissed, or hugged. She had problems in her own relationship because she learned a "cold" way of love. She had difficulty showing it physically. So, I guess it means a lot when you're growing up.

- Thank you for sharing your story. Very inspiring and beautiful. I couldn't agree more. I know every situation is different, and I know that the grass can look greener, but you are so right in how having parents in a "cold" relationship can impact you. I really wish both of my parents could've had your experience and found true love instead of staying together for 56 years in bitterness. I truly never saw them touch. No affection whatsoever. So sad.

- I'm going one step forward and two steps back. I'm in a weird place right now, but at least I don't live in denial anymore. I'm the second child in my family. My parents stayed together because of my mom. She's the one that fought for every single thing, and she is possibly the strongest person I know. But, I think that she shouldn't have stayed married to my father. The same thing is happening to me here, and all I'm hearing is "stay for the kids." I don't want to. I don't want this anymore, but I am afraid to take that step. It's complicated.

The Wedding

"Marry me," he whispers.

Christian's unexpected, desperate proposal set in motion another set of issues for the couple. From prenuptials to wedding vows to dresses, logistics and the honeymoon, all of which we discussed and debated with relish.

Another Contract

Why was the marriage contract so important to Christian?

- I don't think it was so much the paper, but then again, he was fond of contracts. No, but I think it was more about Ana proving her commitment to him. It was a concrete expression of commitment.
- Christian seemed very traditional in wanting the marriage vows, ceremony and all the trappings (even though if I recall correctly, he wasn't a person who went to the family church anymore - Anglican or Episcopalian). Perhaps, that is what he thought was "expected" when one commits to a marriage. He saw tradition in his parents' and grandparents' weddings. I think he had some unrealistic ideas about the "contractual" value of the wedding vows in that, if Ana said them, she was bound by them forever, come hell or high water. Again, when I read that part of the book, I shuddered to think what Ana's choice would be if he thought that, and if things didn't go well for her. I think the painful process of agreeing to the vows, and Christian's eventual relaxing his constraints was a valuable lesson for him. He had to learn to trust that the paper was just paper, the words were just words, and that what really mattered was Ana looking him in the eyes and vice versa, and believing from the heart that they would be a faithful, loving married couple.
- I think initially the contract was Christian's security blanket.

- According to E.L. James, Christian was a "lapsed Catholic."
- Maybe I read that in one of the fanfiction stories.
- Short and sweet. By marrying him, she'd be his forever. Signed, Sealed and Delivered.
- One word: Control.
- He wants control, and that was a way he could have it over Ana.
- I thought the same. Christian's biggest problem was Ana not saying that she'd obey.
- The marriage contract was sacred to him, even more so than any contract he entered into with any of his subs. To him, it meant that legally Ana was his, and he was hers...forever. Sadly, he had to learn that a marriage contract does not give him the right to control her, but rather that marriage is a partnership, not something to exert one's control over the other.
- To make Ana his officially and forever, and he'd be hers forever. They were now legally bound together. A normal relationship.

Thou Shalt Not Obey

So - what did you think of Ana's pushing back on the vows, especially "obey?"
For those who have been married, did you keep the traditional "obey" language? Did it bother you at all?

- What makes this complex is that it was so important to Christian. I would've probably teased him about it, but I also probably wouldn't have argued the point.
- I would've probably made him say it, too!
- That would be really funny - to hear Christian say he'd "obey" Ana!
- The way he acted, I would've stood my ground about not saying it, like she did. I'm stubborn like that!
- To tell you the truth, I sometimes still hear "Oh, I don't wear any make-up, or no nail polish." My husband doesn't like it, or want me to wear it. It's incomprehensible to me.

- I've thought back to when I said my vows several times. We recited the traditional ones, but that was what was expected. But, that is definitely no longer the case. That's why many brides want to write their own vows and eliminate that word. Now, have I adhered to it? well...
- I don't really remember if I said the word "obey" in my traditional vows. I'm certain I'd do quite the opposite.
- I didn't say it when I got married. I told my husband that I would only say it if he did. I told him that I was an equal partner in this marriage, and he agreed. We'll be married for 15 years this coming December and we are still equal partners.
- Sorry. No for me. I'd skip those words. Isn't a relationship to be equal parts? What if one just doesn't obey a small simple rule, or forgot about it? I'd prefer to skip that word.
- We did omit those words from our vows because neither one of us felt that those words defined our relationship. We felt that we are both equal partners and neither one of us should have to obey the other.
- I totally understand about Ana's resistance to the word "obey." I think, in her mind, that word brings her back to the submissive contract, which she had huge problems with. Perhaps, if she had explained her rationale to Christian (maybe she did?) maybe he MIGHT have seen her POV and maybe they would have found middle ground without Christian having those awful nightmares.
- Oh, but we'd miss the clever banter between them! The continuing tension! And remember, this happened only 2-3 months after they met. They didn't have much time to "grow up."
- I don't think they "grew up" until Ana told Christian she was pregnant with Teddy. Until then, I think they BOTH behaved like a couple of spoiled and stubborn brats.
- Why was he so adamant about one damn word? Didn't he know her well enough by now to know she was not going to obey him? I think he still had hope that once

she married him she'd "fall into her place" and obey his wishes. Boy, was he wrong!

- I think he was hoping that since he couldn't get her to sign the submissive contract, he'd get her submission the next best way - become his wife, where she'd contractually be obliged to obey him. Don't get me wrong, he did love her with all of his heart, but he always seemed to find a way to get what he wants (he boasts about it often enough!). So, in his mind, getting married would ensure that she'd obey him in the same way as the sub contract would have. Again, he was so wrong!
- He is a very shrewd businessman. I guess he felt he could do what he always does in business, and try to control her the way he controls everything.
- I'm not certain if we said obey, when we first got married 20 years ago, but when we renewed our vows this June, the Orthodox Christian ceremony had no mention of obey.
- I've said this before: Getting married was his way of getting Ana to "sign a contract." If he could do that, he thought he'd have control over her. Boy, was he wrong!
- I'm not the most obedient person. To tell you truth, I do the exact opposite of what people ask me, or tell me to do. In few things, you can obey when you know they're making right decision. But, when you know what's best and right for you, you should stand up for yourself. I can obey, but not in everything.
- I would only say it, if he did, too.
- I think Christian only wanted Ana to keep the "obey" part because of his past experience with her not listening, and ending up getting in trouble (except when she wasn't in his penthouse when Hyde broke in - which was just luck on her part). My husband and I wrote our own vows.
- Personally, I think that was her way of keeping her independence, and Dr. Flynn did tell her not to change. Christian was head over heels, and that was the girl he fell in love with. Keep doing what you are doing.
- We married in Mexico, and not even in English. My husband used to tell everyone we were married by a taxi

driver. I have no idea what was said, and being so young (17 and 18), it probably wouldn't have mattered (in 1970). But, now I'd never do it, I have my own opinions and my own voice.

Dream Wedding

This made me wonder if Ana had dreamed of her wedding as a little girl, and how she might have envisioned it. We're assuming she was a baby for her mom's wedding to Ray, and a teenager when she married husband #3 (Steve), as well as when she married Bob. I wonder how seeing her mother's marriages affected her dreams. What do you think?

- I wonder if she ever thought of marriage at all. She was such a romantic, and she might've wanted it, but when she contrasted the concept of marriage to her mother's life, she might've rebelled, and never gotten married. Certainly not to someone she wasn't certain about.
- I guess Ana dreamt of a wedding. But, seeing her mother married a couple of times had to have an impact on her wanting to be married. Then Christian came along and, well, things changed.
- Well, she said her mother was a born romantic.
- I think Ana was the born romantic, not her mom. She just put that label on her mom because she didn't want to see that her mom was the "I need to have someone in my life to fill the void, no matter who they are" type. Ana was the one who wanted to be swept away, like in a book. But, I don't think her mom was that way. Then again, I don't recall reading a whole lot about the psychological workings of Ana's mother. So, maybe she was a romantic. But it just seemed to me that Ana was the romantic, not her mom.

Anniversaries

How do you think Ana and Christian spent their anniversaries? Did they save cake from their wedding?

- I don't think it mattered to either Ana or Christian. Grace may have frozen the top layer for them to have on their first anniversary.
- I believe that they do have some of their wedding cake frozen in their freezer. Ana is extremely sentimental and with Ana's influence, Christian also became sentimental. The cake represented the most special day in their lives when they really became each other's "Mine." The "hearts and flowers" theme would be the design. It would be a chocolate cake (which is Christian's favorite), with white vanilla icing (ironic eh?). They'd enjoy it again on their first anniversary.
- Christian's style was classic, clean, not complicated. Ana wasn't fancy, she was simple didn't like over the top so I think they would have had it simple but romantic and elegant. I think the cake would be white, fillings, of course vanilla bean alternating with chocolate ganache. I'm posting a few I really like.
- I think Grace would suggest they freeze the top!! Mia probably would, too.
- And a Charlie Tango cake for Christian.

Cast of Characters

While the story centered on Ana and Christian's relationship, the influence of other characters rounded out the story. We loved discussing and musing over the lives and motivations of Taylor and Jack, Jose and Kate and the others nearly as much. Well, nearly.

Jack

We find out that Jack's father died in a brawl and his mother "drank herself into oblivion." We have compassion for Christian's sad childhood. Why don't we also feel compassion for Jack?

- We don't feel compassion because Jack uses threats and blackmail to get what he wants from women. Christian does not.
- I don't think I'd say Christian didn't use threats. He did, and often. Just in a different, more suave way.
- Well, if he did use threats, they weren't on the same level as Jack's threats.
- You've got that right! I do think it's interesting to look at their similarities. It always makes you wonder.
- I've said that for a really, really long time. I'm not convinced that pointing out their similarities is a coincidence. In stories like this, there always seems more to the story than meets the eye. I believe there's more to both being from Detroit and ending up in the same foster home together. It really should be explored.
- Both (apparently) liked rough sex. Christian just channeled it into BDSM with consensual partners, while Jack took by force and manipulation. (Okay, Christian used some manipulation too). Both had a lot of suppressed anger. The big difference between the two men is that Jack lacked a conscience, while Christian was laden with guilt.
- Jack had always done it with dark intent, with no regrets whatsoever. Yes, Christian used it too, but most of the

time it was for good reason, such as getting Ana to open up sexually, or as a Dom, with a contract and consent.

Jack Attract

Do you think Jack was sincerely attracted to Ana, or do you think he just wanted to control her?

- I think he wanted control, and when he connected the dots regarding his past with Christian, he wanted to take Ana from him. I think, in his twisted mind, he believed that if he'd been the one adopted he'd be in Christian's shoes.
- I think Jack was a predator. He didn't know Christian was her boyfriend when he first started hitting on her. I also believe he made unwelcome advances to other women at the company.
- I believe you're right about him being a predator.
- Am I wrong, but did the lady who hired staff make a comment about it after he left? Or, am I thinking about *MOTU*?
- I think he liked a challenge, and Ana was definitely one. But, I think when he realized she was connected to Christian, it enticed him more.
- He had Donald Trump's syndrome, and felt entitled to grab "the thing" because he had the power to do so. But, when he realized she was Grey's, he was jealous and tried marking his territory.
- I think he was attracted to her, but not enough to want to pursue her. He seemed like the type to want to stick "it" in anyone who would let him. He got the impression that Ana was a goody-two-shoes, and when she rejected him, sparked something within him. He viewed her as a challenge, and one he wasn't intending to lose.
- Just reaching Christian through Ana.
- I believe that in the beginning, like Christian, he was intrigued by Ana, but, I think he was more into the chase. If (God forbid), she would've fallen for him, the chase would've been over and he'd discard her like a used tissue.

- Neither! He was just a sick twisted ass who preyed on women.

That Could've Been Me

"'What do you want?'
"'I want his money. I really want his f*cking money. If things had been different, it could've been me.'"

What did Jack mean when he said that? That they'd both been orphaned and in foster care? Or, something more?

- He thought the Greys should have adopted him instead of Christian.
- I always felt that he hated Christian for more than being adopted by the Greys. Maybe there was something happened in the foster home that was never mentioned.
- The Greys adopted Christian instead of Jack. He also thought he was smarter and more deserving of the things Christian accomplished.
- Do you think if Elena had met Jack instead of Christian he would've turned out differently?
- He might've become more violent. He would've lashed out more at the abuse she would've put him through. His mind was different than Christian's. I think it would've taken him deeper into instability. It also would've given him a larger pool of fish, and more women to abuse.
- I don't think there was deeper meaning to his words. He was jealous of Christian, in all aspects - the Greys, the wealth, and Ana.
- I believe this goes back to my theory that Jack and Christian are half-brothers. Jack harbored extreme anger that his half-brother (Christian) was adopted into a nice family and he wasn't. So, he feels if things had been different he would've been adopted by the Greys too, and that he'd have the same life that Christian had. He didn't know that Christian's life after the adoption was anything but wonderful. Christian had demons to work through too.

- True. Still, we wonder what might've happened if he hadn't had such understanding parents. And, good or bad, if he hadn't met Elena.
- I think he'd be a lot like Jack. That's another reason for my theory.
- If the Greys adopted him instead of Christian.
- Are they really half-brothers?
- In the books, there's so many similarities between the two that I have a theory (and it's ONLY a theory) that they are, and that they have the same father. I think if another book is written maybe that could be addressed in some way.
- Okay, thank you. That would be a twist!

Pot Meet Kettle

When Christian tells Ana "he likes it rough," and when talking about Jack, it appears that he is judging men about "being rough" during sex. Where would you draw the line on "assertive" versus "aggressive?"

- The line for me is when I say "stop" - if he doesn't, then he's crossed from assertive or aggressive...to assault.
- Being completely selfish, not regarding my wants and needs, at all.
- Ignoring my pleas to stop, making it all about his pleasure, and not mine.
- So Jack pretty much raped these women, right? They were unwilling participants? or, at the very least they were being blackmailed. That's the line. That, and not stopping when told to.

Gross Moral Turpitude

Christian warns Ana that if Jack, "makes one move, you tell me. It's called gross moral turpitude—or sexual harassment." Have you ever been sexually harassed at work? How did you react?

- Let's just say I've had my share of flirtations with a boss, or two.
- Isn't the key distinction whether the advances were wanted or reciprocated? If the advances are rejected, then it's harassment. Otherwise, it's just flirting or dating (at least to me).
- Exactly! Harassment is unwanted attention.
- No, but there was a guy who I worked with who told some people there that he had sex with me. Me! Ugh! I was a virgin until marriage - one partner. I didn't find out what he did until he stopped working there. I was pissed! It still pisses me off!
- Grrr! I want to kick his sorry ass!
- You and me both! Girl power!!
- Funny enough, yes, I was harassed at work. I was 18 years old, and working in a department store in the Menswear Department. It was a part-time job, and we had a manager and assistant manager. The manager was great and I really liked reporting to him. His assistant manager, on the other hand, was a complete nightmare. He thought he was God's gift to women, and loved it when the other girls in the department gave him attention. I wasn't the slightest bit interested in him, and he made my life miserable. He messed with the schedule and didn't tell me one day that I was scheduled to work, so I was at home when my phone rang, and he demanded to know why I wasn't at work. I explained that I wasn't aware that I was on the schedule, but since I lived literally two minutes away, I could be right there. He told me not to bother and that he was firing me. He told me that I had a bad attitude and constantly gave him lip (so not true! I was 18 and very Ana-like!). It so happened that my aunt's dad was the tailor for the department, and he wondered why he hadn't seen me for a while, and the next thing I know, I'm getting called into work and asked for my side of the story. The manager was really pissed about what the assistant did, and he wished I had come to him about this. Of course, I didn't know any better. The manager offered me my job back and the assistant was transferred to another store. It was

quite the experience and I hope no other girl was subjected to the a-hole's disgusting behavior. The experience really taught me a lot.

- No, thankfully
- It happened to me. I was 22 or 23, and promoted into a new job, against my boss's will. It was his boss who promoted me. He hated that I was doing the job that people 10 or 20 years older were doing. He made my life miserable, but when I started really excelling in the job, he started liking me because it looked good for him. One night, I was out with him and one of his peers, and he made a pass at me. It was while I was driving in the car, and he leaned over to make a pass. I should add here that he was not only unattractive, but had a wife and five children. It was disgusting. My only move was to lean over and turn the radio on really loud. It stopped him, but he made my life a living hell from that moment on.
- What an ass!
- Yes, I was. I had a summer job working for a man who asked me to go to the drug store and purchase condoms for him. I was embarrassed. I felt like I had to do it or be fired. This was in the days when that could easily happen. I think he asked me to do this to embarrass me, and to watch my reaction. He was interested in me, but I was not interested in him. I was young, going to college and was only interested in making money to use at school. I made sure I stayed clear of him, and never told my parents.

Elena

"'Look, we don't have long,' she says hurriedly. 'It must be obvious to you that Christian is in love with you. I have never seen him like this, ever.' She emphasizes the last word.
"What? Loves me? No. Why is she telling me? To reassure me? I don't understand."

Why did Elena tell Ana this? What was her intent?

- My initial reaction was that Elena was being Ana's friend. That was, until she followed with the threat. Elena is a master manipulator. She's one of those people who pulls you in for a hug so she can stab you in the back. She used this opportunity to lure Ana in and then scare her away. At this point, Ana was still rebuilding trust with Christian, and here she was, being threatened from her nemesis. I felt sorry for Ana – and wanted to kick Elena's ass!
- Hmmm I never thought about that. She was telling her she couldn't leave. She also didn't expect Ana to stand up to her.
- Elena probably doesn't expect anyone, much less mealy-mouthed Ana to stand up to her. I loved it when she did.
- She wanted to see Ana's reaction; and to try to see what Ana's intentions were.
- I wonder if she was trying to be a real friend to Christian, or, if she was trying to undermine him. The first few times I read the books I thought she was being genuine. (I'm too trusting and literal sometimes.) But the more we've discussed her, I think her intentions were selfish.
- I think Elena is very jealous of Ana! She's jealous because Ana attracted Christian, and won his heart, and Elena doesn't like it!
- Elena was trying to scare Ana off, in case Christian was taking things too fast for her.
- I think Elena told Ana that Christian loved her as another thing to rub in Ana's nose - something that Elena had figured out/knew, that Ana was too stupid/naive to have figured out for herself.

Jose

Do you think Kate had any idea how Jose really felt about Ana? Do you think she encouraged him to go for it? What would she think about the way Jose attempted to take advantage of her at the bar? What if Kate was the one to find them instead of Christian. What would Kate have done?

- Ana did tell Kate about what Jose did, and her reaction was "what? Jose and Christian Grey??? Boy, Ana, your pheromones must be working overtime!" I hoped that Kate would've had a more protective reaction towards Ana. I don't think Kate had any idea really that Jose felt that way about Ana. Yet, when Christian comes over after leaving Ana, after the spanking, and returns to see what's going on, Kate goes completely ballistic. Kate drives me nuts

- Yes! Kate is very observant, and she always knew when Ana was upset, or something wasn't right. She knew Jose had a thing for Ana, and it was like a hammer. Hell, Christian knew just by seeing how Jose looked and smiled at Ana at the photo shoot.

- I don't think Kate encouraged Jose. I was very put off by Jose, and his way of going about things, even if he was also drunk.

- I think Kate probably had a very difficult time gauging Ana's wants.

- I feel that Ana was a much better friend than the other way around. I have a love/hate relationship with Kate, because I appreciate the way she defended Ana at Christian's birthday party. But, I feel if she had paid more attention to Ana, she probably would've had an idea of what was going on beforehand.

- I don't blame Kate. Ana probably preferred her privacy and let Kate have the spotlight. They were a good complement to each other.

- I don't think she knew, or would have encouraged him. I think if Kate saw him, she would've gone off on him. Honestly, I didn't get that upset with Jose because he was drunk; she was also drunk. I think most of us have done things in that state we wouldn't do otherwise. I know I have - more than once - twice - okay, more.

- It seemed that until that moment, Jose was a good guy, and a good friend. Both Kate and Ana trusted him. Did he act inappropriately? Perhaps. But he was human and drinking. It happens. It's not like he forced himself on Ana. (Okay, maybe a little).

- Jose was nice, but clueless.
- I'm not sure I agree. I think Ana had given him enough signs for him to think she was open to a kiss.
- I do think Kate would've done something. She had lived with Ana all through college and never saw her interested in a guy, until Christian. But, if Christian wasn't around, I think she might've encouraged Ana to go out with Jose.
- I'm sure Kate knew how Jose felt. He wore his heart on his sleeve. But, I don't think Kate thought anything of it. It was the drink that made him try kissing Ana - he was brave. I think Kate would've told him off, if she caught him with Ana while she was saying "no."

Tell Her You Love Her

What if, upon trying to kiss Ana, and Christian walking up, Jose had not walked away? What if he stood up and said "Ana, you know I love you. We have known each other for years, and shared many special moments. We are drunk tonight, but I care about you so much. Let's sober up and have dinner tomorrow. This man doesn't know you, and doesn't deserve you. I love you Ana." Then what? If he had found his voice and spoken up, what would've happened? I think Jose had the best of intentions. Don't we all need a man who will fight FOR us, not AGAINST us, no matter what the reasons?

- I think, despite Jose's best intentions, Ana just didn't feel *that* way for him. He was just a very good friend, like Ethan; almost like a brother. There was no spark there; meanwhile, between Ana and Christian, there was that instant pull / electricity.
- Isn't it sad that so often, we women reject the "nice guys" like Jose? The ones who make our life easier? Instead, we go for the "bad boy" or the one we can "fix." Jose would've done anything for Ana.
- Maybe there was a chance for Ana and Jose, if it wasn't for Christian who was already on the scene. He definitely ruined her for all the men in this world!

- I don't think it was there for Jose and Ana. He may have been in love with her, or the idea of her, or since they had known one another for a long time, thought it was meant to be, but it wasn't going to happen. Just a gut feeling. I think if Ana had allowed Jose to kiss her, she would've regretted it, and Jose would've been broken-hearted. Ana needed someone to knock her socks off, and Christian was the one to do that!
- I think if he has 'been a man" and stepped up, he would've had a chance. He was too much of a wimp to deserve her.
- Christian would've punched Jose! Christian knew then Ana was his! Jose had no chance!
- She just didn't feel that way about him.
- I have zero sympathy for him. He knew her for years and didn't tell her how he felt? If he had, I think they could've been happy together. Their fathers would've been thrilled. She might've missed that "spark," but she could've been happy. BUT - he didn't have the freaking guts to go for it. So he didn't deserve her.
- Jose is the ultimate of friend-zoned. Ana never saw him that way.
- I think it would've made no difference. Ana didn't have those kind of feelings for Jose. She sees him as a brother. He's had years to work on her, if he wanted to. Besides, no one would beat Grey in that competition. I think every man would feel less man in his presence.

I Get the Picture

What about Jose's show, and not asking Ana for permission to display such private and candid photographs? I took it as being very creepy and invading Ana's privacy. He said he forgot to ask, but do you think he knew she wouldn't agree, and then his show wouldn't be as successful? On some deeper level, it seemed like he "used" her.

- Oh, most definitely, and he knew exactly what he was doing.

- I was just thinking something along the same lines. Who did he expect to buy the pictures? Would someone buy portraits of a stranger? It's kind of creepy.
- I hadn't thought of that. It is a little invasive, if not creepy. Besides, if someone was putting my pictures on display like that, I'd want to know – and give my approval (or disproval). Okay, now I'm pissed at Jose!
- He's in love, or lust with Ana, but I'd say it's a little creepy. More, because Ana had no idea he had taken them.
- Unfortunately, I think, for most of her life, Ana was a push over. Something about her relationship with Christian awakened something in her, and all that began to shift. So, yes, I do believe he didn't ask on purpose. He knew her well.
- Maybe he didn't expect anyone to buy them. Maybe it was just serving as an homage to Ana. It would explain why he was so excited for her to be a part of it, and to share the news of the exhibit with her.
- I never thought about who Jose thought would buy them. Wow! If he had not wanted them up for sale because he planned to keep them, then maybe Christian wouldn't have been able to buy them. (Unless he used his money to influence the sale.) I would've been so pissed, if I were Ana. I wonder if she ever discussed this with Jose later. Yep. "Creepy" and "intrusive" are great words to describe him. I don't think I like him as much now.
- I think it's downright creepy. But, it also is his way of declaring his love for her, without actually coming out and saying it. I can't really blame Christian for buying up all the photos. Jose kept that torch going, even at the wedding. No guy should ever tell a bride, on her wedding day, that he'll be there if she needs him. Sorry, but that was way over the line.
- I've always thought Jose was kind of creepy.
- If Christian hadn't purchased them, what would Jose do with them? Hang them in his apartment? Definitely weird.
- He knew what he was doing.

- He knew, but was delusional in thinking that they could be more than just friends. Deep down, he was hoping that Ana would dump Christian and come running to him. I also don't think he was joking every time he'd take a dig at Christian and his wealth. That really, really bugged him, and he was convincing himself that was what Ana was drawn to. Not just creepy, but a creep too!
- He *was* obsessed with her.

Lookin' Gooood!

Did anyone notice how Ana said that Jose had a suit on at the photo show, and that he looked "good?" I read it that she was attracted to him. I wonder if she felt that way, or if she just meant "different."

- I had the same reaction.
- Maybe, seeing Jose dressed up, and not in his jeans or school attire, for the first time, she noticed him as being an attractive male, rather than Jose, a good friend.
- She also commented on the fact that Jose had a few beautiful girls hanging around him. Hmmm...
- It might've sparked a little jealousy in Ana, perhaps.
- Maybe she was thinking, "What if...?"
- She's probably never seen him in a suit. She's only seen Christian in a suit. It was novel for her, and she's just reacting to that novelty.
- Now that her libido has been awakened, she's more aware. The Reticular Activating System.
- I think she was expressing brotherly caring. He was "all grown up."
- Exactly what I was thinking.
- I thought maybe she was just admiring him. Really coming into his own, with the whole exhibit. She was simply appreciating his good looks, nothing deeper.
- I also think it's important for her as an author to let us know Jose is handsome. Since it's in first person, we have to get her POV.
- I think it was just appreciating that he looked nice in a suit, compared to jeans and a shirt; like one woman

would think about another woman looking pretty in that dress.

- I think she was just amazed by how nice he looked in a suit. Ana has never seen Jose as anything other than a brother, and I figure since they have only been in everyday clothes, without the need to dress up to go to school, maybe it's just a reaction to how her brother looks.

Jose's Soulmate

Ana and Christian. Kate and Elliot. Mia and Ethan. Grace and Carrick. Taylor and Gail. But what about poor Jose? Did he ever find his soulmate?

- Oh yes! He got super successful as a photographer for National Geographic, and then met a woman in Iowa, while he was taking pictures of covered bridges.
- I never really liked Jose, but I do hope he eventually found his own happiness.
- I'm being funny here, but he married Phoebe, just like Jacob married Renesme. On a serious note, I think he did find the one for him. He deserved to be happy too.
- I think the bridges were in Madison County
- I'm going to be mean by saying this. Jose probably had some casual flings but they never measured up to Ana. My hope is that he found happiness, but my gut is telling me he probably just loved Ana from afar.
- That's very sad. I hope he got over her and moved on.
- I actually like that Jose wasn't paired off by the end. For a lot of reasons. It would have been too pat a solution. Everyone meets a life mate within a 3-month time frame? Plus, he's only 21!
- I wouldn't have expected him to be paired up in three months, but it might've been nice to have a brief mention of him, and his wife, and children at the end of *Freed*.

Kate

I've never really thought Ana and Kate were a good fit. Even in the epilogue, when Ana mentions Kate had a baby as well, I rolled my eyes because Kate did not seem like the "motherly type" to me. It just felt like she had a baby because Ana had a baby. Am I wrong? Thoughts?

- Well, they say opposites attract. Even in *Grey*, Christian thought it was a strange friendship too. But people change and Kate matured. She married a year after Ana, and had a baby two years after Ana did, so that would put her at 24 or 25. Hopefully, some women are ready to have children at that age, and Kate had a chance to learn about taking care of a baby, with Teddy on board.
- I think, in a lot of ways, mentally, they're a lot alike. They lived together for four years, and then moved to Seattle together. Ana and Christian found each other, and Ana started maturing very fast. She had to, and she did a great job. She knew what she was doing every time. Kate is a force to be reckoned with. She was born with a silver spoon in her mouth and she's not afraid to say what she means.
- My best friend in high school was most definitely a "Kate." Sometimes, she was abrasive and blunt, but always had your back, and was loyal to a fault. When I moved to a small town in North Dakota, in the seventh grade, she took me under her wing and made me feel like I'd always lived there. I was so shy and awkward, so that was no small feat considering most of the kids knew each other from birth. We are still good friends today- 26 years, and half a continent later.
- That's a lovely story.
- I think they were good friends. Kate was a little more outgoing than Ana, but I believe she cared for her, and she worried whether Christian was treating her right. Then she had Elliot, so they were with brothers. I think she had a baby because that just happened, but not really sure.

Kate to the Rescue

"'What's he done to you?' Kate asks, ignoring Christian. She looks so apprehensive. I flush as a myriad of erotic images flit quickly across my mind.
"'That's none of your business, Kate.' I can't keep the exasperation out of my voice."

Do you think your safety is your friend's "business?"

- I definitely think so. Your friends are there to help protect you, and defend you, and be there for you when/if you make a mistake. I cheer Kate for stepping in to make sure her friend was okay.
- I'd rather my safety not be anyone's concern, but I hope my safety would be a concern to my best friend; not a random friend.
- Your best friend is always going to be concerned about your well-being. I think Kate's heart was in the right place, but her delivery was a tad overbearing.
- Of course, it is. They were best friends and lived together for four years. I'd expect nothing less. Also, Kate knew Ana was a virgin and inexperienced. That would make her feel even more protective.
- Your best friend is always going to look out for you.
- Yep, I think that is what a true friend does - protect her from harm.
- That's what real friends do, isn't it? Yeah, to a point, I understand Ana's hiding all that. It was a heavy load, but she should have shared with Kate.
- This is a conundrum for me to answer. While the old "Ana" pre-Barbados vacation with Elliott might've made Kate feel she needed to put on her protective role, Kate really didn't know how much Ana had come into her own, grown up, if you will, and learned to act and think for herself without Kate's help. Ana's rebuttal of Kate's help made me think how much she trusted and believed Christian, and in Christian. That is really necessary in a strong love.

- Girlfriends are absolutely necessary; however, Ana was way beyond needing a girlfriend at that point in her journey with Christian.

None of Your Business

It really bugged me when Ana yelled and glared at Kate when Kate confronted her on Christian's birthday (after finding the BDSM contract). Ana had been completely elusive to her best friend and now gets angry when her friend is trying to protect her? I can see how she might be worried/concerned, but angry? Am I the only one who thinks Ana is the unreasonable one?

- Ana has grown and shown her independence. She probably thought it could've been brought up at another time, besides Christian's party. That's what pissed her off, not the fact that Kate confronted him.
- I think it's a combination of things. In a very short time, Ana grew up, beyond recognition. She is also bound by the NDA, so couldn't really discuss much about their very personal life. She wanted to keep this part of her life private and only known to her and Christian. She felt protective over Christian, even if it was her best friend who "attacked" him. I think she shifted from having only one relationship with her best friend to having two. She tried to find her footing in all of this. It was all so new to her.
- Clearly, Ana chose her man over her friend, in this case. I could maybe understand that because Kate was just doing her job, as her friend. If I put myself into Kate's place, I would've done the same thing. I can't even imagine what she must have been thinking. She knew how Ana was; that she was a virgin, and naïve, and innocent. She could read Christian, too, and how overwhelming, and domineering he was. Add that to Ana's secrecy, and "BAM!" you've got the recipe for a blow-up.
- I always thought her anger came from the bad timing in which she confronted them. I mean, it was Christian's

birthday party at his parents' house, and Kate came at them in a very indiscreet way. I feel like she could've chosen a different time to ask about what she found, but then, the book wouldn't be as interesting, right?

- True. Also - I don't think Kate had many opportunities to get to Ana. And I suspect she'd only recently seen the contract.
- Right. Ana is off with Christian 24/7. When else could she have talked to her?
- I thought she was, but Ana was just reacting to shut her up. She was worried about what Christian would say.
- I think they should have talked in private, and that confronting her at Christian's party is what pissed Ana off.
- I think Ana was more upset about the timing of being confronted. I think Kate, at some point, should've had a conversation with Ana about the e-mail, but not at the party. It was completely inappropriate. The conversation could've waited.

Kate Knows All

Three weeks before the wedding, Ana says she'd finally told Kate "everything." Do you think Ana told Christian that she told Kate everything? How do you think Kate reacted? Anger? Shock? Understanding? Do you think we will see this scene in the movie? I bet Ana and Kate are much closer since having that conversation. I can only imagine the relief Ana felt being able to share the events leading up to their marriage with Kate.

- I'm not sure Christian believes that Ana told Kate every detail. But if she did, Christian would have cause to be upset. There are some things that are private. If it happened to me, it would've been a serious breech in trust.
- I can't imagine how stunned Kate must have been!
- I can envision the scene. Shock, horror, curiosity, and anger. Hopefully, with a little laughing, too! Like 'He did *what*?" I'd love to see Kate's expression when she

finds out Ana's doing things Kate hasn't ever experienced!

- At least they can joke about it now.
- I can see them laughing about, "You asked him 'What are butt plugs," Ana? Couldn't you figure that out, with your 4.0 GPA?"
- I think Kate had many reactions. I think she was initially shocked by what Ana told her about Christian, and the lifestyle he introduced Ana to. Then, she probably got very angry at Ana, especially after the whole scene at the party, when she confronted Ana and Christian about the email. Then, after Ana would've reassured her again, Kate would've been happy that Ana found her happily ever after. There's no way in hell she'd ever tell Christian that she told Kate everything - he would've gone ballistic!
- At first Kate would've had a shock, just hearing Ana telling her all that she's into. Then after Ana calmed her down and explained to her that it's something she has agreed on, that she likes all that's been done so far, then Kate would be cracking up, listening to all the questions Ana had asked Christian!
- I don't think Ana would tell Christian the truth about what she told Kate. She'd find a way to get off the hook from Christian's inquisition. But, she'd explain to him that it was good for her to get the point of view of someone she loves, even though Christian hated Kate knowing about their sex life.

The Men in Grey

Thinking about Christian and Elliot. What challenges will Ana and Kate have after they get married?

- The Grey men are a complete mash-up of all these types. They share many of the traits as described, but don't really fit the mold of any one in particular...at the end of the day, honestly, I think that Kate is going to have the roughest time...Elliot's eye tends to wander, and I'm not

385

entirely convinced that he'd remain 100% faithful to Kate, and I don't think she'd forgive or forget so easily.

- I think both Elliott and Christian have elements of several of these types of men. But the I think a lot of men have bits and pieces - that they grow out of.
- I don't know that I agree about the "grow out of" part. Men don't grow out of anything. They are who they are, and us women will *never* change them. Trust me!
- A lot of men experiment with a lot of women until they settle down. A lot are selfish until they have kids.
- Case in point: one of my best friends. He was on a dating frenzy until he married. Instant change.
- I think many men grow up and out of these behaviors. Some grow out of them and then back into them for their midlife crisis. I also think a huge amount of men don't grow out of them. I don't think we can say all. It isn't fair to paint all men with the same brush. It does take longer for most men to grow up than women, but many do.
- I think the player and the Chase not the Prize fit Elliott well at least before Kate. The Fixer Upper seems to fit Christian and Ana. She just thought or hoped she could love him out of his Fifty Shades. He is also the Non- Communicator. He also has a touch of manipulator/narcissist.
- My ex fiancé was definitely the Player and the manipulator/narcissist. He was horrible! He was the bad boy. After being with him, I wanted the exact opposite and I married the opposite.
- He and my ex must have been friends in another life to learn from one another!

Do You Like It Deep?

Coming Soon! Get the Fifty Shades Deeper t-shirt!
www.50ShadesDeeper.com/fun/

Learn More and Follow us

Our website:
www.50ShadesDeeper.com

Facebook Page:
https://www.facebook.com/FiftyShadesDeeper/

Twitter:
https://twitter.com/FSOGdeeper

Pinterest:
https://www.pinterest.com/brownelllandrum/deeper/

Follow Brownell

Goodreads:
- https://www.goodreads.com/author/show/3387210.Brownell_Landrum

Facebook:
- https://www.facebook.com/brownell.landrum.author/

Twitter:
- https://twitter.com/BrownellLandrum

Pinterest:
- https://www.pinterest.com/brownelllandrum/

Follow Kaydee Fergus

Facebook:
https://www.facebook.com/KaydeeFergusAuthor

Twitter:
https://twitter.com/KaydeeFergus901

Go Even Deeper with Brownell

Did you enjoy this book? Want to read something even *DEEPER*? Check out Brownell's books!

DUET Stories Novels – Volume I - IV

The DUET stories novel series is what Brownell calls a "metaphysical love story" spanning centuries and lifetimes. The books are available in both PG and Adult versions, and all are available on Amazon.
http://duetstories.com/

- DUET stories Volume I: The Song Begins
- DUET stories Volume II: The Tempo Builds
- DUET stories Volume III: A Chorus of Voices
- DUET stories Volume IV: Repercussions

Reasons Why

Brownell is also the author of the book, *Five Reasons Why Bad Things Happen: How to Turn Tragedies Into Triumph*.
http://reasonswhy.com/

Wonderactive Books!

Looking for a "deeper" book for children? Look for Brownell's two children's books in the Wonderactive Books! series: *Sometimes I Wonder* and *This Isn't My First Time*.
http://wonderactivebooks.com/

Coming Soon!

And more books are coming soon!
http://duetstories.com/more/